Campus Violence:
Kinds, Causes, and Cures

Campus Violence: Kinds, Causes, and Cures

Leighton C. Whitaker, PhD
Jeffrey W. Pollard, PhD
Editors

The Haworth Press, Inc.
New York · London · Norwood (Australia)

Campus Violence: Kinds, Causes, and Cures has also been published as *Journal of College Student Psychotherapy*, Volume 8, Numbers (1/2) (3) 1993.

The development, preparation, and publication of this work has been undertaken with great care. However, the publisher, employees, editors, and agents of The Haworth Press and all imprints of The Haworth Press, Inc., including The Haworth Medical Press and Pharmaceutical Products Press, are not responsible for any errors contained herein or for consequences that may ensue from use of materials or information contained in this work. Opinions expressed by the author(s) are not necessarily those of The Haworth Press, Inc.

The Haworth Press, Inc., 10 Alice Street, Binghamton, NY 13904-1580 USA

Library of Congress Cataloging-in-Publication Data

Campus violence : kinds, causes, and cures / Leighton C. Whitaker, Jeffrey W. Pollard, editors.
    p.   cm.
    Also published as v. 8, nos. 1-3, of Journal of college student psychotherapy.
    Includes bibliographical references and index.
    ISBN 1-56024-568-9
    1. Campus violence–United States. 2. Universities and colleges–United States–Security measures. 3. College Students–United States–Crimes against. I. Whitaker, Leighton C. II. Pollard, Jeffrey W.
LB2355.C36 1993
378.1'88–dc20   93-35657
                                                 CIP

INDEXING & ABSTRACTING

Contributions to this publication are selectively indexed or abstracted in print, electronic, online, or CD-ROM version(s) of the reference tools and information services listed below. This list is current as of the copyright date of this publication. See the end of this section for additional notes.

- *Applied Social Sciences Index & Abstracts (ASSIA)*, Bowker-Saur Limited, Maypole House, Maypole Road, East Grinstead, East Sussex RH19 1HH, England

- *Contents Pages in Education*, Carfax Information Systems, P.O. Box 25, Abingdon, Oxfordshire OX14 3UE, United Kingdom

- *Educational Administration Abstracts*, Sage Publications, Inc., 2455 Teller Road, Newbury Park, CA 91320

- *Higher Education Abstracts*, Claremont Graduate School, 740 North College Avenue, Claremont, CA 91711

- *International Bulletin of Bibliography on Education*, Proyecto B.I.B.E./Apartado 52, San Lorenzo del Escorial, Madrid, Spain

- *Inventory of Marriage and Family Literature (online and hard copy)*, National Council on Family Relations, 3989 Central Avenue NE, Suite 550, Minneapolis, MN 55421

- *Mental Health Abstracts (online through DIALOG)*, IFI/Plenum Data Company, 3202 Kirkwood Highway, Wilmington, DE 19808

- *Psychological Abstracts (PsycINFO)*, American Psychological Association, P.O. Box 91600, Washington, DC 20090-1600

- *Social Planning/Policy & Development Abstracts (SOPODA)*, Sociological Abstracts, Inc., P.O. Box 22206, San Diego, CA 92192-0206

- *Social Work Research & Abstracts*, National Association of Social Workers, 750 First Street NW, 8th Floor, Washington, DC 20002

(continued)

- *Sociological Abstracts (SA)*, Sociological Abstracts, Inc., P.O. Box 22206, San Diego, CA 92192-0206

- *Special Educational Needs Abstracts*, Carfax Information Systems, P.O. Box 25, Abingdon, Oxfordshire OX14 3UE, United Kingdom

SPECIAL BIBLIOGRAPHIC NOTES

related to indexing, abstracting, and library access services

☐ indexing/abstracting services in this list will also cover material in the "separate" that is co-published simultaneously with Haworth's special thematic journal issue or DocuSerial. Indexing/abstracting usually covers material at the article/chapter level.

☐ monographic co-editions are intended for either non-subscribers or libraries which intend to purchase a second copy for their circulating collections.

☐ monographic co-editions are reported to all jobbers/wholesalers/approval plans. The source journal is listed as the "series" to assist the prevention of duplicate purchasing in the same manner utilized for books-in-series.

☐ to facilitate user/access services all indexing/abstracting services are encouraged to utilize the co-indexing entry note indicated at the bottom of the first page of each article/chapter/contribution.

☐ this is intended to assist a library user of any reference tool (whether print, electronic, online, or CD-ROM) to locate the monographic version if the library has purchased this version but not a subscription to the source journal.

☐ individual articles/chapters in any Haworth publication are also available through the Haworth Document Delivery Services (HDDS).

Campus Violence: Kinds, Causes, and Cures

CONTENTS

ABOUT THE EDITORS

Leighton C. Whitaker, PhD, a Diplomate in Clinical Psychology of the American Board of Professional Psychology (ABPP), is Director of Psychological Services for Swarthmore College, Pennsylvania, and Clinical Adjunct Professor for the Widener University Institute for Graduate Clinical Psychology. He is Editor of the *Journal of College Student Psychotherapy* and consulting editor for mental health of the *Journal of American College Health.* His own publications include about sixty articles, book chapters, and editorials on college mental health, social issues and schizophrenic disorders, as well as the *Whitaker Index of Schizophrenic Thinking* (WIST) and the 1992 book *Schizophrenic Disorders: Sense and Nonsense in Conceptualization, Assessment, and Treatment* (Plenum Press). Dr. Whitaker also maintains a private practice.

Jeffrey W. Pollard, Guest Editor, received his PhD from The University of Virginia in 1978 after completing a Clinical Psychology Internship at the Eastern Virginia Graduate School of Medicine, Norfolk, VA. Prior to graduate training, he was a probation officer and addiction counselor. After completing graduate training he served on the staff of the counseling center at Villanova University, Villanova, PA. In 1982 Dr. Pollard was appointed Director of Counseling Services, Denison University, Granville, OH. In 1987 he was appointed Adjunct Assistant Professor of Psychology, Denison University and in 1989 Director of Counseling and Health Services at Denison. He is licensed as a Psychologist in Pennsylvania and Ohio and is a Certified Chemical Dependency Counselor III. Dr. Pollard serves on the State of Ohio Department of Human Services Family Violence Prevention & Services Grant Review and the Domestic Violence Advisory Committees. He is a member of the Licking County, Ohio Battered Women's Advisory Committee and chaired the Batterers' Treatment Programming Subcommittee for Domestic Violence in the 80s Conference.

Preface

The United States has become an increasingly violent society in recent decades and, inevitably, so has campus society. Our larger society's increase in both externally directed and internally directed kinds of violence, epitomized by higher rates of youth murder and youth suicide, inevitably influences our colleges and universities. Lest we be passive bystanders who allow our campus cultures to be destructively influenced, we must determine the nature of these influences and what to do about them. If we respond to the "Violencing of America" as an opportunity to educate, we can enhance the essence of educational leadership: educating for a better society.

Campus violence has become a topic of such great concern in recent years that the traditional "ivory tower" has given way to another image: campuses as microcosms of a larger increasingly violent society. New violence trends in our society, especially as they are now affecting children, are forging future college students. For example, weapon carrying, shooting people, "car jacking," and ethnic and sexist violence are being taught to children. Females, besides being the principal victims of campus violence currently, are being trained increasingly in perpetration as well as victimization.

We have tried to stimulate the reader to ask and to try to answer major questions applicable to their schools, whether primary, secondary, or colleges and universities. What programming will work to deconstruct and to counter outside negative influences on your campus? What are generalizable elements of particular campus programs which can be used on other campuses in customized ways? What role should the campus judicial system play in prevention efforts? Should institutions of higher education use society's mod-

[Haworth co-indexing entry note]: "Preface." Whitaker, Leighton C., and Jeffrey W. Pollard. Co-published simultaneously in *Journal of College Student Psychotherapy* (The Haworth Press, Inc.) Vol. 8, No. 1/2, 1993, pp. xi-xiii; and: *Campus Violence: Kinds, Causes, and Cures* (ed: Leighton C. Whitaker and Jeffrey W. Pollard) The Haworth Press, Inc., 1993, pp. xi-xiii. Multiple copies of this article/chapter may be purchased from The Haworth Document Delivery Center [1-800-3-HAWORTH; 9:00 a.m. - 5:00 p.m. (EST)].

xi

els or should they promote and even insist on a "higher" standard for student behavior? Can academic institutions assume the responsibility to face the problem of violence on campus and through research, community action and cooperation, consensus building and intervention, make change? Most of all, how can we develop a constructive spirit?

What is the institution's responsibility to minimize violence and provide treatment for victims and survivors of violence on its own campus, and how does that responsibility impact the institution's response to perpetrators? Currently, 83% of campus counseling centers mandate counseling for perpetrators (Gallagher 1991), often as a requirement for the student to remain in college. Is this practice unduly intrusive psychologically, ethically and legally? Or is bringing perpetrators into counseling and psychotherapy, even under pressure, a justified policy to prevent recidivism?

The authors have explicated many of the problems and suggested many answers but have also raised many questions. We hope that readers will provide even more questions and answers.

This volume is devoted to highlighting important kinds, causes and cures of violence destructive to living and learning in colleges and universities. We believe that the chapters herein have strong implications not only for institutions of higher education but also for primary and secondary schools, which are the training grounds for college life. We solicited chapters from many distinguished contributors to what is, arguably, the most pressing topic in education: how to nurture and develop atmospheres for learning, respect and constructive action in the midst of increasingly destructive influences.

Our first four chapters address the broadest and most far-reaching views of campus violence: the conceptualization of campus violence, administrative perspectives, the commercial promotion of mindless violence as it invades campus culture, and the destructive concoction of alcohol, other drugs and morbidity.

Chapter 5 speaks to the pressures on and limitations of college counselors and psychotherapists called upon to deal with disruptive students.

Chapters 6, 7 and 8 address specific kinds of violence as seen in urban crime, racism, and in violence toward lesbian and gay students.

Chapters 9, 10 and 11 focus on the most frequent immediate perpetrators of campus violence, male college students, and how their behavior can be dealt with and improved. Notably, we have focused more on perpetrators than victims because the previously existing literature focuses very largely on victims whereas perpetrators are more causally important. But we emphasize also how "victimization training" sets up students to become victims.

Chapters 12 and 13 describe actual major campus tragedies in which members of campus communities were murdered and how these tragedies were handled. Lastly, we have discussed in Chapter 14 the nature of resistances to reducing violence and how colleges and universities can proceed to reduce violence if we want to.

Leighton C. Whitaker, PhD
Jeffrey W. Pollard, PhD

REFERENCE

Gallagher, R. (1991). The Annual National Survey of Counseling Center Directors. The University of Pittsburgh, pp. 1 & 5.

Chapter 1

Conceptualizing Campus Violence: Definitions, Underlying Factors, and Effects

Mary L. Roark

SUMMARY. A conceptual framework is provided in this chapter for understanding violence in college and university settings. The types of violence common to campus environments are identified and definitions of key words such as "campus," "violence," and "victim" are given to form a base from which the interventions discussed in the remainder of the publication can be viewed. Also addressed to aid in planning prevention activities and counseling services are the identification of underlying factors and the effects of campus violence.

College campuses are part of American culture, and many of the activities, both positive and negative, that take place in the broader community are found also in institutions of higher education. Vio-

Mary L. Roark, EdD, NCC, is Associate Professor and Counseling Program Coordinator, State University of New York College at Plattsburgh, Plattsburgh, NY 12901. She originated and chaired the American College Personnel Association Commission I Task Force on Campus Violence, is a member of the Board of the Campus Violence Prevention Center, and was a panelist on the 1992 national teleconference, "Campus Violence Redefined."

[Haworth co-indexing entry note]: "Conceptualizing Campus Violence: Definitions, Underlying Factors, and Effects." Roark, Mary L. Co-published simultaneously in *Journal of College Student Psychotherapy* (The Haworth Press, Inc.) Vol. 8, No. 1/2, 1993, pp. 1-27: and: *Campus Violence: Kinds, Causes, and Cures* (ed: Leighton C. Whitaker and Jeffrey W. Pollard) The Haworth Press, Inc., 1993, pp. 1-27. Multiple copies of this article/chapter may be purchased from The Haworth Document Delivery Center [1-800-3-HAWORTH; 9:00 a.m. - 5:00 p.m. (EST)].

1

lence between strangers, among acquaintances, and in relationships is present on college and university campuses as in society. In light of institutional commitments to education, development, and personal safety of individuals, acts of personal abuse in the college setting are particularly damaging. Persons and the institution are harmed, sometimes in irreparable ways. On campuses across the nation, happenings in a variety of relationships are leaving people victimized by abuse, assault, harassment, rape, and other behaviors inappropriate to a civilized society and destructive of a learning environment.

The campus response to violence typically is instigated and informed by counselors who share with other student affairs professionals a heritage of concern for student welfare and well-established skills of responding to student needs through crisis, remedial, developmental, and preventive outreach activities. The development of the whole student has long been the theoretical and philosophical base of student affairs professionals, with extensive practical applications of this developmental perspective to all aspects of college life. The prevention of violence, while never easy or simple, is not basically different from developmental interventions already made by counselors and administrators in other areas of student growth, maturation, and concerns. Thus, the mechanisms necessary to counter-act violence and victimization are not unique; they are generally available and need only to be focused on the problem at hand. Progress in the elimination of campus violence will be due more to a core of knowledgeable and committed persons than it will be to innovations in types of activities.

The purpose of this chapter is to provide a conceptual framework for understanding campus violence. This framework begins with a discussion of types of violence, considerations about the collegiate setting, and definitions of campus and of violence. The last sections of the chapter focus on factors underlying violence among traditional-aged college students and on the effects that such violence induces. This knowledge can be used to help institutions create intervention programs and to help individuals build or rebuild personal strengths. For students and staff members, knowledge can heighten urgency and commitment to eliminate violence in personal settings and relationships.

TYPES OF VIOLENCE

The kinds of violence on the college campus include a broad range of activities. One category is that of rape with its varieties of perpetrators–strangers, acquaintances, dating partners, and gangs. Rape is defined by specific state laws, usually as intercourse forced on a person against his or her will; the gender of the parties, the specific behavior, and the degree of force vary in legal definitions. Another type of violence is non-sexual physical attack, including assault, fighting, mugging, and other forms of physical and interpersonal violence. The latter is called by a variety of names–"relationship abuse," "dating violence," or "courtship battering"–and is the equivalent of domestic violence among married partners. Similarly, hazing and sexual harassment may lead to varied levels of violence. Bias-related violence refers to harmful acts directed against certain persons and groups of persons because they are members of particular ethnic, cultural, or religious groups or because of their sexual/affectional preference. Casual violence, random violence, and wilding are terms used in media reports to portray violence that has neither an identifiable purpose nor an apparent specific reason for choice of victim. Coercive sex and sexual exploitation are general terms sometimes useful as "umbrella" coverage for a variety of sexual offenses. It is important to note that rape, assault, and harassment are crimes, as defined by state law and federal regulations; many state laws also make hazing illegal. Suicide and homicide, as extreme forms of physical violence against self or others, are further kinds of campus violence.

Other abuse situations of concern in higher education institutions are those which are more purely psychological: academic harassment (intimidation and humiliation of students by professors); expressions and manifestations of bias against persons with disabilities; emotional abuse in relationships; inappropriate teasing and joking; and verbal harassment by peers. Making false accusations about incidents of violence also can victimize members of the campus community.

For purposes of this chapter, violence will be discussed as an interpersonal act rather than an act against property and will emphasize current active forms. It is recognized, however, that many students come to campus already victimized by past situations and carry ramifications of this earlier abuse within them.

Any and all categories of persons–heterosexual women and men, gays and lesbians, members of varied ethnic, racial, religious and socioeconomic groups, students, staff, and faculty–can become targets for campus violence, some more than others. Women are predominantly the targets of sexual assault and sexual harassment. Men, more than women, are affected by hazing and fighting. First year students, women students, members of ethnic groups, gays and lesbians, and persons with disabilities are more likely than their counterparts to be seen as less powerful and hence more vulnerable to exploitation.

THE COLLEGE SETTING

Violence is threaded through many aspects of American life, but it is perhaps most out of place in an institution devoted to education and development. According to the National Association of Student Personnel Administration Task Group on Safety and Security,

> A safe campus environment is one in which students, faculty, and staff are free to conduct their daily affairs, both inside and outside the classroom, without fear of physical, emotional, or psychological harm. Personal safety is a basic human need that must be preserved if the mission of the university is to be pursued. (1989, p. 2)

In spite of this desire to maintain a safe setting, a campus environment provides a culture in which violence can ferment. As noted earlier, all the forces of the larger culture are present on a college campus. In addition, the very nature and developmental status of college students may contribute to their victimization by others. Irresponsible actions are not uncommon and are even predictable among adolescents. Youthful indiscretions and lack of judgement are present; predators exist. In one of the earliest articles acknowledging campus violence, Brown (1983) pointed that while the public media present a romantic portrayal of college life, getting through college can be a cruel and demanding experience due to the harshness of the campus environment, the grading system in higher education, and the stresses of collegiate life.

Institutions of higher education differ from other environments in terms of expectations, ambitions, operating principles, and values. Colleges and universities have commitments to the values of free inquiry, intellectual honesty, personal integrity, tolerance of diversity, and respect for human dignity. Freedom of expression on the college campus usually translates into freedom of experimentation relevant to personal life styles. Judicial opinions have consistently moved away from *in loco parentis* responsibilities (Gulland and Powell, 1989); the goal of higher education now is to educate and enlighten, not to control.

A campus is a relatively open and free place, physically as well as academically. It can rarely be closed to the public; generally, it would be considered inappropriate to do so. Service to community as a stance of higher education means that campus boundaries are not firm and that many buildings are kept open for public use.

A college is not a self-contained system, with all of its important variables and conditions available to manipulation and control. Unlike the prison system, security is not the main mission; hence, public safety is only one of the subsidiary goals of an institution of higher education–The campus community comprises a wide range of societal habits, ethnic customs, cultural norms, and individual and family histories. Some of these habits, customs, norms, and histories include abuse of and by others.

Other unique features of a campus community also may contribute to persons becoming victims of violence and to victimizing others. Large campuses with thousands of students in classes, residence units, dining halls, activities, and recreational pursuits can be very impersonal and thus add to a sense of insignificance. At the other end of the size spectrum, small institutions may find rumor mills and a "pressure-cooker" intensity which can feed violence and reactions to it. Optimistic assumptions about security and safety may characterize any campus community, and individuals may be putting their trust in an untrustworthy environment.

Like all other collections of humans, institutions of higher education are both notably similar to and different from one another, so that no simple typology is adequate. We know, however, that setting-specific conditions are crucial to understanding and presenting violence on individual campuses.

DEFINING CAMPUS VIOLENCE

Naming the realities of campus violence is essential to intervention work, whether of a preventive or developmental nature. Once we name something, we can move beyond vagueness to clarity that favors efforts at prevention and control. Words are powerful, and naming gives us an ability to describe, to discuss, to understand, and eventually to make changes. The terms "bias-related violence," "date rape," "courtship violence," and "sexual harassment" are all relatively recent nomenclature, even though the behaviors have been around as long as people have been in relationships of unequal power. Until the naming took place, it was difficult to justify interventions after the incident and even more difficult to educate about the behavior and its prevention.

I will now discuss definitions related to the campus and to the concept of violence in order to provide perspective for the chapters that follow. Definitions of campus violence are necessarily somewhat fluid, even when broken into component behaviors of rape, assault, harassment, and hazing and into the categories of physical, sexual, and psychological abuse. Both the definition of campus and of violence are less than clear-cut.

Campus. A typical dictionary definition of campus is "the grounds of a school, college, university or hospital" (*The American Heritage Dictionary of the English Language,* 1992, p. 227). However, "campus" can be a mind-set as well as physical property. There is no ready answer to how far to go beyond specific geographical markings to include perceived and psychological communities as part of the college campus. Campus boundaries are relatively permeable, and the limits of the word "campus" are not easily established. One issue is whether to consider only actions within the geographical boundaries of institutions of higher education as campus violence or whether to consider also actions among, against, or by its constituents in any setting, such as off-campus commercial establishments and personal residences.

It may help an institution to determine its responsibility and priorities by looking at a system of levels of where and to whom violence can take place:

1. Violence which happens to anyone within the geographical boundaries of the campus, regardless of whether a constituent (student, staff, or faculty member) or an outsider is the target or the offender. Example: A spectator at an athletic event who is not affiliated with the campus is assaulted in a parking lot by another unaffiliated spectator.
2. Violence which happens between its constituents in their institutional and social roles, outside of institutional boundaries. Examples: a gang rape of a student by other students in an off-campus party setting or unwanted sexual attention by a faculty member directed to a student at a community drinking establishment.
3. Violence which seriously affects institutional roles even though it happened to constituents outside both institutional boundaries and institutional roles. Example: A student assaulted by a family member.
4. Violence which constituents inflict on others beyond their institutional roles and beyond the institution's boundaries. Example: A student assaults a family member.

Most college administrators would agree that actions on the first level clearly come under the institution's direct concern while actions in the last category may not. As one moves outside the institutional boundaries and roles, responsibility is less clear and may be more a matter of legal parameters, specifics of the situation, educational and moral concerns, and the institution's self-chosen response. Institutional responses vary in accord with criminal charges, campus disciplinary processes, medical and counseling services, educational efforts, and other.

Violence. The word "violence" is highly charged, and defining it is even more difficult than defining campus boundaries. Definitions of violence, like the issues related to it, vary by time, community reaction, and individual subjectivity. Legal terminology (usually state-by-state specific), social use, research language, and dictionary definitions are useful, limited, and do not always match.

Violence is a culturally determined label applied to behavior and injury patterns as an outcome of a social judgment on the part of the observer. Margaret Mead defined the word violence as behavior "which is experienced by other members of the same culture as a positive violation of culturally patterned interpersonal behavioral norms" (1969, p. 227). From their social judgment perspective, Garbarino and Gilliam stated:

> The meaning of most actions is determined by the environ-ment in which they occur, including (1) the intention of the actor, (2) the act's effect upon the recipient, (3) an observer's value judgment about the act, and (4) the source of the stan-dards for that judgment. (1980, p. 5)

An important consideration in defining violence is whether to include actions beyond the physical, such as verbal or psychological violence. Dictionary definitions usually stress the physical aspects of violence but allow other meanings. *The American Heritage Dictio-nary of the English Language* (1992) defines violence as:

> (1) Physical force exerted for the purpose of violating, damag-ing, or abusing. (2) The act or an instance of violent action or behavior. (3) Intensity or severity, as in natural phenomena; untamed force. (4) Abusive or unjust exercise of power. (5) Abuse or injury to meaning, content, or intent. (6) Vehemence of feeling or expression; fervor. (p. 1994)

The Random House Dictionary of the English Language (1987) defines the same term as:

> (1) swift and intensive force, (2) rough or injurious physical force, action or treatment, (3) an unjust or unwarranted exertion of force or power, as against rights or laws, (4) a violent act or proceeding, (5) rough or immoderate vehemence, and (6) dam-age through distortion or unwarranted alteration. (p. 2125)

A broad definition of violence is taken by Gregg, who claimed, as cited by Bickmore (1984), that any adequate definition must include not only physical acts but verbal, psychological, symbolic, and spiritual attacks, with many forms taking on a combination of characteristics. Gregg defined verbal attacks as those that demean and humiliate, symbolic attacks as those that evoke fear and hostility, psychological violence as attitudes that deny one's humanity and equality, and spiritual violence as displays of hostility and hatred or postures that communicate racism, inferiority, and worthlessness. He includes both acts and inactions and that which was done directly to people or indirectly to them through what they esteem.

The term violence can be used to describe either *overt* or *covert* and either *offensive* or *defensive* behaviors which involve the use of force toward others. Thus, four types of violence can be identified: (1) overt violence is visible, such as fighting; (2) covert violence is either not acted out, such as threat, or is concealed; (3) aggressive violence is initiated for gain, such as mugging; and (4) defensive violence is undertaken for self-protection (Douglas & Waksler, 1982).

Douglas and Waksler believe threat behavior plays a significant role in attempts to gain compliance and is much more pervasive than overt violence:

> Threat behavior communicates to others the supposed intention to use overt violence *if* necessary. The one issuing the threat need not *really* intend to be violent; others need only believe in the truth of the threat and the threatener's ability to carry it out. (1982, p. 232)

Violence was defined by Iglitzin (1970) as "coercive behavior which results in harm and destruction to others. . . It may be evidenced by overt physical action or by intangible psychological or mental behavior" (p. 166, 167). Iglitzin stated that the definition of violence must be "broad enough to include not only specific actions deliberately intended to injure others, but also intangible behavior, even non-action, which has the same result" (p. 168). She indicated that the most obvious form of violence is overt physical assault and identified covert psychological violence as an assault on another's self-esteem and dignity.

Lystad (1986) defined violence as "an act carried out with the intention of, or perceived as having the intention of, physically hurting another person" (p. 52). It can be (1) instrumental (to some other purpose); (2) expressive (an end in itself); (3) legitimate (culturally permitted); or (4) illegitimate (counter to cultural norms). Lystad further defines violence as behavior that involves the direct use of physical aggression against others which is against their will and detrimental to their growth potential.

Another categorization includes (1) physical violence, whereby bodily harm is done; (2) interpersonal violence, whereby one is treated as a nonperson or as an object; (3) institutional violence, when the institution or organization violates human rights, dignity, and freedom to choose and when it treats persons as objects; and (4) intellectual violence, whereby knowledge is treated loosely, in a biased way without some form of objectivity or by outright lying (O'Neil, 1985).

In speaking to student affairs professionals, Orzek (1989) presented commission and omission as two means of violence. Commission is actively doing something to or against a person, and omission is neglecting to provide what is necessary for growth or recovery. Her categories of violence perpetrated by students is divided according to these means of violence and their target groups and gives a unique perspective on campus violence. A chart of this material, as adapted from later presentation by Orzek (1991), is shown as Figure 1.

The definition of violence which I have formulated for use in my educational, research, and consulting work on the topic of campus violence is *behavior which by intent, action, and/or outcome harms another person.* This definition, a clarification and expansion of that given in an earlier work (Roark, 1987), sets the stage for situation-specific responses to concrete happenings. The phrase contains three essential elements which can be emphasized differentially in terms of interventions, namely intent addressed through education, actions through judicial processes, and outcomes through counseling and other services.

I view both physical (including sexual) and verbal (including psychological) abuse as violence, with physical abuse referring to attempts to hurt others by use of physical force and verbal abuse referring to deliberate acts to hurt others by words or symbolic actions. In both verbal and physical abuse, there are degrees of force and degrees of harm, consideration of which may affect value judgments and judicial processes. It is important to note that cam-

FIGURE 1. Violence Perpetrated by Students

	TARGET GROUP				
	Self	Partner/ Dating	Residential Community	Members of Out-Groups	"Unknown Others" "They/Them"
O M I S S I O N OR N E G L E C T	Withholding Mainte-nance Self-Sabotaging	Withholding Support Passive-Aggressive Actions Sabotaging	Failure to Live up to Responsibil-ities	Lack of Recognition or Support for Existence/ Philosophy	Failure to Take Needs into Account for Policy Planning, Etc.
C O M M I S S I O N OR A B U S E	Alcohol Drugs Eating Disorder Suicide	Insults Slapping Punching	Harassment Stealing Hazing	Rape Harassment Verbal Threats Physical Harm Property Damage	Harassment Property Damage

Adapted from Orzek, A. (1991). Campus violence and campus discrimination. In A. L. Reynolds and M. von Destinon (Eds.). *Campus violence manual* (pp. 10-11). Washington, D.C.: American College Personnel Association.

pus judicial processes can differ from educational processes, particularly in the realm of attention to verbal violence.

Victim. Paralleling the attention given to the difficult task of defining violence is the need to clarify terms used to refer to the recipient of violent acts. "Victim" is commonly defined as a person to whom a crime has happened. According to Kent (1982), a victim is a person who is injured, harmed, or abused physically or psychologically. Victims can suffer economic, social, medical, or legal indignities. They may have been chosen because of their vulnerability. The process of becoming a victim is termed victimization.

Some sexual assault counselors object to any use of the word "victim" on the grounds that labeling the assaulted person a victim reinforces a sense of powerlessness. Those holding this view prefer to call the person a survivor, which can have an empowering effect and be viewed as a more positive term. "Victim mentality" indicates a pervasive sense of lack of control whereas "being a victim" indicates a situational, time-limited condition.

The word "target" is often useful to bypass the emotionally laden concept of victim and the sometimes artificial and forced use of "survivor" when applied to situations other than rape. In my educational efforts and writing, I use the words "victim," "survivor," and "target" interchangeably to refer in general to persons who have been made the object of another person's harmful behavior. None of the words is meant as a lifetime label but rather as a useful description until the ramifications of the behavior inflicted upon the person are resolved. College services are designed to remove effects of victimization as quickly and completely as possible and move the former victim beyond the survivor state to positive developmental growth. Rarely do I use any labels when working as an advocate or counselor with a specific person who has been the object of assault, abuse, or harassment.

The definitions of campus, violence, and victims necessarily remain fluid but difficulties in establishing definitions should not stop us from examining the problems and finding solutions. As Garbarino and Gilliam (1980) noted when discussing abusive families,

> There are many things in life that we cannot define precisely and yet deal with nonetheless. Lack of a precise definition of time does not prevent us from using our watches. Nor does our inability to produce a conclusive definition of love stop us from loving. Neither time nor love has been defined satisfactorily, yet each exists and supports a body of scientific evidence. So it is with abuse. (p. 5)

UNDERLYING FACTORS OF CAMPUS VIOLENCE

Because all acts of violence are events of the same order and have a similar base, an examination and understanding of common elements can give direction to intervention efforts. The ultimate causes of violence are difficult to discern since they are part of larger, interconnected problems in society. A concept of single-event causation is more simplistic than realistic, and a stimulus/response paradigm may be outdated. Hoff stated:

> There is no single cause of violence. Rather there are complex, interrelated *reasons* that some individuals are violent and others are not . . . A violent response is not inevitable; it is chosen. The choice of violent behavior is influenced by the social, political, legal, and belief and knowledge systems of the violent person's cultural community. (1984, p. 228)

Like any dysfunctional behavior, violent behavior is caused by an interaction of personality, biology, environment, and social acceptability. The latter two are emphasized in the following material. Explanations of factors underlying all campus violence are not to be viewed as excuses for abusive action nor as an all-inclusive list. Campus violence incorporates a web of issues, among them the following linked and overlapping phenomena discussed below:

Vulnerability of traditional-age college students. College students typically create a population at risk for victimization. In terms of crime statistics, they are in the age group (16-25) that comprises the most frequent offenders and the most frequently offended against. Students' stages of psychosocial development during the late teens and early twenties are a factor in their victimization on campus. They are in transition from direct parental supervision to eventual autonomy, usually in new settings and always with a variety of environmental stressors. Sexual impulses and cultural expectations make insistent demands. Peer pressures are heavy, competencies only partially established, and mistaken beliefs about personal invincibility abound. They live away from old support systems, among others who are experimenting with new freedoms. They may be socially immature and naive about the world. They may feel themselves to be under a heavy burden of competition for available jobs, income, and status.

While some of the stresses and strains on college students are unique to the times in which we live, others have always been a part of campus life. Joseph Katz and Nevitt Sanford, writing in 1965 about the causes of the student revolution, pointed out that:

> We are aware how far from truth is the stereotype of the happy-go-lucky, golden college years. The time between seventeen and twenty-one is often one of nagging self-doubt, of intense conflict in relations with other people, of painful and sometimes rebellious struggles for independence from one's parents, of an uneasy search for one's eventual occupational and sexual roles. Such emotional struggles and discomforts upset the individual's equilibrium and thus free considerable energy for either creative or destructive acts. (p. 64)

Societal legitimization of violence. American culture includes many pro-violent values and behaviors, as demonstrated in our history, forms of entertainment, wide-spread fascination with guns, and until recently, a hands-off stance toward domestic abuse. Relationship violence typically has not been viewed in America as criminal, and there has been an acceptance of abuse in courtship, marriage, and patenting. As Mario Cuomo noted:

> For too many men, the masculine ideal is the silent, tough, even brutal hero who wins confrontations with guns and fists. They can be gentle with their women and their kids as long as it's clear who's boss–and as long as things go well. But in the real world, things frequently go badly. There are pressures and disappointments, moments of tension and embarrassment. In those moments, the smaller and physically weaker–women and children–become targets for the rage and frustration that society has not taught men to ventilate through self-reflective speech and analysis. (1986, p. 11,12)

In addition to violence against females and children, male violence toward other males is seen in three major areas: criminal assault, sports, and war.

Entanglement of sexuality and violence. There is confusion about sex and sexuality, adding to a pro-violent attitude in society. When sex and violence are mixed, the result is usually the creation of a victim. Pornography is one example of this mixture, linking male-defined and imposed sexuality, violence, and the physical and sexual abuse of women. Pornography can be distinguished from erotic materials by its themes of hatred, pain, and humiliation. Media images that combine sex and violence promote an ideology that justifies the abuse and domination of women, children, and others perceived as less powerful. The Attorney General's Commission on Pornography (1986) found that violent pornography can affect negative attitudes toward women and teach people that coercive sexuality and aggression are acceptable in relationships.

Sex role socialization processes. Rigid sex role stereotypes socializing males to be aggressive and females to be submissive are part of the underlying factors of violence on campuses. Sexism in society may contribute to violence in relationships, because abuse is deeply rooted in views of what constitutes a woman's "place," her role, and her relationship with men. It is equally dangerous to have persons in a community who ignore the rights of others and persons who deny their own rights. Our society seems to be in transition from earlier, more definite role prescriptions to more fluid, self-defined roles, and times of transition are typically confusing and unsettling. Some violence may be an expression of distorted relationships between the sexes and an attempt to keep rigid sex roles in place; hence, homophobism and sexism go hand in hand. The social and cultural mechanisms for defining, shaping and constraining sexuality are a fundamental element in male power over women. Violence on campus may be fueled, in part, by macho sex roles encouraged by some aspects of the fraternity system.

Hierarchical patterns of dominance. Closely interwoven with the societal legitimization of violence and sex role socialization processes are hierarchical patterns of dominance. The inappropriate use of personal, physical, or institutionally-based power appears to be part of many demands and commands which lead to victimization. As has been determined about rape, most violence is a power issue rather than a sexual or aggressive matter. Most forms of harassment are based on incorrectly used power. Patriarchal systems and paternalism serve most women *and* most men poorly. According to David and Brannon:

> Violence and male supremacy have been companions in the course of civilization. The domination of women by men has been the prototype of the control men have tried to exercise over other men–in slavery, in war, and in the marketplace . . . That game says that to be a man one must possess, control, dominate–and that domination must be assured by force and violence. Masculinity is interpreted to *demand* male supremacy . . . the masculine game cannot have a winner unless it also has a loser. The rules of the game require that the losers be reduced to humiliation and powerlessness–to the classic status of women. (1976, p. 13)

Abusive use of substances. Many violent acts occur while persons are under the influence of alcohol or other substances. Perhaps from 50% to 80% of campus violence involves the use of alcohol, according to Smith (1989) and confirmed by many campus judicial reports. (Also see Chapter 3.) Results from the 1985 College Alcohol Survey (Gadaleto & Anderson, 1986) showed that college administrators believe alcohol is frequently involved when problem behaviors happened on campus, with 60% of violent behaviors involving the use of alcohol. Being under the influence of alcohol is used by perpetrators to rationalize behavior, reduce personal responsibility, and present a socially acceptable excuse to engage in otherwise prohibited behavior. Many of the deaths among the college age group are due to alcohol abuse. The continuing problem of alcohol abuse becomes more apparent as the problems pass from one generation to the next. In addition to alcohol, other drugs such as cocaine, crack, and steroid use may lead to aggressive acts against others.

Denial. Silence is the voice of complicity. While not a causative factor of violence in the first instance, violence is made possible by denying and down-playing its existence. Denial, ignorance, and intentional hiding of the facts are contributing factors in the continuation of violence. The kinds of violence under discussion are very personal, and the behaviors usually happen in private settings. It is easy to claim that what was not witnessed by others may not have taken place. Members of the campus community are frequently unaware of the nature and extent of the problem or do not want to admit its existence. The shame and self-blame of the victim, the "I won't do it again/please forgive me" syndrome of the offender, and bystanders looking the other way have led to much secretiveness about personal violence. The victims, the perpetrators, and those with responsibilities to both parties may have an interest in keeping quiet about behavior that does not serve the community as a whole. Hanson, Turbett, and Whelehan (1986) stated the opinion that:

> Faculty and staff, fearing possible job recriminations, the specter of witch-hunts or believing that incidents are either misrepresented, distorted, or hearsay, tend not to see or know of the violence, and that interpersonal violence is underreported, underprosecuted, and underpunished, thus allowing it to occur in secrecy, ignorance, and shame. (p. 14)

Cuomo (1986), quoted earlier in regard to societal legitimization of violence, said that by turning away we absolve the violator and condemn the abuse. In addition, denial allows us to avoid drawing painful conclusions "about the images of dominance and power in our culture, about an economy that crowds women into undervalued and underpaid occupations, and about the psychological toll of brutality" (p. 12).

Inequality and prejudice. I see at the root of violence the perception that others are of less value than oneself. A lack of mutual respect for those different from self, maintaining discriminatory stereotypes, and acting on the basis of personal prejudices creates potential victims of other persons. The usual targets of aggression are undervalued classes and groups; people considered equals are rarely exploited. When violence is directed to those who are devalued, it in turn contributes to the devaluation. Hatred spawns violence, and violence reduces the dignity of both the target and the perpetuator.

Heightened anxiety, particularly among previously advantaged groups, may lead to violence in both dramatic and subtle ways. As Lee Daniels noted in a *New York Times* (1989) article, a fear of competition from previously disenfranchised populations may make the former oppressor now feel oppressed. Reactive violence which is rooted in fear, prejudice, misinformation, and misperception has self-preservation as its real or imagined aim.

EFFECTS OF CAMPUS VIOLENCE

Violence differs in type and in intensity; physical, psychological, and sexual abuse can be carried out by words and/or by actions that have varying outcomes, degrees of impairment, and human and economic costs. As the Bureau of Justice Statistics of the United States Department of Justice identified (Wolfgang, Figlio, Tracy, and Singer, 1985), the seriousness of an event can be assessed by its consequences. Chief among these are the extent and nature of physical injury, the extent of psychological trauma, and the monetary cost of victim expenses and institutional services. In addition, the extent and type of force or intimidation used and the relationship between victim and offender can affect how the victim reacts to the event. Explicating levels of bodily harm, these authors proposed a scale from (a) minor harm, injury requires or receives no professional medical attention; (b) victim treated and discharged, receives professional medical treatment but is not detained for further medical care; (c) victim hospitalized, requires in-patient care in a medical facility or out-patient care for three or more clinical visits; and (d) individual killed, dies as a result of the injuries.

All categories of persons–heterosexual women and men, gays and lesbians, members of varied ethnic, racial, religious and class groups–can be targets for and suffer the effects of all types of criminal activity; rape, assault, harassment, and hazing are of primary concern on the college campus. Women, more than men, are the targets of acquaintance rape and sexual harassment; men, more than women, are affected by hazing and fighting (Roark, Poveda, & Scanlon, 1992).

The effects of violence, experienced by individuals and by institutions, usually cause damage beyond the original harm. Indeed, incidents of violence can have a lingering, profound, sometimes lifelong impact. Violence can leave both visible and invisible scars. These effects are similar regardless of the location of the violence: in campus residence units, at the library, in classrooms, and around activity areas; off campus in apartments, on the streets, and in entertainment establishments. The effects also are similar across types of violence; while outcomes may differ in intensity and nature, little of this difference is due to the type of violence which was perpetrated. Rape, assault, and harassment all leave damage in ways that are predictable in general although variable for individuals.

Effects of violence on individuals. The key point in the discussion of effects of violence on campus is that harm is created by the incident. Effects of violence on individuals can be in the cognitive, effective, or behavioral domains. Extremes in thought patterns, emotions, and actions are normal reactions to an abnormal event. These effects, while separated for purposes of discussion, interact with one another in ways unique to the individual, based on his or her experiences. The response may vary according to the severity of the crime, its significance for the victim, the extent of its impact, the availability and effectiveness of the victim's support system, his or her coping skills, previous experience with traumatic events, and the relationship of the involved parties. The effects are not all felt originally or simultaneously; reactions can come in stages and cover a variety of impacts.

Any of the effects discussed below may also be experienced by those close to the victim, such as roommates, floormates, friends, and family. In addition, unknown persons who identify with the victim on the basis of shared group characteristics (gender, ethnicity, religion, sexual orientation, disability) may vicariously perceive themselves to be threatened. Persons can be affected by being, caring for, treating, reading about, hearing about, or fearing becoming a victim. Violence is a shared threat, even when it is not a shared experience.

Cognitive effects are those that change basic thinking about self and situations; as such, they may be devastating to future functioning. One pervasive effect of having been the target of a violent act is a loss in one's sense of personal control, accompanied by lessening of confidence in one's ability to assess and manage situations. While it is impossible to cite in advance the "worst" effect of violence, one of the key results of victimization is the loss of self-esteem. Self-esteem is frequently damaged by incidents of personal abuse. Persons who have been abused and/or who see others of their group abused for long periods of time may internalize a sense of "secondary citizenship" and believe themselves to be less worthy than their abuser. Both the loss of real and perceived control and the erosion of esteem lead to a less secure sense of self-identity.

Another frequent and serious cognitive effect of violence is a diminished sense of personal safety, which may or may not be a valid assessment of reality. The *perception* of lack of safety has an impact on behavior as forceful as does a realistic assessment of an unsafe situation.

One of the most troublesome cognitive effects is the tendency of the target of the violence to blame self for all or part of the incident. This thought-pattern is often internalized from a societal inclination to blame the victim and from wanting to believe that one could have been, and therefore now is, in control. The roots of this blaming, in part, lie in thinking such as: "It must be your fault, because if it isn't, if you were in no way to blame, then this could happen to anyone; it could happen to me or to persons important to me."

According to Pinderhughes (1972), blaming and devaluing victims serves both offenders and the public by reducing the pain which would otherwise be experienced through identification. This spares one the guilt and need for reaction and, at the same time, gives indignation a target which is unlikely to strike back in its weak and wounded state.

On the part of the victim, the belief that nothing can or will be done leads to both inaction and feelings of demoralization.

Behavioral effects include all the actions taken in response to violence. A frequent behavioral effect is to withdraw socially, emotionally, and/or academically. The shock of a violent crime can lead to an immobilization and inability to remember what happened during the event. Missing or dropping classes and leaving school are frequent behaviors after a traumatic event. For some time after the event, the target of violence may be distracted from important tasks and disorganized in everyday routines. Typically there is difficulty in concentrating and there is an impaired ability to study, followed by lowered academic performance. Achievement in classwork or other areas becomes secondary to survival and to maintaining self-integrity. A generalized inhibition can be present, with reduced participation in activities and in socializing. Impairment in sexual functioning can be a long-term effect of having been sexually abused or assaulted. Eating or sleeping disturbances and somatic symptoms of headaches and stomach problems may be present.

The victim may react to "trigger events," such as the anniversary date of the event or seeing the offender or someone who looks like the offender. Any of the effects of the original crisis may be re-experienced by such reminders of the original trauma.

Actions taken against an aggressor may or may not be in the victim's long-range best interests, depending sometimes on the nature and legality of the action. Even the action, considered positive by most college personnel staff, of reporting the event and/or bringing charges against the offender may lead to emotional and cognitive outcomes which are as difficult to manage as were the original effects of the violence. Some of the problems of victims are created or intensified by treatment in the justice system that is disrespectful, disbelieving, or unduly cumbersome, or even by too eagerly retributive therapists.

Feelings run high after incidents of abuse and assault. Affective reactions may range from slight embarrassment to utter demoralization, with an endless variety of emotional nuances in between. There may be irrational guilt and shame, as well as misdirected anger at self and legitimate anger at the offender. Indeed, anger may be too mild a word to describe the combination of rage and despair directed at self and others. Feelings of isolation, hurt, and grief are present as a reaction to a variety of losses. Among these are a loss of trust in others, in the environment, and in one's own judgment. Other pervasive losses may be loss of relationships because of the inability to relate in the same way as before the crime, loss of physical mobility or dexterity because of injury, and loss of a sense of justice in the fairness and "justness" of the world.

Anxiety can be pervasive and fear prevalent. Energy can be consumed by worries about repetition of the behavior, about retribution or retaliation if the abuse is reported and recourse is sought, and about revictimization by processes intended to address the incident. Anxiety about the safety of self and others and a feeling of vulnerability may be present. The victim may fear being blamed by others. Because of fear, past targets of violence may modify current activities and behavior, sometimes in self-limiting and self-defeating ways.

The effects of some acts of violence on some individuals are sufficiently devastating to merit the diagnostic label of post-traumatic stress disorder, one of the anxiety disorders categorized in the *Diagnostic and Statistical Manual of Mental Disorders, Third Edition-Revised* (American Psychiatric Association, 1987). The essential feature of this disorder is "the development of characteristic symptoms following a psychologically distressing event that is outside the range of usual human experience" (p. 247). The stressor producing this event is usually experienced with intense fear, terror, and helplessness.

Impairment may affect every aspect of life, in mild to severe forms. Symptoms of depression and anxiety are common with this disorder; impulsive behavior can occur, evidenced by sudden changes in life-style. Interference with personal relationships, phobic avoidances, emotional extremes, guilt, self-defeating behaviors, and suicide may result. When the stressor is of human design, as opposed to accidental and natural disorders, the disorder is apparently longer lasting and more severe. The symptoms usually begin immediately or soon after the trauma and can resurface months or years later.

Trauma symptoms, according to assessments by Brom, Kleber, and Defares (1989) include fears, negative emotional experiences, tensions, concentration and memory disturbances, lack of interest in the external world, and sleep disturbances.

Another framework for examining the effects of campus violence is to consider them as inhibitions in growth along the dimensions of the vectors for college student development proposed by Chickering (1969). These seven vectors are: developing competence; managing emotions; gaining autonomy, revised to gaining interdependence (Chickering, 1984); establishing identity; freeing interpersonal relations; clarifying purpose; and developing integrity. Personal involvement in violence can negatively affect development in each vector, for both victim and perpetrator. Violence damages a sense of personal competence in intellectual, physical, and social realms. In a campus setting, it is frequently due to mismanagement of emotions and self and leaves emotional issues to be resolved. Violence can ruin interdependence and impair the establishment of identity. It can damage the capacity for intimate relationships and affect the setting of life goals. It calls one's integrity and values into question. Thus, on all developmental fronts, violence is much more likely to affect progress negatively rather than positively.

Violence targeted at a person because of ethnicity, religion, or sexual orientation may cause victims to attempt to hide these significant characteristics, with subsequent costs in dignity, identity, and empowerment. Bias-related violence has the effect of keeping intimacy at bay.

When women are the objects of abuse, they may receive a message that they are not equal to men and not valued as people, with a subsequent undermining of academic, vocational, and personal goals and difficulty in forming trusting relationships with men (Hughes & Sandler, 1988). Similar dynamics may take place for any target of bias-related violence.

Effects on the perpetrators of violence depend on their sense of responsibility for their actions. Anger, guilt, erosion of self-esteem, confusion about identity, and fear of future ramifications can upset a perpetrator's healthy academic and personal development, just as it does that of a victim. When men abuse women with impunity, the implication is that such behavior is acceptable, and this may make it difficult for a man to form a healthy relationship with a woman. In discussing peer harassment, Hughes and Sandler stated that, "Men who do not respect women as individuals and do not take women seriously . . . are not well prepared for the working world, where women are increasingly likely to be their colleagues" (1988, p. 3). The same could be said about disrespect for members of the ethnic, racial, religious, gay and lesbian, and disability identified groups.

Violence also has an effect on the staff of a college or university. Incidents of violence drain staff energy as well as the energy of targets of the violence. Staff are not immune from becoming victims themselves. While some college staff come to be involved with issues and services related to campus violence out of their own experiences as earlier victims and others because of work assignments made for them by supervisors, most staff do so essentially out of a commitment to the developmental growth of college students.

O'Neil (1984), who observed that our society is an increasingly violent one, discussed how violence affects staff members delivering direct services:

> My personal experience with professionals working with victims is that they have been profoundly touched. It is more than another professional issue for them to explore; it is intensely emotional and personal. Those who have studied victims and particularly those doing therapy with victims have seen human pain, fear, suffering and trauma in most vivid ways. They have seen how the human spirit has been sometime permanently damaged. . . it is a topic of intensity, vulnerability, and pain. (p. 4, 5)

Effect of violence on institutions. The costs of victimization and violence to an institution as well as to individuals are high, and the institution, too, can become a victim when violence takes place within its boundaries. The college or university loses the time and capacities, at least temporarily, of students and staff who become occupied with the ramifications of violence. The institution also suffers loss of positive image, often with an accompanying loss of students through withdrawal of current students and non-matriculation of potential ones. The disruption of an academic institution's learning environment is a serious matter. Loss of student developmental potential damages the institution and the campus climate becomes contaminated if violence is rampant.

All of these negative effects have a monetary cost, as well as a moral one. Adverse publicity may affect public and private funding. There may be the threat or reality of legal action against the institution for negligence regarding personal safety. The inability to provide a living and working environment in which its members are and feel safe is a basic failure for a college or university community.

In a classic work about violence, Arendt (1969) commented that, like all actions, the practice of violence changes the world, with the most probable change being a more violent world. Parallel effects may well take place for individual perpetrators and for institutions, community, and society.

CONCLUSION

This chapter has offered definitions and descriptions of campus violence, precipitating factors, and possible effects involved in acts of personal abuse in the college environment. Such knowledge can be used to design interventions which indirectly and directly affect the outcomes and the circumstances of campus violence. These interventions can be of a primary, secondary, or tertiary order in which are addressed, respectively, developmental considerations for the entire population, educational efforts to reduce prevalence for an at-risk group, and remediation for damage already done. In an earlier article (Roark, 1987), examples of these types of interventions were discussed in some detail. Lyddon's work, while not on the topic of campus violence, gives a framework for understanding the types of changes that can be addressed through institutional programs, namely first-order change to address specific behaviors and second-order change to alter the fundamental structure of the system (Lyddon, 1990). Because the problem of campus violence is multifaceted, multidimensional intervention efforts are needed, of which a variety are presented in the chapters of this volume.

REFERENCES

American heritage dictionary of the English language, Third Edition (1992). Boston: Houghton Mifflin Co.

American Psychiatric Association (1987). *Diagnostic and statistical manual of mental disorders,* Third Edition–Revised. Washington, D.C.: Author.

Attorney General's Commission on Pornography (1986). *Final report.* Washington, D.C.: U. S. Department of Justice.

Bickmore, C. (1984). *Alternatives to violence.* Cleveland, OH: Alternatives to Violence Committee, Cleveland Friends Meeting.

Brom, D., Kleber, R. J., & Defares, P. B. (1989). Brief psychotherapy for posttraumatic stress disorders. *Journal of Consulting and Clinical Psychology, 57* (5), 607-612.

Brown, R. (1983). Reality, madness and our responsibility. *Developments 10* (3), 1.

Chickering, A. W. (1969). *Education and identity.* San Francisco: Jossey-Bass Inc., Publishers.

Chickering, A. W. (Ed.) (1981). *The modern American college.* San Francisco, Jossey-Bass Inc., Publishers.

Chickering, A. W. (1984). Education and identity revisited. *Journal of College Student Personnel, 26,* 392-399.

Chickering, A. W. (1984). Education and identity revisited. *Journal of College Student Personnel, 26*, 392-399.

Cuomo, M. (1986, April 15). Speech at conference on domestic violence, Albany, NY.

Daniels, L. A. (1988, October 31). Prejudice on campuses is feared to be rising. *New York Times, 138*, p. A12.

David, D. S., & Brannon, R. (1976). *The forty-nine percent majority: The male sex role.* Reading, MA: Addison-Wesley Publishing Company, Inc.

Douglas, J. D., & Waksler, F. C. (1982). *The sociology of deviance.* Boston: Little, Brown, & Company.

Gadaleto, A. F., & Anderson, D. S. (1986). Continued progress: The 1979, 1982, and 1985 college alcohol surveys. *Journal of College Student Personnel, 27* (6), 499-509.

Garbarino, J., & Gilliam, G. (1980). *Understanding abusive families.* Lexington, MA: D. C. Heath and Company.

Gulland, E. D., & Powell, M. E. (1989). *Colleges, fraternities, and sororities: A white paper on tort liability issues.* Washington, D. C.: American Council on Education.

Hanson, D., Turbett, J. P., & Whelehan, P. (1986). Interpersonal violence: Addressing the problem on a college campus. In J. Kalas and C. J. Lott (Eds.), *University Symposium on Personal Safety* (pp. 7-26). Albany, NY: State University of New York.

Hoff, L. A. (1984). *People in crisis: Understanding and helping.* Menlo Park, CA: Addison-Wesley Publishing Company.

Hughes, J. O'G., & Sandler, B. R. (1988). *Peer harassment: Hassles for women on campus.* Washington, D.C.: Project on the Status and Education of Women / Association of American Colleges.

Iglitzin, L. B. (1970). Violence and American democracy. *Journal of Social Issues, 26* (1), 165-186.

Katz, J., & Sanford, N. (1965, December 18). Causes of the student revolution. *Saturday Review,* pp. 64-66, 76, 79.

Kent, C. A. (1982). *No easy answers.* Minneapolis, MN: Illusion Theatre.

Lyddon, W. J. (1990). First- and second-order change: Implications for rational and constructive cognitive therapies. *Journal of Counseling and Development, 69*, 122-127.

Lystad, M. (Ed.) (1986). *Violence in the home: Interdisciplinary perspectives.* New York: Brunner /Mazel, Inc.

Mead, M. (1969). Violence and its regulation. *American Journal of Orthopsychiatry, 39* (2), 227-229.

National Association of Student Personnel Administrators (1989). *Preliminary Report: Task group on campus safety and security* (Brochure). Washington, D.C.: Author.

O'Neil, J. (1984, April). Societal violence, oppression, and victimization: Implications for college student professionals. Paper presented at the convention of the American College Personnel Association. Baltimore, MD.

O'Neil, J. (1985, March). Campus victimization: Relevance, psychological response, primary prevention. Paper presented at the convention of the American College Personnel Association, Boston, MA.

Orzek, A. (1989, March). Campus violence and campus discrimination. Paper presented at pre-convention workshop of the American College Personnel Association, Washington, D.C.

Orzek, A. (1991). Campus violence and campus discrimination. In A. L. Reynolds & M. von Destinon (Eds.), *Campus violence manual* (pp. 10-11). Washington, D.C.: American College Personnel Association.

Pemberton, G. (1988). *On teaching the minority student: Problems and strategies.* Brunswick, ME: Bowdoin College.

Pinderhughes, C. A. (1972). Managing paranoia in violent relationships. In Usedin, G. (Ed.), *Perspectives on violence.* New York: Brunner/Mazel, Inc.

Ramazanoglu, C. (1987). Sex and violence in academic life or you can keep a good woman down. In J. Hanmer and M. Maynard (Eds.), *Women, Violence, and Social Control.* New Jersey: Humanities Press International.

The Random House dictionary of the English language, Second Edition (1987). New York: Random House.

Roark, M. L. (1987). Preventing violence on college campuses. *Journal of Counseling and Development, 65* (7), 367-371.

Roark, M. L., Poveda, T., & Scanlon, J. (1992). *A survey of campus safety at SUNY Plattsburgh.* Plattsburgh, NY: President's Advisory Committee on Personal Safety, SUNY Plattsburgh.

Smith, M. (1989). Students, suds, and summonses: Strategies for coping with campus alcohol abuse. *Journal of College Student Development, 30* (2), 118-122.

Wolfgang, M. E., Figlio, R. M., Tracy, P. E., & Singer, S.I. *The national survey of crime severity.* Washington, D.C.: U. S. Department of Justice, Bureau of Justice Statistics, 1985.

Chapter 2

Administrative Perspectives on Disruptive Student Conduct

Diana K. Conklin
Norman W. Robinson

SUMMARY. The very nature of the university–its ethos–is the surest touchstone for defining student misconduct and determining responses to it. Every important campus constituency should be involved in discussing how students are expected to conduct themselves, and should come away with a clear understanding of the guiding principles that underlie those expectations. Students should be encouraged to focus not on a list of do's and don'ts but on the principles that they need to grasp in order to determine for themselves, in any setting, what is the right thing to do. While it is important to know what the usual kinds of student misconduct are, it is also true that each case will require its own analysis to determine the nature of the misconduct and who and what an appropriate response to it will involve. The mission of the university is to teach its students, and they may learn the most important lessons of all by grappling with matters of principle, moving from principle to practice, and developing in the process the habit of thoughtful reflection on issues of importance.

Diana K. Conklin, MA, is Associate Director of Residential Education and Norman W. Robinson, PhD, is Associate Dean of Student Affairs, both at Stanford University, Stanford, CA 94305.
The authors wish to thank Sally Cole, Judicial Affairs Officer at Stanford, for her editorial assistance.

[Haworth co-indexing entry note]: "Administrative Perspectives on Disruptive Student Conduct." Conklin, Diana K., and Norman W. Robinson. Co-published simultaneously in *Journal of College Student Psychotherapy* (The Haworth Press, Inc.) Vol. 8, No. 1/2, 1993, pp. 29-44: and: *Campus Violence: Kinds, Causes, and Cures* (ed: Leighton C. Whitaker and Jeffrey W. Pollard) The Haworth Press, Inc., 1993, pp. 29-44. Multiple copies of this article/chapter may be purchased from The Haworth Document Delivery Center [1-800-3-HAWORTH; 9:00 a.m. - 5:00 p.m. (EST)].

Increasing attention is being given to the issue of dealing with disruptive students in the nation's colleges and universities. Like most large and complex organizations, however, colleges and universities are not monolithic in responding to their issues and problems, including disruptive students. Many individuals, perspectives and often conflicting interests come into play when colleges attempt to deal with such students: deans, faculty, mental health professionals, medical staff, police and other security personnel and legal staff, to name a few. Given the number of individuals, offices and perspectives that often become involved, it is crucial that all have a reasonable level of understanding of what will happen and why. All of the players need to be familiar with what everyone else's role is. In addition, they should know not only the specifics of the institution's policy but, perhaps more importantly, the principles that inform that policy.

In order to assure that students are treated equitably and consistently in both the process and outcome of any university action in response to disruptive behavior, it is imperative that everyone be guided by the same principles and assumptions. Dealing with disruptive students is one area in which the left hand and right must know what the other is doing. Knowledge by all players of the roles, responsibilities and likely actions of the others will, to the greatest extent possible, avoid both the appearance and the fact of random, arbitrary, inconsistent and unprincipled university treatment of students who find themselves in violation of some standard or regulation. This article will present some issues and concerns that college and university administrators confront in this arena and suggest some possible responses.

The first step that any administration must take is to be certain that the definition of "disruptive" is articulated, disseminated and generally understood and accepted by the community. That may mean that as much attention is paid to the process by which the college develops its definition and response as is paid to the substance. As with other issues, it is essential that the institution's general policies and specific procedures for dealing with disruptive student conduct be direct reflections of the values, goals and prevailing ethos of the institution (Conklin, Robinson, and D'Andrea, 1987.)

In developing a workable definition of disruptive behavior, several elements should be considered, even if they are ultimately not included in the definition. Must the action of the individual or individuals be visible to others in the community? Must there be a victim? Must the action take place on the property of the institution? Did the behavior violate an institutional norm, standard or rule and/or was it a violation of the laws of the government? Were others in the community precluded from carrying out their business or were they merely inconvenienced? How does one distinguish between the two? Was the behavior physical or verbal? If verbal, what is the institution's policy regarding freedom of expression? Was the offending behavior part of an ongoing pattern or was it an isolated event? These and other factors must be considered as colleges and universities develop and refine their policies to deal with disruptive student conduct.

Amada (1986), citing the California Community College Chancellor's Ad Hoc Committee on Disruptive Student Affairs, provides an example of a definition of the disruptive student. Such a student is described as one who "verbally threatens or abuses college personnel, physically threatens or assaults others, willfully damages college property, misuses drugs or alcohol on college premises, habitually interferes with the learning environment by disruptive verbal or behavioral expressions, or persistently making inordinate demands for time and attention from faculty and staff" (Amada, 1986, p. 222).

This specific definition may not be appropriate or adequate for some institutions, but it does provide a useful example of the kinds of issues that a definition might address. It is a definition that focuses on behavior. It is also notable for what it does not contain–for example, there is no reference to the student's psychological condition or to underlying causes. Those issues may come into play later, however, when an institution is determining the appropriate response to the behavior of a disruptive student.

An institution's response to student conduct, then, depends on its own definition of disruptive conduct, and that very much depends on the nature and characteristics of each institution. It is likely, therefore, that different institutions will respond differently to identical circumstances and events because each institution has its own goals, values and guiding principles. The importance of each institution's own context cannot be overstated because that context is what determines if, why, how, when and who within the institution will respond to instances of student misconduct.

THE NATURE OF THE INSTITUTION

Not all colleges and universities are alike; not all have the same goals and objectives; not all interact with their students in the same way and quite obviously not all have the same definition of acceptable, or unacceptable, student conduct. Is the institution public or private? Is it residential or non-residential? Is it primarily for undergraduates or graduate students? Is it two-year or four-year? To what degree is its student body domestic or international? Is the institution religious or secular? Single sex or coeducational? Urban or rural? What is the degree of homogeneity or heterogeneity of the student body?

All of these factors influence how the institution defines and responds to disruptive student conduct. For example, public institutions may have different legal obligations from private schools. Constitutional guarantees of freedom of expression may be explicitly granted to students attending public institutions while private schools have much greater latitude in setting limits on expression. The current debate over how to deal with the issue of discriminatory harassment highlights this difference. Whether a private institution chooses to exercise its ability to prohibit certain kinds of speech will depend on many of the other factors that help shape and define an institution's character.

Institutional action may invite the attention and involvement of those outside. Public schools are subject to influences that private institutions may be able to ignore. Politics and the role of legislatures in appropriating funding are obvious examples, as is the role of other elected and appointed bodies. Private institutions are often shielded from such direct influences although other forces like parents, alumni and Boards of Trustees may have similar impacts.

Schools with a particular religious affiliation often find themselves limited by the tenets of that religion and its governing bodies. The beliefs and codes of a particular religion may determine the codes of conduct of affiliated colleges and universities. For example, on one campus it may be perfectly acceptable for students to disseminate information about such issues as birth control, condoms or abortion while on another campus, such behavior would be considered a breach of acceptable student conduct.

Likewise, the degree to which a school is comprised of domestic or foreign students and other dimensions of homogeneity and heterogeneity may influence how it deals with issues of student misconduct. The background of students, the kinds of communities in which they grew up, the amount of freedom that they had before enrolling at a particular school–these should influence that school's approach to matters of student conduct.

Finally, whether an institution is residential or not may affect the definition of what constitutes a violation of that school's code and how that violation is addressed. What one does in the privacy of one's home away from the campus might be of no interest whatsoever to the institution, whereas similar behavior in student housing could invite an institutional response.

THE NATURE OF BEHAVIOR CODES

The characteristics of an institution determine the code of conduct that it will have and therefore what constitutes an act of student misconduct. The specific route that a school chooses to follow in developing its code and the actual nature of that code can vary widely, but two basic approaches can be taken.

An institution can approach the matter of student conduct in a general, conceptual way or it can use a more specific, rule-oriented approach. Sally Cole, in a paper presented at the March 1992 Rutgers University Conference on Academic Integrity, makes a compelling case, based on educational grounds, for codes of conduct that are short, general statements as opposed to those that consist of lengthy lists of specifically prohibited behaviors. The nature of colleges and universities as educational institutions should, of necessity, argue for conduct codes that require students to think about their behavior and the potential consequences. What does it mean to be a member of an educational community in general? What does it mean to be a member of a particular college? What is expected of each student? How does individual or group behavior affect that community? What consequences accrue to those who violate the norms of that community?

These and other questions are more likely to be considered by students if they are presented directly as issues that require thought and discussion. A clearly delineated set of specific rules, a list of do's and don'ts, is much less likely to generate that kind of contemplation. In fact, when students are confronted with such lists, they very often spend inordinate amounts of time devising ways around the rules rather than thinking about their behavior and its effect on themselves and others.

The above discussion does not mean that there should be no specific rules, regulations and guidelines. Rather it is intended to convey the belief that campus conduct codes should be developed in ways that emphasize the institution's educational mission and its goal of developing individuals who will be thoughtful, responsible members of society. The approach that a college or university takes in developing student conduct codes, and where a particular school's code falls on the continuum from general to specific, will depend in large measure on the particular nature and mission of that institution.

Whatever the approach, however, what is absolutely essential is that there be wide-spread discussion among all members of the community, and particularly among new members, about what is acceptable and unacceptable conduct.

Educational institutions have a compelling interest in making sure that all students (and especially new students) have an opportunity to learn about and discuss the prevailing norms of acceptable and unacceptable student conduct. In keeping with the goals of every educational institution, the aim of such an exercise is to promote thought and learning as well as to create the kind of community that the institution seeks and to reduce (or eliminate) instances of student misconduct. Another reason for wide-spread promulgation and discussion is simple fairness. If students are expected to conform to certain standards and are subject to sanction if they do not, institutions must make reasonable efforts to assure that knowledge and understanding are widespread in the campus community. Finally, widespread knowledge and understanding of

the institution's code of conduct and the likely responses to violations will help assure that all students are treated equitably and in
accord with well thought-out and developed procedures.

Regardless of the nature of the institution and its code of conduct,
all institutions experience violations of that code. The definition of
disruptive student conduct and the appropriate institutional response
are as much a reflection of the nature and characteristics of the
institution as is the code itself.

ASPECTS OF THE PROBLEM

Whatever one's role in responding to disruptive student conduct,
it is important to have some notion of the usual categories into
which such behavior falls and the usual responses that it evokes.
However, it is also true that every instance will require its own
thoughtful analysis to determine who should respond, how, and
with what array of possible sanctions. Aspects of each case that
ought to be considered include means of expression, location,
which and whose rules were violated, nature (content) of the act,
impact, scope, and contributing elements. Depending on the institution, there may be additional aspects to consider as well.

Means of expression. Was the act verbal–that is, written or oral–
or physical? In light of First Amendment guarantees, the institution
is likely to allow considerably greater latitude for verbal expression,
however execrable, than for acts of physical violence. If the act
combined elements of both, then one should promptly sort through
the event and categorize its various parts. Did the verbal elements of
the encounter constitute "fighting words" as that term is used in
constitutional law? If so, does that fact constitute an exoneration or
a mitigating circumstance, suggesting a reduced penalty? Where
does the institution stand on physical violence against property or
people? At one university, for example, the president has gone on
record indicating that physical violence against a fellow student
results in a minimum of a one-quarter suspension. Elsewhere, it
may result in anything from a warning to expulsion.

Location. Does it matter where the incident occurred? Should a
distinction be made between what a student does in a classroom and
what he does in his dormitory? Between what he does in the gymna-

sium and what he does at a downtown pub? Would the university intervene if his misconduct occurred with a group of other students in a remote campground owned and operated by the university? What if the campground were owned by an entity other than the university? And what about a solitary act of misconduct in a remote and unpopulated part of campus? For example, an institution with undeveloped land as part of its campus might treat solitary drunk driving out in the woods differently from the same behavior in the middle of fraternity row on a Saturday night.

Whose rules were broken? Did the student violate university policy, state or federal law, or some combination? If she violated the law, should the university be involved in punishing her? Conversely, if she violated only university policy, should law enforcement agents be involved? If the institution's rules require obedience to the law, then presumably the institution would respond to a legal infraction since that would also constitute a violation of university policy. Some universities take this approach, and others choose to make a separation, wherever possible, between institutional policy and the law, leaving law enforcement to police and the courts. These schools do not act as law enforcers, nor do they try to shield students from the consequences of their own unlawful behavior. Rather, they take as their focus the education of students, defined to include student conduct issues related to the university but not necessarily beyond its delimited mission and boundaries.

On the other hand, if the police are university employees, such separation becomes more difficult. There are likely to be occasions when the role of the administration and the role of the police will be to some degree in conflict. For example, the dean may wish to respond to a given situation with leniency while the police may have no choice but to respond with more severity, under the terms of the law. If both sides are seen as acting as agents of the same entity–the university–confusion and conflict may ensue. For example, a senior with a stellar academic and community service record, upon being betrayed by a long-time friend, suddenly and uncharacteristically breaks several windows in his house. The police respond to a call by arresting the student for vandalism and disorderly conduct–the law is the law. The dean, on the other hand, may respond quite differently–and more informally. It is helpful to make clear to students and others that while police work with and sometimes for the university, they are bound by the law to enforce the law.

Nature of the act. How simple or complex was the act? For example, did it involve apparent racist or anti-homosexual sentiments, or was it a punch in the nose by someone who had had too much to drink? How well-matched were the participants in a fight–was it David and Goliath, or Schwartzenegger and Van Damme? Was the act impulsive or premeditated–did the drunk student simply decide suddenly to throw a chair through a window, or did he go looking for her ex-boyfriend in order to shatter that former lover's window? Was hanging a confederate flag outside his dorm room an act of aggression against other residents, or was student Zeb Stuart VI merely displaying an important symbol of his cultural heritage?

Impact. What was the potential for harm as compared to the harm actually done? What risk did the act present to its perpetrator? To others? For example, driving under the influence of alcohol, at high speed, with a car full of friends, presents a very high risk of injury or death. An intoxicated walk around campus presents a much lower risk. To what extent was the risk realized? Did the sofa that was hurled off the roof actually hit someone? What psychological harm is done to the victim of an acquaintance rape? What are the effects when an American Indian student from a reservation is subjected to harassment because of her choice of a boyfriend? What is the effect on other students in a residence when one of them sabotages the house computer cluster?

It is often difficult, if not impossible, to determine with any kind of confidence just what impact an action has had on others. It is especially challenging when racial, sexual, ethnic, and cultural differences are taken into consideration. For example, it is not always possible to determine from the face of a victim how she is being affected by an act of hostility, especially if she comes from a culture that values stoicism and privacy. No matter how difficult to assess, though, impact is important, and ought to be raised in considering how best to respond to disruptive student conduct.

Scope. A fight between roommates is different from an incident that plunges the whole campus into an uproar. For example, at one university, two drunken freshmen defaced a dorm poster of Beethoven, creating from it a caricature of a black man and hanging it adjacent to the door of a black resident. Their action was in response to an informal house debate over Beethoven's race. The dorm in which this happened was the African-American theme residence, and the reaction to the students' "joke" was widespread shock, outrage and grief. While the ensuing campus-wide uproar gave rise to much fruitful and educational reflection and discussion, those benefits were purchased at a high price in terms of emotional well-being and racial harmony. Friendships were sorely tried and in some cases ended, students' academic work suffered from weeks of debate and turmoil, and the life of an ordinarily unified and congenial student residence was changed, for the worse, for the rest of the year. Although issues of First Amendment rights prevented disciplinary action in this case, the fact remained that the actions of the two freshmen adversely affected hundreds of their fellow undergraduates and themselves for the rest of the school year. What occurred was a clear case of conflicting rights–the right of students to express themselves using symbolic speech (a caricature) and the right of students to enjoy their home free of harassment and fear.

Contributing elements. In deciding on a course of action in response to student misconduct, it is important to identify, in addition to the foregoing aspects, any other factors that may have significantly influenced the student's behavior. Perhaps the most common contributor to conduct that gets students into trouble is the misuse of alcohol or other drugs, alcohol being by far the drug of choice for college-aged people. Misuse of alcohol presents an important teaching opportunity, especially when the student reveals that he somehow expects the fact of intoxication to mitigate any punishment. On the contrary, students need to be helped to understand that alcohol acts to diminish their rationality, making them more difficult to reason with and more dangerous to themselves and others; consequently, the fact of drunkenness is an aggravating–not mitigating– circumstance when penalties are considered. A sober miscreant might come to his senses or be dissuaded by others; the drunken student willfully renders himself beyond reach.

Provocation and "fair fight" questions should also be taken into consideration. Was the student who punched another student in the nose goaded beyond forbearance, or did he simply walk up and land the punch for no apparent reason? Was one combatant a muscular athlete and the other a little guy? Was either of them armed with more than his own fists? In assessing culpability, elements such as these may not be spelled out in the judicial procedures, but those who hear the cases and weigh penalties usually take them into consideration. While provocation does not justify or excuse violence, it still matters.

Perhaps the most difficult element to weigh when a student's conduct has gotten her into trouble is psychological disturbance. There is a continuum: at one end is a student in perfect control of, and responsible for, her behavior and at the other end is a student not accountable or in control, by reason of serious mental disorder. The assessment belongs to mental health professionals, of course, but administrators in charge of student discipline must also grapple with the question in determining appropriate responses to unacceptable behavior.

Finally, a whole array of other possible influences on students' behavior should be considered: a recent death in the family; the breakup of an important relationship; academic failure; and other significant stressors. Because it would be impossible to create a comprehensive checklist of such considerations, it is wise to include in any conversation with a student accused of misconduct a general and open question about what has been going on in her life.

RESPONSES

Determining with as much precision as possible the problem characteristics described above will go a long way toward revealing who should be involved in responding, and what the range of possible outcomes ought to be. For example, a troublesome yet inherently simple roommate dispute need not evoke the full weight of formal institutional action. And conversely, a group fight resulting in serious injuries should not be handled only locally and informally. It could be argued that conduct that strikes at the most important values of the institution, whatever they may be, requires the highest-level and most formal institutional response. These questions, then, must be answered in preparing to respond to disruptive student conduct: who should respond, how, and with what possible sanctions?

Who should respond–the possible players. In general, it is wise to keep involved those who are closest to the misconduct. For example, if a student has disrupted a class, then the faculty member ought to be encouraged to remain involved, or at least informed, for the duration of the subsequent responses. If a student has caused upheaval in his dormitory, disrupting and distressing his fellow residents, then those students should be involved, to the extent possible, in what follows. It can be argued that as victims, these people have a right to know what consequences accrue to the student's misconduct. There is also educational value in letting members of the community know that unacceptable behavior leads to sanctions. Balancing the right to know against the individual's legal and perhaps institutional right to privacy is challenging, but victims' rights must not be overlooked in favor of granting total privacy to the perpetrator.

Determining the relative public versus private nature of the act will help in balancing the rights of victims and offenders. If the incident was quite public–for example, occurring in the main lounge of a busy dormitory shortly before dinner–then the perpetrator can hardly expect to "unring the bell" and have the event treated as a private matter. If, on the other hand, the incident was quite private, she has the right to expect that others will be informed about her situation only according to a narrowly defined need to know. However, even in responding to private misconduct, it is important to convey to the public the consequences that attach to this kind of behavior, especially if it can be done in a way that protects the identities of those involved. For example, for one roommate to destroy another's research computer disks is a private act, but the general consequences ought to be made known to the campus community.

On-campus people who may respond alone or in various combinations to student misconduct include the following:

- Students–the aggrieved party or victim; the perpetrator's own residence group; the students who live in the residence where the incident occurred; the perpetrator's fraternity, sorority, or other important social group; members of a local or University-wide judicial committee; student reporters for the campus paper.
- Faculty–the professor in whose classroom the incident transpired, the department chairperson, the student's House Fel-

low, the student's academic advisor, members of a local or university-wide judicial committee.

- Administration–residence staff of the involved houses, security staff/police, the dean, the legal office, the president.
- Mental Health Staff–the student's own therapist, consultants to the institution.
- Campus Chaplain–the student's own minister, the dean of the chapel or one of her assistants.

The question of the student's right to privacy and the confidential nature of some professional relationships will arise, especially with mental health staff and the chaplain. For example, the student's own therapist, in order to protect the therapist-client relationship, may refuse to be a party to any disciplinary action. The chaplain may choose to do the same. However, both people can be extremely helpful in the overall response to the student's misconduct, in their own private ways and through their own special relationships with the student. No student, however dastardly his conduct, ought to endure the disciplinary process alone and friendless. In fact, if he has no one to go through it with him, the institution ought to provide him with someone who will serve as a steadfast, supportive resource. It is especially in this way that therapists and chaplains can often be helpful in cases of student misconduct.

Students involved in disciplinary action against other students may need to be educated about the institution's values, the importance of ethical and compassionate treatment of people in trouble, confidentiality, the presumption of innocence, and the standard of proof required by the judicial process to find someone guilty. As difficult as it can be for thoughtful and caring people to sit in judgment of others, it is also an extremely valuable learning experience for everyone concerned. Student adjudicators often emerge from the experience humbled and sensitive to the complexities of human motivation and behavior. Indeed, non-students involved in a disciplinary process may also need educating before they enter their first experience of helping to decide another's fate.

Off-campus people who may respond to student misconduct alone or in various combinations (with each other and/or with members of the institution) include the following: police; the courts;

health professionals, including psychologists or other therapists; community crisis centers; family members; neighbors and other members of the community; and alumni.

The extent to which the university will initiate contact or consent to work with any of these extra-institutional entities will depend upon the university's ethos–the values that should undergird its policies and procedures. For example, some schools work closely with parents when a student has gotten into trouble. Others prefer to work exclusively with the student himself, believing that the decision to involve or not to involve his parents belongs to him. (This derives from a related belief that students are adults and as such, are responsible for accepting and coping with the consequences of their own conduct.) On any campus, of course, the student is free to involve his parents himself, and may know best whether that involvement would be helpful or not.

Kinds of responses and possible sanctions. To a large extent, deciding who responds will help determine the kind of response that is made. Some people may be more immediately concerned with punishment while others focus on education or rehabilitation. In any case, the institution should, to the extent possible, ensure that the student involved learns as much as possible from the experience. This may be facilitated by sensitizing all who will be working with the student to the need to help him reflect upon and learn from his mistakes.

Within the university, response to misconduct may be local–that is, as close as possible to the scene of the problem. For example, a residence may have its own judicial board before which come students accused of playing their stereos too loudly, damaging or misappropriating dorm furniture, or just being poor citizens of the residence community. A faculty member with a student who is disruptive in class is likely to try local remedies first, whether through attempts at rational discourse, moral suasion or threats of calling outside agents to respond to the student's behavior. Local responses usually tend to be relatively informal. They may come from the student's roommates, hall mates, friends, residence staff, or the residence judicial board, which may include the faculty resident or residence director. Penalties may range from simple–yet often very effective–private censure to more public confrontation, work or monetary fines, suspension of residence privileges, suspension from the residence for a specified time, to permanent eviction from the residence. Depending on the specific circumstances and the guiding university policy, eviction may be a decision that fellow students are empowered to make, as in the case of a fraternity or sorority house, or it may require the action of a university representative.

It is often appropriate to handle local misconduct locally. Exceptions are likely to include physical violence; racist, sexist, or anti-homosexual conduct; sexual harassment or assault, and the like. In short, if the conduct is not egregious and if it does not strike at the core of the institution's values, then it is probably best handled by those closest to the student and his behavior. There is powerful precedent for the concept of a trial by one's peers.

If the local resource people are not an appropriate adjudicator, then others may be chosen: the student's inter-fraternity or panhellenic officers or another pertinent student group, medical/counseling staff if that is seen as a likely effective avenue of response, administrative action by the dean, or full and formal university judicial action. It will often be the case in more serious situations that the most effective handling requires a combination of response agents.

A word of caution is in order about mandated psychological counseling as part of a student's penalty for misconduct. Although this practice is still common in the court system and at some universities, its efficacy is in serious question. Many argue that mandated counseling is doomed from its inception. The student is present under duress, is likely to view his therapist as just another agent of the university's punishment, and is unlikely to be in a frame of mind to speak openly about his personal problems. Even suggestions that a student voluntarily seek counseling should be made carefully and with understanding that effective therapy does not involve coercion. (See also chapter 5 by Gerald Amada.)

Institutional-level response is usually significantly more formal and, potentially, at least, more serious in terms of the student's standing at the university and its impact on his future endeavors. The response may be mild or severe, but it involves high stakes, in that consequences can extend as far as expulsion from the university. A typical range of sanctions might include private censure–oral, or written which is made part of the student's record–public censure (for a public act), work or monetary fines, suspension of privileges (e.g., to serve as a Resident Assistant or to have a car on campus), removal from a particular residence or loss of campus housing privileges, suspension for a limited time or indefinitely, and expulsion.

Outside the university, the student, because of her behavior, may face arrest and subsequent criminal court action; civil action by her victim(s); mandated psychological counseling; and an array of responses from her family, friends, church and community. For one ill-begotten act, the student may find herself in trouble with a multitude of individuals and organizations.

A great many different individuals and agencies may be involved in responding to a wide variety of student misconduct. If the responses are to be equitable and consistent, and if students are to learn coherent lessons from their experiences, it is important for everyone involved to understand the guiding principles behind the university's code of student conduct and how its provisions are enforced.

REFERENCES

Amada, G. (1986) Dealing with the disruptive college student: some theoretical and practical considerations. *Journal of American College Health*, 34, 5, 221-225.

Cole, S. (1992) Issues and trends in student judicial affairs for the nineties. Speech delivered at the Conference on Academic Integrity, Rutgers University, March 1992.

Conklin, D., Robinson, N., & D'Andrea, D. (1987) The parent-student-university relationship: Issues and principles. *Journal of College Student Psychotherapy*, 2, 1/2, 5-16. Also published as chapter 1 in L. Whitaker (Ed.) (1987) *Parental concerns in college student mental health*. New York: The Haworth Press, Inc.

Chapter 3

Violence Is Golden:
Commercially Motivated Training
in Impulsive Cognitive Style
and Mindless Violence

Leighton C. Whitaker

SUMMARY. Campus violence is strongly determined by our increasingly violent American culture. National increases in violent crime, weapon carrying, drug dependency, eating disorders, and youth suicide rates in recent decades are both reflected by and promoted by commercial interests. Addiction cultivation, whether to cigarettes, alcohol or other drugs, diets, or violence per se is extremely profitable for its purveyors. The large and small screens, magazines and various forms of advertising sell ever more ways to be violent toward oneself and others.

Colleges and universities show generally lower rates of violence than the surrounding culture, but they are inevitably heirs to the culture of violence, especially as it has trained youth both to victimize and to be victimized. Children and adolescents are being subjected to depictions of violence at record rates. Thus colleges and universities must do more to deconstruct and counter the training for violence. Our academic institutions can help by emphasizing their greatest contribution: the cultivation of critical thinking which can be an antidote to the mindless violence promoted by addiction pushers.

Leighton C. Whitaker, PhD, is Director of Psychological Services for Swarthmore College, 500 College Avenue, Swarthmore, PA 19081.

[Haworth co-indexing entry note]: "Violence Is Golden: Commercially Motivated Training in Impulsive Cognitive Style and Mindless Violence." Whitaker, Leighton C. Co-published simultaneously in *Journal of College Student Psychotherapy* (The Haworth Press, Inc.) Vol. 8, No. 1/2, 1993, pp. 45-69: and: *Campus Violence: Kinds, Causes, and Cures* (ed: Leighton C. Whitaker and Jeffrey W. Pollard) The Haworth Press, Inc., 1993, pp. 45-69. Multiple copies of this article/chapter may be purchased from The Haworth Document Delivery Center [1-800-3-HAWORTH; 9:00 a.m. - 5:00 p.m. (EST)].

45

This chapter addresses the problem of destructive behavior on campuses as a reflection of its larger cultural context, with emphasis on commercial culture. The increase in campus violence in recent years is parallel to and a function of the increase in violence in our culture at large. The United States now leads the industrialized nations of the world in murder rates and kindred sorts of externalized violence as well as many kinds of internalized violence including eating disorders and drug dependencies. One of the powerful determiners of these increases is commercially motivated exploitation of violence sensationalism which keeps growing in media presentations including television, movies, and various forms of advertising. Given modern advances in commercial communication technology which gives it ever growing power, the profitability of violence exploitation is also growing. Thus our youth from infancy on up are now subjected to and trained in more violent behavior than ever before.

To reconstruct campus community cultures, we must look at the campus community in terms of the problematic influences in the larger culture that we may otherwise unwittingly accept and perpetuate on our campuses. We can counter and nullify these influences, which otherwise predispose us to resort quickly to both internal and external forms of violence, by cultivating critical thinking, long the hallmark of liberal education, and apply critical thinking to evaluating our society and its influence on us. We can then negate both the explicit and implicit approval we give to those–often commercially motivated–enterprises that exert destructive influences. In essence, we must first deconstruct negative culture in order to construct better campus environments.

The thesis of this chapter is that our culture trains us in many ways, from infancy, to be violent both toward ourselves and others and that the foundation of both kinds of violence is our absorbing and internalizing the violence around us. Numerous studies (Goleman, 1992) are substantiating intuitive hunches that violence in the atmosphere even weakens peoples' immune systems.

Though biological proclivities may have a role in producing violent behavior, perhaps especially in terms of male hormonal make-up, differences between countries and cultural changes over generations in violence proclivities are so great that, obviously, we are not mainly biologically impelled to be violent either toward ourselves or others. For example, "The risk of being murdered in the United States is 7 to 10 times that in most European countries" (Lore and Schultz, 1993, p. 17). And Americans themselves are far more violent today than they were just four decades ago.

THE UNITED STATES AS A CULTURE OF VIOLENCE

Training to be violent is so embedded in our culture as to be almost taken for granted: the supposed heroism and glory of war, the easy proliferation of guns, the thrill of murder, the pervasiveness of scapegoating and bigotry, and the "inevitability" of rape, suicide, drug dependency, and eating disorders. All of these forms of violence, and often our conceptualization of them, involve a mindlessness that omits genuine thinking and promotes a blind, unwitting conformism. It may appear that not all of the phenomena just listed should appear in the category of violence behaviors but a casual, unquestioning attitude toward violence is integral to all forms of violence, whether externally or internally directed. Specifically, allowing oneself to be subjected to violence, however culturally acceptable the medium, is training simultaneously to accept violence from others toward the self, to perpetrate violence toward oneself, and to perpetrate violence toward others. For example, "Although intense aggression toward others and suicide are often considered to represent very different problems, there is a surprisingly strong relationship between the two; violence-prone and assaultive adolescents are at much greater risk for suicidal behaviors" (Lore and Schultz, 1993, p. 16).

On August 4, 1992 a national television network broadcasted interviews with several Los Angeles teen gang members illustrating the inherent togetherness of externally directed violence and internally directed violence, the latter manifested in the extreme constriction of thought that is mindlessness, and the passive acceptance of the "inevitability" of violence both toward oneself and others. Without exception, the youths were all simply resigned to death. They all said that "it" (the gang killings) had always gone on, that "that's just the way it is." No one could imagine an alternative to mindless violence. Though this is an extreme case, in which the constricting circumstances of life in a ghetto promote abject helplessness to prevent violence either against others or oneself, it illustrates a general tendency in our culture to become readily resigned to violence. (In this case, fortunately, some solutions are being sought as youths have been helped to start legitimate businesses and to take genuine pride in themselves.)

GUNS AND GREED

Movies and network television in the United States have escalated to ever greater amounts of violence programming with special emphasis on guns and the development of guns into weapons of mass destruction. Significantly, in the decade from 1979 through 1989, the homicide death rate for youths ages 15 through 19 increased 61%. Nationally, "The number of firearms has nearly quadrupled over 40 years–from 54 million in 1950 to 104 million in 1970 to 160 million in 1980 to 200 million now" (Hollman and McCoy, 1992, p. E1) To illustrate the importance of this increase: "In 1988 nearly two-thirds (61%) of homicide victims were killed with a firearm, 75% of these with a handgun" and the 54% rise in homicide among black males (ages 15-24) from 1985 to 1988 is 99% due to firearms (Centers for Disease Control May 22, 1992, p. 1). And just as gun-implemented homicides have increased with gun availability and gun glamour, gun-implemented suicide rates have increased. The next generation of college students is especially affected. According to the Centers of Disease Control, in 1988 one in twelve high school students has already attempted suicide and one in four has carried a weapon (Centers for Disease Control, October 16, 1992).

In the United States now there are approximately four guns for every five people, including children. By contrast, in Canada where guns are less available, the homicide handgun rate was less than 15% of the United States rate in 1990 (Hollman and McCoy, 1992). Or compare the U.S. with Japan which has about as many firearm murders in one year as New York City often has on a single weekend (Larson, 1993). Or, looked at another way, consider that in 1991 for example, "69 percent of the 177 New York City workers who died of injuries sustained on the job were victims of homicide"

(*New York Times*, 1993, p. B1). The relative lack of gun availability *thus far* on college campuses probably helps to account not only for their lower rate of homicides but also for the 50% lower rate of suicide among college students compared to their non-college peers (Schwartz, 1990; Schwartz and Whitaker, 1990). But college-age youths have become much more vulnerable. For example, "In 1987 America's civilian guns were used to murder 3,187 young men aged fifteen to twenty-four, accounting for three-fourths of the annual homicide rate of 21.9 per 100,000 people" (Larson, 1993, p. 50).

Violence promotion means big bucks for the promoters. Who are they? They include the movie and television industries, magazine and book publishers, and the manufacturers, distributors and sellers of lethal weapons, all working in close harmony. Gun publicity affords a good example of how they work together. Most obviously, America's macho heroes promote violence, especially among young males and especially since they combine hero images with violence in a way that justifies violence as virtue. John Wayne, Clint Eastwood, Sylvester Stallone all made their fortunes by glorifying their weapons and the murders they committed on screen. Only recently has Clint Eastwood, with his movie "Unforgiven," decided that "Demythologizing 'people who portray violent behavior and indulge in violent behavior is an important item now'" (Spillman, 1993, p. 3D).

As of this writing, a huge 75 foot blow up balloon figure in New York City shows Arnold Schwarzenegger with an automatic weapon in one hand and dynamite in the other. The twin towers of the World Trade Center have been massively bombed with dynamite a few days ago, however. So the City of New York–eager for the movie industry money–has made a small concession: the dynamite in Mr. Schwarzenegger's left hand is being replaced with a badge (thus giving his gun the blessing of the law). The balloon straddles the Armed Forces Recruiting Center in Times Square. Columbia Pictures' Mark Canton explains "We want to make a strong statement about supporting the right people at this time. After all, Arnold's character is a hero" (Hevesi, 1993, p. B3). The government support of this advertising of the movie "Last Action Hero" by both the U.S. military and New York City will directly inconvenience about 12,000 drivers per day for seven days, but city officials believe the filming is financially worth the inconvenience. The clear lesson here is that violence is not only acceptable but it is enormously desirable if it makes big bucks. In this case, the movie offers a lame excuse. It is called a spoof on gun violence films. Perhaps its subtitle ought to be "A Gun is Fun." The message is always the same: violence is good entertainment.

Also as of this writing, the Waco, Texas standoff continues many deaths later as federal law enforcement officers, according to one official, were outgunned by a heavily armed religious sect in the 77-acre compound where the followers of David Koresh remain holed up. This is the state–Texas–whose residents own 68 million guns, an average of four guns per person, where there are no gun registration laws, and in which a person can become a gun dealer for $30. Not so surprisingly, Texas is the only state in which more people were shot to death in 1991 (3,692) than were killed in car crashes (3,180) and Houston ranks as the nation's capital for gun dealers while San Antonio ranks second in the nation (Potok, 1993, p. 3A).

Hollywood, however, is pushing its own state of California toward the gun morbidity award. Michael Douglas in the movie "Falling Down" portrays a middle-aged, seemingly acceptable guy who takes a massively lethal stroll through Los Angeles with his big gun. "Falling Down" quickly became the nation's No. 1 box-office hit (Green, 1993, p. 5D).

How do we know that such gun publicity spurs gun sales and murders? We know that not only violence movies promote violence behaviors but that even guns used in actual publicized grisly crimes gain popularity thereby.

> After the assassination of President John F. Kennedy, sales of the otherwise undistinguished Mannlicher-Carcano rifle used by Lee Harvey Oswald soared. Even the murder of schoolchildren can increase sales. After Patrick Edward Purdy opened fire on a school yard in Stockton, California, with an AK-47, sales of the gun and its knock-offs boomed. Prices quadrupled, to $1,500. Guns Unlimited felt the surge in demand. "I didn't sell an AK until Stockton in California; then everybody wanted one," James Dick said in a deposition (Larson, 1993, p. 72).

Our movies and TV shows do far more damage than simply

enhancing the appeal of exotic weapons, however. They teach a uniquely American lesson: When a real man has a problem, he gets his gun. He slaps in a clip, he squints grimly into the hot noon sun, and then he does what he's gotta do. (Larson, 1993, p. 74)

Manufacturers, distributors and sellers of guns have been supported most liberally by money interests, including through the lobbying of legislators. Erik Larson (1993) has documented this collusion from his standpoint, that of a gun dealer. In showing how a gun became a murder weapon, he "provides a clear example of the culture of nonresponsibility prevailing in America's firearms industry; it is but one example of how their commercial ethos governed the gun's progress from conception to its use as a murder weapon in a Virginia Beach classroom" (Larson, 1993, p. 50). The gun, the Cobray M-11/9 was advertised by its producer as "The gun that made the 80s roar."

INSTITUTIONAL TRAINING IN MINDLESS VIOLENCE

Our own sponsored campus activities often help train students to be violent. Miriam Miedzian (1991) illustrates the inherent togetherness of mindlessness, internalized violence and externalized violence in the common training to become a violent football player, as distinct from just learning how to be courageous and to withstand pain.

. . . when a high school football player is shot up with novocaine in order to play, when he plays with injuries that if aggravated could lead to permanent damage, he is learning much more than to withstand pain. *He is learning to sacrifice his body unnecessarily and to hide all feelings of fear and vulnerability, however warranted they may be. He is also being taught to sacrifice the bodies of others.* For if he is willing to risk serious injury to himself, then why shouldn't he be willing to risk injuring others seriously? If he is not allowed to feel sympathy for himself when he is injured or justifiably frightened, why should he feel empathy for anyone else? (Miedzian, 1991, p. 201)

Images of athletic achievement, as well as health, are especially likely to be paired with commercial advertising of debilitating products. The 1992 Olympics television coverage subjected viewers dozens of times to linkages of alcohol with Olympic caliber athletic achievements. "Swimmers" in beer commercials swam powerfully to reach beer, a "discus thrower" threw a discus that became a beer bottle cap, and "the alcohol drink of the future" was glorified, though it is merely the kind of alcohol spritzer already popular with 8th graders. And sentimental ads appeared featuring the most popular singers who declared the sacred bonding of all nations of the world when linked by drinking a certain caffeinated soft drink. Similarly, we are targeted by Virginia Slims cigarettes which sponsors and advertises at women's tennis tournaments (thus managing to get around the ban on television cigarette advertising). Why shouldn't these Virginia Slims tournament backdrops feature in equally large print "Tobacco is the single biggest cause of premature adult death throughout the world" and "Smoking-related deaths of women are predicted to double in 30 years" (Nullis, 1992). Heinekin produced the "official beer" of the U.S. Open tennis tournament. Why not add to their ads: "Alcohol is the number 1 cause of premature death in the 16 to 34 year age range" (Koop, 1991).

The connotation of the ads' oxymoronic pairings is that smoking cigarettes or drinking alcohol or caffeine (combined with refined sugar or a possibly damaging sugar substitute) causes positive personal attributes, just the opposite of the real consequences: impairment of health and strength, damaged teeth and gums, prematurely aged skin, pregnancy damage ad infinitum. Nor do deeply meaningful personal relationships occur as a consequence of imbibing these substances.

Many institutionalized forms of training for sports competition involve learning to be self-destructive as a necessary condition for competitive activity which itself may damage any and all players both physically and psychologically. James Michener (1976) has written about the often inherent connection between competition and violence when coaches teach it that way. He quotes the fabled Vince Lombardi: "Football isn't a contact sport, its a collision sport. Dancing is a contact sport." "To play this game you must have fire in you, and there's nothing that stokes fire like hate" (Michener, 1976, p. 420). Meanwhile, Lombardi extolled religion, the player's family, and the Green Bay Packers as the highest priorities in that order, thus injecting a seeming (but contradictory) alliance between hatred and violence on the one hand and religion and the family on the other. Author David Looney wisely rebutted Lombardi: "He admitted that competition appeared to be a natural component of human life, but argued that it was best when one competed against oneself rather than against another human being whom one wished to destroy" (Michener, 1976, p. 422). Of course, popular culture has often paired religion with wars, moralizing away the contradiction by declaring "holy wars" or, at the very least, a catchall appeal to "patriotism" and the flag. But "holy wars," "ethnic cleansing," and "the ends justify the means" are more oxymoronic than wise.

Such mindlessness is not a natural condition; it has to be learned through violent enforcement because all children, otherwise, are naturally endlessly curious until they are forced to stop being curious and to give up their capacity to be imaginative, thoughtful and creative. The Los Angeles gang members had become so intimidated by their own institutionalized violence (and the prejudice that creates ghettos) as to resign themselves to mindlessness and its inevitable associate, mindless violence. They no longer had the freedom or security, externally or internally, to be thinking persons. Similarly, soldiers and football players are often coercively taught mindless violence.

IMPULSIVE COGNITIVE STYLE
AND THE COMMERCIAL VIOLENCE CURRICULUM

A recent television beer commercial presents an interpersonal dilemma between a young man and a young woman. Before there is any time to think about the dilemma as such, or the cause of the dilemma, or any way it can be resolved, a voice says "Why ask why?" whereupon the dilemma is dissolved immediately by the two parties drinking beer. The commercial thereby denies the dilemma as such, short-circuits the critical thinking that would be needed to understand and resolve it, and provides an immediate means of escape in the form of the temporarily anxiety-reducing drug, alcohol, which is associated with the majority of violent behaviors. So both the opportunity and the motivation to solve a problem are quickly sacrificed in favor of impulsively ingesting a mind-altering, weakening drug which short-circuits thinking and facilitates violence. Naturally, it is youth who are thus targeted by adults for profit.

What is most often recommended by purveyors of unhealthy substances is that one not really think at all but simply be suggestible and wish for consequences that are the opposite of the realistic consequences. Such advertising campaigns involve vast budget enterprises to implement the necessarily tricky business of convincing people of gross falsehoods. The size of the advertising budget is usually inversely proportional to the healthfulness of the product advertised. For example, cigarette advertisers spent approximately four billion dollars in 1990 pairing–in visual images–cigarette smoking and young people with vibrant health, glistening white teeth, perfect skin, exemplary good looks, and superb social skills (The Advocacy Institute, 1992). The alcohol industry spends two billion dollars per year on advertising (National Council on Alcoholism and Drug Dependency, 1992). The males in both nicotine and alcohol ads are handsome and strong and the females are beautiful. But cigarettes are the number 1 cause of premature death in the world and alcohol is number 2, befitting the sizes of their advertising budgets. Alcohol, however, is not only the number 1 cause of premature death in the 16 to 34 year age group (Koop, 1991), but college grades are strongly inversely correlated with the amount of alcohol drunk per week (Presley & Meilman, 1992).

Selling substances that demand "an acquired taste," such as nicotine or alcohol, requires cultivating the individual's tendency to self-destructiveness together with what Shapiro (1965) labeled impulsive cognitive style. Passivity is a basic ingredient of impulsive cognitive style though, superficially, this style may impress one more with its activity; but it is a kind of passively acquiesced-in activity that one is drawn into more than one deliberately chooses and "owns." Its passive quality correlates with abnegation of personal responsibility both for initiating the action and being accountable for consequences. Impulsive cognitive style excludes thinking about consequences and deliberately making decisions. In contrast, thinking is an active process which Webster's Third New International Dictionary (1986) defines as "the *action* of using one's mind to produce thoughts" (italics mine).

Thus impulsive cognitive style represents the opposite of the responsible educational process which teaches the entire cognitive sequence that deserves the name "thinking," the active, critical process enabling both inhibiting unwarranted actions and taking *deliberate, actively wished for actions.* As Shapiro notes, impulsive cognitive style is captured in the doers non-explanation: "I just *did* it–I don't know why" (Shapiro, p. 135). In this style, thinking per se is short-circuited. The person really wasn't thinking. The common motto in impulsive cognitive style is simply accepting the impulse to "Just do it!" In other words, "Don't think: *just* act!" The denial of the need to think is conveyed by the beer ad: "Why ask why?"

MINDLESS VIOLENCE GOES TO COLLEGE

The phenomenon of increasingly violent and disrespectful behavior in and around college and university campuses is inextricably related to the larger culture which has become more accepting of violence in recent decades. Students come to campuses not only from influential family settings but from institutionally sanctioned programming of a commercial sort. Thus the new student is not a tabula rasa merely to be written upon by the civilizing influence of the formal education curriculum. Nor can counselors and psychotherapists prevent the psychological problems that students bring with them, including those featuring destructive behavior. These problems inevitably emerge on campuses. Rather, each entering student has already been written upon, sometimes seemingly indelibly, both by her or his family (or the lack of it) *and* an increasingly pervasive and influential popular culture effected by an exponentially growing communications technology. College educators and psychotherapists cannot prevent what has already been done but must help students to learn ways to undo destructive influences and their internalizations and to counter further destructive influences. We cannot ignore past and present influences and simply begin our work on top of them; we must deconstruct them and then help ourselves and students to learn different orientations.

In most young lives, what we call education, exemplified by formal schooling, is greatly outweighed by the combination of television, the principal baby-sitter, movies both on television and on the big screen, video games, and magazines. These entertainment vehicles constitute the overwhelming educational curricula for the young as well as most of their elders. They are relentless trainers of the psyche. They firmly establish models of appearance, attitude and behavior by generally sensational means. This commercially-motivated education is vastly more pervasive, aggressive and intrusive than formal education. Besides being trained in how to destroy oneself through cigarettes, alcohol, diets, pill popping, and misuse and disuse of one's mind, the passive viewer is shown ever more sensational, mindless forms of committing violence on others and, more subtly, on oneself. So it should not be surprising that entering college students have been well trained generally in mindless violence toward themselves and others.

It is tempting, nevertheless, to believe that highly intelligent college students will readily dismiss violence sensationalism. But as I write this I see a college schedule of events for the weekend. Friday night's only movies are "Lethal Weapon" followed by "Lethal Weapon II." On Saturday night students may see "Dead Again" in the early evening or late evening. No other movies are offered. Meanwhile, "Lethal Weapon" and "Lethal Weapon II" are promoted as "Super Duper Double Feature Delivers Twice the Fun for Your Money" and the reader is told of a "night of laughs, suspense, action, and downright fun!" The shootings and an explosion are advertised as especially entertaining.

Sexual interests and activity in such films are rarely shown without some form of admixed violence let alone in the context of a strong mutual love relationship. Typically, in popular movies, guns are made a symbol of male potency, quite as if guns have anything but a negative effect on genuine sexuality.

By the time young people get to college, they have been thoroughly trained, as it were, in impulsive cognitive style through popular commercial culture in the form of television, movies, magazines and newspapers hawking various modes of internally directed and externally directed violence. The training is of a hypnotic kind with the trainers motivated not by a positive value system but by greed. Nicotine and alcohol pushers are not interested in benefitting consumers; they are trying to make money and are willing to do so by any means that will "succeed," including preaching the exact opposite of the truth even though that means destroying people both with the products they are selling and the means of selling. Often, it is difficult to tell which is the more destructive: the product or the means; what is certain is that the combination is powerfully harmful.

DOES VIOLENCE PROGRAMMING HELP THE VIEWER?

By now it should be clear that the ever greater programming of violence in our culture does not really serve benign cathartic purposes as apologists have claimed. The truth is that our culture is motivated by commercially profitable cultivation of addictive life styles–including addiction to violence–because inducing addictions generates huge amounts of money for the pushers. Screen writers now have a solid formula for (commercial) success: provide ever larger doses of violence to (temporarily) gratify the consumer addict (Whitaker, 1989). Violence viewing and behavior thus become addictions since more and more are required to achieve the "same degree of entertainment." That our society is exceptionally violent, that its violence is increasing and that violence portrayals in the media are increasing are meaningfully related facts. One might argue that the media only reflect our violent culture but, if one believes they have any influence, they certainly also promote violence (Phillips, 1977; Phillips, 1983; Larson, 1993).

Though males commit 88% of violent crimes in the United States (Miedzian, 1991), females have become more violent, a trend now reflected by and seemingly endorsed by television. Women "in jeopardy" TV films and series are now being abetted and replaced by women who try to kill and do. According to CBS Vice-president Peter Totorici, "these programs were being produced in part because of success of reality-based shows coupled with the fact that women are the principal viewers of prime-time television" (Killer Women on TV, 1992). The term "reality-based" is a euphemism for violence portrayal, similar to the euphemism "action picture."

Theoretically, violence programming may not have a destructive effect. As Bettelheim (1990) has argued:

> There is plenty of violence and crime in Old Testament stories, as well as in fairy tales. There is a lot of cruelty, enmity within the family, homicide, and even patricide and incest in Greek drama, as there is in Shakespeare's plays. This suggests that people have always needed a fare of violent fantasies as an integral part of popular entertainment. Aristotle said that such fare is required for catharsis–for the relief of our emotional tensions. Children need as much that relief as adults do–perhaps more–and they always will. (Bettelheim, 1990, p. 151)

He goes on to acknowledge that while seriously disturbed children may become more violent after watching violent cartoons, that "The decisive factors are not the type of events shown on the screen but the child's own personality (which is formed in the home under the parents' influence) and, though to a much smaller degree, the child's present situation" (Bettelheim, 1990, p. 152).

He says to help children "develop the right attitudes toward violence": "What is necessary is for parents to explore with the child what he, all on his own, made of what he saw and heard. We must let the child tell us what he got from the program, and start there in helping him sort out which impressions came from within himself and which from the program, which were good and which were not, and why" (Bettelheim, 1990, p. 155).

He would require that the adult watch along with the child, and that parents spend more time with their children so that children would become more discriminating in their viewing and spend less time in front of the TV. This is excellent advice. But most parents generally leave their children unaccompanied for many hours per day watching the tube, which means that the critical examination and thinking necessary to discrimination are not being done. Furthermore, Bettelheim acknowledges that television and movies lend themselves more to entertainment than education and they are inherently more passive experiences. He notes:

> In the art experience I was always present and active, but in the experience of an absorbing movie, I simply existed while I

saw and heard. In art experiences which were deeply meaning-ful, my experience was that of being at the height of selfhood. In the movies, there was no self-awareness, no selfhood, just the experience of events happening on the screen.

This tremendous and unique power of the movies, to lift the spectator out of his selfhood, is what makes them so fascinat-ing. (Bettelheim, 1990, p. 115)

The question remains: how can we nurture selfhood, that develop-ment of an actively aware self able to evaluate, plan, and behave wittingly instead of merely react?

TEACHING CRITICAL THINKING

While impulsive cognitive style and its obliviousness to harmful consequences may characterize much of infantile behavior, children of even elementary school age show eagerness and ability to devel-op critical thinking. In fact, some of the most effective deterrents to cigarette smoking have been created by children. For example, Melissa Antonow of Our Lady of Hope School in Queens, New York produced the "Come to Where the Cancer is" cartoon, a takeoff on the Marlboro Country cigarette ads. Her cartoon shows a skeleton of a man riding a horse alongside tombstones marked variously "lung cancer," "heart disease," and "emphysema." Melissa's "ad" now appears in all New York City subway cars. Simi-larly, Caheim Drake of Public School 112 in the Bronx produced an anti-smoking ad showing a "Pack of Lies," a cigarette pack with each cigarette bearing a label such as "Fun," "Relaxation," "Safe," "Cool," "Mature," and "Popular" (Howe, 1992).

If children, with the aid of their adult teachers, can cut through denial and engage in effective critical thinking which gets to the truth, formal education can serve to immunize children from the adult-instigated propaganda that exploits all consumers. This nurtu-rant educational process requires that *we*, the adult teachers, engage in the critical thinking processes we have been trained to abnegate in our own commercialized upbringings. We will need to stop being so suggestible as to smoke cigarettes, to drink alcohol to the point of intoxication, and to participate actively or passively acquiesce in externally directed as well as internally directed mindless violence. We, as adult professors, counselors and therapists, will have to *actively criticize* all aspects of the cigarette, alcohol, and weapons industries, instead of passively accepting them.

Some communities have recently demonstrated how adults can decrease the gross intrusion of destructiveness training. A largely black community within the city of Philadelphia found itself targeted by an advertising campaign designed to addict black people specifically to a new brand of cigarettes that was given a suave, cool image. Their protest resulted in the cigarette advertisers, i.e., drug pushers, calling off the campaign. In Perth Amboy, New Jersey, a neighborhood group sent its young people out on the streets to demonstrate how easy it *was* for persons under 18 to buy cigarettes (Teltsch, 1992). The young people were able to make underage cigarette purchases in 63 of the 94 stores they visited. The community of Perth Amboy was selected for such a drive against child and teenage smoking because it was saturated with billboards urging tobacco and alcohol use for black and Hispanic residents. The advertisers know whom to prey on just as the regular, more obviously dis-respectable street drug pushers do: target those with less power. But those with apparently less power, including minorities and the young, can protest effectively, as in these cases.

We will also have to take a more critical attitude toward certain "sports" which have the primary aim of causing physical harm, such as boxing or, in many cases, ice hockey and football. For example, instead of merely extolling football at all levels, perhaps we should point out the recently accumulated evidence that the violent collisions characteristic of football playing are associated with an average reduction in longevity of 12 years per professional football player. Likewise, we may caution gymnasts and wrestlers that training pressures may induce eating disorders. And we should point out that diets promoted by the nation's huge commercial diet industry not only do no good but promote eating disorders.

Most basically, we can foster better child care, including changing children's television programming. A federal law enacted in 1990, the Children's Television Act, requires broadcasters to provide educational programs for children in order to renew their lucrative licenses every five years. But broadcasters have tried to pass off shows like "G.I. Joe" and "The Flintstones" as educational (Andrews, 1993, p. A1). Furthermore, the law does not affect cable broadcasting which is just as violence-filled as the regular network television which is notorious for violence programming aimed at children. We could support better programming under this law in the interest of country and campus.

APPLICATIONS FOR PSYCHOTHERAPY

Charles Tart and Arthur Deikman (1991) have addressed how mindlessness is considered a central problem to be dealt with in both Eastern and Western ways of promoting personal growth, or what I would call the development of selfhood. They focus on use of meditation practices in terms of Eastern tradition, and psychotherapy in terms of Western tradition.

> These disciplines are based on the recognition that people are often not clear about the actual state of affairs they find themselves in, what they are doing and why—we are all too mindless. Such mindlessness causes immense amounts of human suffering, suffering which is stupid and unnecessary, because if you knew what you were doing and why you were doing it, you would have the possibility of acting more adaptively. (Tart and Deikman, 1991, p. 29)

When psychotherapy works, it is an intriguing process, especially when therapist and student work well together in figuring out how the student's developmental issues evolved (Whitaker, 1992a). Students can become quite fascinated with discovering how their needs and expectations have been formed, including by the culture. In particular, the therapist can help the student to recognize how independent thinking has been discouraged in favor of a mindless conformism motivated by commercial profit and passive acquiescence in the lowest common denominator of mental functioning.

> By the time Jane was 13 she was becoming alcoholic, a not unusual condition among her high school peers, and she began to use virtually any street drug that was available. Her

"friends" showed their disapproval if she outdid them academically or athletically, and they showed that they were threatened by her natural good looks. Jane learned early to disavow her positive attributes by engaging in whatever self-destructive behavior seemed to appease her contemporaries and to fit in with "popular culture." She soon added an addiction to cigarettes to her alcoholism and developed an eating disorder. By the time she was 16 she "fit in" with her peer and popular culture quite well. An inpatient stay in a rehabilitation center and participating in Alcoholics Anonymous helped her to finish high school. But her eating disorder, cigarette addiction, and generally self-defeating orientation continued.

At age 20 she was managing to work as a secretary but really wanted to go to college. She began psychotherapy which focused not only on the enabling aspects of her family dynamics but also on the cultural influences that shaped her orientation from childhood on. A central issue developed: was she going to continue to conform or was she going to think critically and independently? She carried the notion from childhood that she was "too dumb" to go to college; the therapist interpreted her notion as "You're too afraid to not be dumb." Her lifelong peer and cultural influences were discussed in terms of this insidious notion. Discussions sometimes focused on cigarette ads, popular movie and television depictions of women, and the manipulative ads for diets, all with emphasis on learning to criticize them and to develop a kind of constructive self-love or normal narcissism in their place. As she understood that she had been trained to be self-destructive and self-deluding so that the manufacturers and sellers of the world's number 1 destructive drug could make money off her, she stopped thinking of smoking cigarettes as a pleasure and managed to do what she had thought impossible; she kicked cigarettes out of her life.

Her new pattern of assertive rejection of cultural nonsense carried into her beginning college career. But she was confronted early in her first semester by another woman student who stridently denigrated their woman professor for the professor's serious devotion to teaching. Jane was faced with either giving in to the other student, who was very aggressive, or standing up for her own convictions, i.e., herself. She chose to stand up rather than continue to be intimidated. So she boldly told the aggressive student that she disagreed.

Despite her own originally dire predictions, Jane proceeded to excel academically and finished her first year with virtually straight A's, in stark cognitive dissonance with her previous "dumb" self-image. Similarly, instead of acquiescing in destructive kinds of sexual relationships, which had given her little or no real pleasure, her developing self-respect began to enable her to change the nature of her relationships with men into ones of greater mutual respect.

> But not all was smooth. She encountered disrespectful men, felt out of "adjustment" with her previous friends, as well as some relatives whose problems had not been so obvious before, and was tempted to give up on account of "loneliness," especially as she was transferring to another, more challenging college. She needed emotional support to compensate for what she was "losing." A big question arose: could she maintain her excellent progress in the face of such alienation? The conflict was resolved in large part by allowing herself to be sad and to grieve her past; she was then able to be more consistently enthusiastic about her new life since she was able to give up the old, comfortable conformism. She then excelled at the more challenging college. And instead of continuing to be bulimic she discovered that she had been acting as though she had to "purge the thought" when she had bright ideas. She then stopped purging.

It would be misleading to depict destructive behavior in college students as solely the product of influences in the popular culture. Most typically, family and cultural influences interact powerfully. But weaknesses in family upbringing become severe vulnerabilities to destructive cultural influences. Often, the destructive behavior is modeled, as it were, by the parents and/or the parents are enablers; they support behaviors that the culture may eventually punish in the long run but surely encourages in the short run.

> Charley grew up with an alcoholic and manic-depressive father. During his manic phases, father would beat up mother and threaten to beat up Charley if he interfered. As Charley entered

college he was beginning to see his father as abusive because of his mental disturbance but he saw no causal link between father's abusiveness and his, Charley's, own alcoholism. Charley joined a fraternity and found jovial male companions used to drinking heavily. Drinking alcohol became the social thing to do. He watched sports with them on TV and associated the alcohol ads with being macho, and thereby felt socially accepted by his macho male peers and the world of outstanding male athletes.

He was insufficiently aware that alcohol would inevitably release in him a great proclivity for violence, especially toward authority figures, violence that he had pent up in the course of his relationship with his father. He was only dimly aware at all that he was ever out of line even after he had sobered up on the days after he had scuffles with other students. Drinking still remained the "in-thing" to do until the night he punched out a security guard. After that he was strongly urged to "attend counseling sessions."

Though even strongly urged, much less mandatory, counseling or psychotherapy often does not work and may be inadvisable for ethical and legal reasons, Charley tolerated gaining insight into how the admixture of the relationship with father, the fraternity atmosphere and his own alcohol use unleashed a fury in him. He became able to acknowledge how much he had missed having a father who was genuinely fathering, and he was able to cry over his history and not merely resent having to be in counseling. He recognized his own personal need not to drink and there was no further violent behavior. He did not, however, choose to explore his dynamics to the point of thorough understanding.

LEGALISM VS. THE SPIRIT OF RESPECT

Society has turned out to have scarce defence against the abyss of human decadence, for example against the misuse of liberty for moral violence against young people, such as motion pictures full of pornography, crime and horror. This is all considered to be part of freedom and to be counterbalanced, in theory, by young people's right not to look and not to accept. Life organized legalistically has thus shown its inability to defend itself against the corrosion of evil. (Alexander I. Solzhenitsyn, 1978 commencement address at Harvard University)

In the face of escalating rates of campus violence and disrespectful behavior, some colleges and universities have imposed rules against behaviors that are clearly injurious physically and/or psychologically to others. This kind of regulatory system is literally a court of last resort.

We have a compelling urge in our society to resort to legalistic solutions which are usually partial and temporary; they do not get at the heart of the matter, and they do not address the spiritual problem. People *may* then begin to behave themselves, as it were, but only under external duress. Thorough solutions require certain kinds of psychological and spiritual development. As Solzhenitsyn pointed out in his address, as soon as there is a power shortage in our cities, the looting and vandalism begin. At best, campus rules and regulations are merely *some* of the important starting points. Colleges and universities are learning that legal solutions are sharply limited by First Amendment rights, even as related to quite egregious emotional abuse. Already adopted "hate speech" restrictive codes designed to protect minorities at United States public universities have come under scrutiny. For example, the Supreme Court ruled that a St. Paul, Minnesota ordinance restricting cross burning and swastika displays violated freedom of speech. Pending legislation would also give students the right to challenge in federal court private university codes that punish speech (American College Health Association, 1992).

Such limitation of restrictions on free speech is especially evident in advertising where little other than blatant outright direct and immediate threat to life may be restricted, as we know from decades of struggle to ban cigarette advertising. In a recent case (Smothers, 1992) that raised First Amendment issues, a Federal Court of Appeals was needed to uphold a ruling against *Soldier of Fortune* magazine for printing this ad: "GUN FOR HIRE: 37 year old professional mercenary desires jobs. Vietnam veteran. Discreet and very private. All jobs considered." The ad was linked subsequently to a murder conspiracy resulting in a man being shot to death. The defense argued, at first successfully, that a conviction could threaten commercial free speech.

But many clearly legal measures are available that may go overlooked by administrators and faculty alike because they are ambivalent about trying changes. In some cases, the adults may personally tacitly approve. For example, some colleges and universities still sell cigarettes in their campus book stores or other buildings, regularly provide alcohol at social functions attended by underage students as well as their adult leaders, and turn the other way when students come back drunk and disorderly from faculty houses. They allow fraternities, sports teams, and other official campus organizations not only to serve alcohol to underage students but allow public drunkenness at a level that would not be tolerated off campus. In these cases, both fear of student disapproval and ambivalence about one's own alcohol use may stifle interventions that would legally reduce the conditions conducive to problematic behavior, for example penalties for disorderly conduct.

Certain other interventions could also be undertaken with no apparent legal hazard, so that students and the entire campus community could benefit immediately. For example, some campuses have tried alcohol-free parties with great success, and some have found great demand for alcohol-free dorms. In fact, about one-third of college and university students express a preference that alcohol not be available at all on campus (Presley & Meilman, 1992). These changes appear no more difficult to instigate than "quiet dorms" of various kinds, or certain room uses for clubs and committees. Importantly, such changes would satisfy student desires and not just administrative needs.

More assertive educational efforts could directly counter widely held erroneous assumptions that are relentlessly hyped in advertising and other commercial ventures. For example, a course in practical logic could deconstruct the nonsensical but sensational appeals to young people to use this or that drug (tobacco or alcohol), to go on a commercial diet, or to revel in mindless violence movies. From the standpoint of logic exercises, the instructor and students could have a field day. Psychology courses dealing with abnormal conditions of the mind could provide highly useful perspectives by illustrating those forms of mental morbidity common to commercial culture, for example the "schizophrenic thinking of everyday life" that is cultivated in advertisements for harmful substances (Whitaker, 1992b). Similarly, sociology as well as psychology courses could focus on how women's weight and beauty issues are used against them (Wolf, 1991), on violence training for men (Miedzian, 1991; Whitaker, 1987) and use and produce videos and films that explicate the training for victimization such as "Killing Us Softly."

Let us also feel free to give clear messages in educational posters, brochures, newspapers and journals; we can exercise our own free speech rights. The National Institute of Dental Research and the National Cancer Institute (NCAA News, 1992), for example, have collaborated on producing posters which show vividly just what damaging substances you are internalizing by using snuff, the smokeless tobacco: polonium 210, acetaldehyde, lead, formaldehyde, cadmium, N-nitrosamines, uranium 235, nicotine, and benzopyrene. Similarly the California state health authority now has posted on street corners large ads of its own against cigarette advertising, such as "500,000 women a year are seduced by the cigarette industry." We can also counter destructive kinds of advertising. Our efforts can show that adults, as well as children, can dare to counter commercial nonsense by telling the truth.

REFERENCES

Advocacy Institute (1992). Federal Trade Commission Report to Congress, 1990. Personal communication, October 13, 1992.

American College Health Association (1992). Freedom of speech: The debate continues. *Action*, 31, 5, pp. 1, 5, July/August/September.

Andrews, E.L. (1993). "'Flintstones' and programs like it aren't educational," F.C.C. says. *New York Times*, March 4, 1993, p. A1.

A New Worry: Going To Work Can Be Murder (1993). *New York Times*, February 25, 1993, p. B1 and B4.

Bettelheim, B. (1990). *Freud's Vienna and other essays*. New York: Knopf.

Centers for Disease Control. Homicide surveillance, 1979-1988. In *CDC Surveillance Summaries*, May 29, 1992. *MMWR* 1992; 41(SS-3), 1-33.

Centers for Disease Control. Behaviors related to unintentional and intentional injuries among high school students–United States, 1991. October 16, 1992. *MMWR* 1992; 41(41), 760-772.

Goleman, D. (1992). New light on how stress erodes health. *New York Times*, December 15, 1992, pp. C-1, C-12.

Green, T. (1993). Douglas' walk on the illogical side. *New York Times*, March 5, 1993, p. 5D.

Hevesi, D. (1993). In latest bigger-than-life role, Schwarzenegger is disarmed. *New York Times*, March 3, 1993, p. B3.

Hollman, L. & McCoy, C. (1992) The growing urban arsenal: Are rising handgun sales only a reflection of the problem, or a cause too? *The Philadelphia Inquirer* Review and Opinion, August 2, 1992, pp. E1, E4.

Howe, M. (1992). M.T.A. panel approves cut in cigarette advertisements. *New York Times Metro*, p. B 3, 6-17-92.

Killer women on TV (1992). *New York Times* Word and Image, October 12, 1992, p. C20.

Koop, C.E. (1991) *Koop*. New York and Toronto: Random House.

Larson, E. (1993). The story of a gun. *The Atlantic Monthly*, 271, 1, 48-78.

Lore, R.K. & Schultz, L.A. (1993). Control of human aggression. *American Psychologist*, 48, 1, 16-25.

Michener, J.A. (1976). *Sports in America*. New York: Random House.

Miedzian, M. (1991). *Boys will be boys: Breaking the link between masculinity and violence*. New York: Doubleday.

National Council on Alcoholism and Drug Dependence (1992). Personal communication, October 6, 1992.

NCAA News (1992), 29, 43, Education Newsletter Winter supplement p. 4.

Nullis, C. (1992). Smoking-related deaths of women are predicted to double in 30 years. *Philadelphia Inquirer*, April 2, 1992.

Phillips, D.P. (1977). Motor vehicle fatalities increase just after publicized suicide stories. *Science*, 196, 1464-1465.

Phillips, D.P. (1983). The impact of mass media violence on U.S. homicides. *American Sociological Review*, 48, 560-568.

Potok, M. (1993). Waco standoff reopens debate in "gun country." *USA Today*, March 8, 1993, p. 3A.

Presley, C.A., & Meilman, P.W. (1992). *Alcohol and drugs on American college campuses: A report to college presidents*. Carbondale, Illinois: Southern Illinois University.

Schwartz, A. (1990) The epidemiology of suicide among students at colleges and universities in the United States. *Journal of College Student Psychotherapy*, 4, 314, 25-44. Also published as chapter 2 in Whitaker, L. C. & Slimak, R.E (Eds.) (1990) *College student suicide*. New York: The Haworth Press, Inc.

Schwartz, A.J. & Whitaker, L.C. (1990). Preventing college student suicide. Chapter 12 in *Suicide over the life cycle*. D. Kupfer and S. Blumenthal (Eds.), pp. 303-340, Washington, D.C.: American Psychiatric Press, Inc.

Shapiro, D. (1965). *Neurotic styles*. New York: Basic Books, Inc.

Smothers, R. (1992) Magazine held liable for killing as result of ad. *New York Times* National Report, August 19, p. A18.

Spillman, S. (1993). Directors' call: Eastwood. *USA Today*, March 8, 1993, p. 30.

Tart, C.T. & Deikman, A.J. (1991). Mindfulness, spiritual seeking and psychotherapy. *Journal of Transpersonal Psychotherapy*, 23, 1, 29-52.

Teitsch, K. (1992). Keeping teenagers smokeless. *New York Times* Metro Section, August 18, pp. B1, 4.

Whitaker, L.C. (1987). Macho and morbidity: The emotional need vs. fear dilemma in men. *Journal of College Student Psychotherapy*, 1, 4, 33-47.

Whitaker, L.C. (1989). Myths and heroes: visions of the future. *Journal of College Student Psychotherapy*, 4, 2, 13-33.

Whitaker, L.C. (1992a). Psychotherapy as a developmental process. *Journal of College Student Psychotherapy*, 6, 3/4, 1-23. Also published as chapter 1 in Whitaker, L.C. & Slimak, R.E. (Eds.) *College student development*. New York: The Haworth Press Inc.

Whitaker, L.C. (1992b). *Schizophrenic disorders: Sense and nonsense in conceptualization, assessment, and treatment*. New York: Plenum Publishing Corp.

Wolf, N. (1991). *The beauty myth: How images of beauty are used against women*. New York: William Morrow & Co.

Chapter 4

Violence, Alcohol, Other Drugs, and the College Student

Timothy M. Rivinus
Mary E. Larimer

"College kids?" said Francis. "Drunk? On drugs? On this guy's land in the middle of the night?"

"You were on his land?"

"Well, apparently, said Henry. That's where the paper said his body was found . . ."

"Really. I wonder if you understand what sort of state we were in. Scarcely an hour before, we'd all been really, truly, out of our minds. And it may be a superhuman effort to lose one's self so completely, but that's nothing compared to the effort of getting one's self back again."

–Tartt, 1992, pp. 165-166

Timothy M. Rivinus, MD, is Chief of Mental Health Services, Harvard Health of New England, 400 Bald Hill Road, Warwick, RI 02886-1617. Mary E. Larimer, PhD, is affiliated with the Addictive Behavior Research Center, Department of Psychology, N 1-25, University of Washington, Seattle, WA 98195.

The authors gratefully acknowledge help from Susan Lundgren, Leslie Penn, Helen Perryman, and Toby Simon while retaining responsibility for all errors of fact or interpretation.

[Haworth co-indexing entry note]: "Violence, Alcohol, Other Drugs, and the College Student." Rivinus, Timothy M., Mary E. Larimer. Co-published simultaneously in *Journal of College Student Psychotherapy* (The Haworth Press, Inc.) Vol. 8, No. 1/2, 1993, pp. 71-119: and: *Campus Violence: Kinds, Causes, and Cures* (ed: Leighton C. Whitaker and Jeffrey W. Pollard) The Haworth Press, Inc., 1993, pp. 71-119. Multiple copies of this article/chapter may be purchased from The Haworth Document Delivery Center [1-800-3-HAWORTH; 9:00 a.m. - 5:00 p.m. (EST)].

Violence in its arbitrariness [is] taken for granted and therefore neglected; no one questions or examines what is obvious to all.

–Arendt, 1969, p. 8

The Elephant in the Living Room

–A common definition of Substance Abuse (or Dependence) among professionals.

INTRODUCTION

In this era of a rapidly rising incidence of aggressive acts associated with substance use and intoxication, it is timely to concentrate on these issues as they relate to the college student. College students are the youthful elite of our society and the teachers and leaders of the next generation. Their issues cannot be cynically written off, as do the biases of sexism, classism, and multiple environmental risk factors that plague groups less fortunate in our society. For the college student, violent acts are not child's play, although violent behavior is often overlooked and forgiven in the college student.

College student alcohol and other substance use/abuse is big business. National figures estimate that in 1992 college students spent 5.5 billion on alcohol alone–more than the amount nationally budgeted for alcohol and other substance use research alone (Eigen, 1991). The college and university years (ages 18 to 30 generally) are a time of extremely high risk for mortal accidents, rape, suicide, and other untoward events related to substance use and abuse (Rivinus, 1992).

Substance use and its disorders are a microcosm in college of the same problems with psychoactive chemicals in society at large. One in ten students has or will have during college a problem with psycho-active substance abuse (Eigen, 1991). The student may also, in college, learn that substance use and aggressive acts may be tolerated as acceptable ways of coping. Or, alternatively, they may be dissuaded from or unlearn these ways and make a commitment to self-care and communication leading to higher levels of deportment and problem-solving.

Newspaper articles commonly report substance abuse and violent related events on campuses and in fraternities (see for example, Matthews, 1993). One only need consider the reflections in a recent letter to the *New York Times* by a researcher of college student violence. Commenting on the remarks of a U.S. Navy admiral in the recent highly publicized Tailhook incident, the author noted that the Admiral's public statements openly demonstrated sexism, misogyny, and tolerance of the drunken naval pilots' assault on women. The author also noted that the navy incident has "much in common with [college] fraternities," and that

> In attempting to explain sexual assault by otherwise "decent" men . . . that high prestige male organizations are almost always misogynist . . . [the assaults are] expressed in various ways from humor to exploitation and felony assault. This is variously motivated, or at least facilitated, by competition among men, a pornographic view of sexuality, and hostility toward outsiders and intruders (as women are, by definition). (O'Sullivan, 1992)

The Tailhook incident and the recently publicized cases of William Kennedy Smith and Michael Tyson suggest that we need to look not only on gender-related, racial, minority group, and cultural factors as motivators of violent acts; we also need to focus on *the central facilitating role of intoxicating substances in these incidents–a subject rarely directly reported or addressed.*

Developmental Issues of Substance Use and Violence

Late adolescence and early adulthood are stages of rapid physical, sexual, psychological, and moral development. Levels of aggressive biological urges and cultural expectation peak simultaneously at these ages. These are times when sexual activity begins to achieve a high plateau that does not diminish until decades later. Levels of testosterone (which are associated with aggressiveness) are at their peak in men (Maccoby & Jacklin, 1974; Treadwell, 1987). Our culture also expects young men and women to be strong and aggressive: militarily, athletically, academically, interpersonally, vocationally and sexually. Youthful men are often mustered and sent to war to defend their country. Young men and women are also negotiating and experimenting with the social stereotypes of dominance and submission between genders.

Although many young people are superficially aware of equal rights between individuals, the use of intoxicating substances tend to facilitate regressive behavior, particularly in courtship and competitive relationships (Rabow et al., 1987). A high association of courtship violence with alcohol and other substance use has been noted in college student research throughout the forty years in which these phenomena have been studied (Straus & Bacon, 1953; Kanin, 1957; Kirkpatrick & Kanin, 1957; Makepeace, 1981; Bloch and Ungerlieder, 1986; Koss et al., 1987; Koss & Dinero, 1989; Abbey, 1991). Numerous other psychoactive substance use/abuse-related acts of aggression and violence are now well-documented in college students (Bausell et al. 1991; Koss and Dinero, 1989; O'Sullivan, 1991). Table 1 lists some of the common aggressive acts related to substance intoxication or abuse commonly seen on college and university campuses.

DOCUMENTING LINKS BETWEEN VIOLENCE AND SUBSTANCE USE

Accurate statistics relating aggressive acts and use of intoxicating substances at colleges and universities are hard to obtain. Researchers who examine such data note that the incidence of substance use and substance intoxication is grossly underestimated (Bausell et al., 1991). Most universities do not yet have laboratory access, quality-controlled breathalizer analysis, and mandatory substance measurement procedures that would accurately estimate the association of problem behavior with substance use.

At Brown University, for example, between January 1, 1990 and October 31, 1992, three categories of data were recorded (see Table 2). The recorders of the Brown data note a large number of criminal and noncriminal reports for which no reliable information was gathered regarding the association of substance use with behavior (65%). Specific types of misdemeanors, such as fighting, and reports of date rape are notably associated with alcohol and/or other drug use. Of the five cases of acquaintance rape one case documented that *both victim* and the *victimizer* were under the influence

TABLE 1. Types of College Violence Associated with Alcohol and Other Drugs

I. Violence against property
　　1. Malicious mischief (vandalism)
　　2. Vehicle theft and driving to endanger
　　3. Breaking and entering
　　4. Use of firearms or other weapons to endanger or to cause property damage
II. Violence against persons
　　1. Verbal harassment or assault
　　　　a. Scatological
　　　　b. Racist
　　　　c. Sexist
　　　　d. Homophobic
　　　　e. Mixed
　　2. Physical assault and/or battery
　　　　a. Male-male assault
　　　　b. Assault with dangerous weapon
　　　　c. Male-female assault
　　　　d. Female-female assault
　　　　e. Group violence (including post-game or town-gown fights, gang rape, etc.)
　　　　f. Violence in the name of hazing
　　　　g. Homophobic attacks
　　　　h. Interracial assaults–individual or group
　　　　i. Driving under the influence (therefore driving to endanger)

of intoxicating substances. Substance use was suspected but not specifically tested for in three of the four remaining cases.

Revealing statistical associations between college student substance use and violence have been achieved by researchers from Towson State University (Bausell et al., 1991). Between 1989 and 1990 more than ten thousand U.S. college and university students nationwide responded to a questionnaire (27% response rate) exploring the relationship of violent behavior and substance use.

TABLE 2. Brown University Statistics Relating Alcohol to Criminal and Non-criminal Reports January 1, 1990–October 31, 1992

Alcohol-related noncriminal reports filed	9%
Simple assault	15%
Noise disturbance	8%
Verbal harassment	7%
Alcohol-related criminal reports filed	8%
Simple assault	14%
Verbal harassment	5%
Malicious mischief (vandalism)	5%
Alcohol-related acquaintance rape reports	20%

Thirty-six percent of respondents reported having been a victim or a perpetrator of a physical or sexual assault. Victims and perpetrators used alcohol and other drugs in significantly higher quantities and frequencies than did controls (students who were neither victims or perpetrators). Perpetrators used intoxicant substances significantly more frequently than controls and than victims. The substances included alcohol, marijuana, sedatives (including methylqualone), cocaine, and amphetamines. Steroid use, unaccountably, was not correlated with higher degrees of violence. Students who committed multiple offenses tended to use alcohol and other drugs more frequently than students who committed a single antisocial act. *Perpetrators* were more often male, athletes, or fraternity members, and had slightly lower grade point averages. Alcohol and other drug use before entering college was more frequent in victims *and* perpetrators than in other students. *Victims* were more likely to be female, use nicotine, own a car, have a job, live off campus, be a fraternity/sorority member, be slightly older, and use illicit drugs and alcohol more frequently than controls. Students who had been victimized more than once reported significantly more alcohol and other drug use than one-time victims. The most common crimes reported in the study were theft, vandalism, physical and sexual assault. Alcohol was the most commonly used drug associated with crime and violent acts. The study concluded that the risk of student victimization and perpetration of crime, in part, is predictable, is directly related to quantity and frequency of alcohol and other drug use, and is quite possibly *preventable, particularly if interventions focus on student substance use and abuse* (Bausell et al., 1991).

MODELS LINKING GANG VIOLENCE AND SUBSTANCE USE

Models of the relationship between substance use and violence suggest that a violence threshold is breached as a result of the accumulation of predisposing or disposing factors of which psychoactive substance use and the behaviors associated with it are one. Figure 1 proposes an accumulation of background or distal factors related to an individual's past history, personality, and traits and Figure 2 proposes an aggregation of proximal factors which contribute to a violent outcome. In each case we have purposefully constructed the diagram to suggest that substance intoxication, withdrawal, or abuse (and the expectations and behaviors associated with these conditions) may contribute to breaching the threshold of violence, for a perpetrator, victim, or both.

Individual and Environmental Factors

Certain individuals have a high temperamental (or *trait*) tendency toward irritability, impulsiveness, acting out, and destructive acts toward others or toward property, particularly under the influence of intoxicants. These traits may be related to genetic factors, central nervous system deviations or injuries (Slaby & Roedell, 1982; Lewis et al., 1982). Childhood disorders such as attention deficit disorder/hyperactivity disorder and conduct disorder are associated with aggressiveness and later substance use disorder. Jerome Kagan (1984) maintains that "the aggressive seven year old is likely to be an adolescent bully." Personality trait disorders (e.g., antisocial, narcissistic, explosive, borderline) are also correlated with risk-taking, substance use, substance use disorder, and violent, aggressive, or destructive acts (Jessor & Jessor, 1977; Meyer, 1986; Cloninger, 1987; Stone, 1990).

FIGURE 1. Past, Personality and Trait-Related Factors

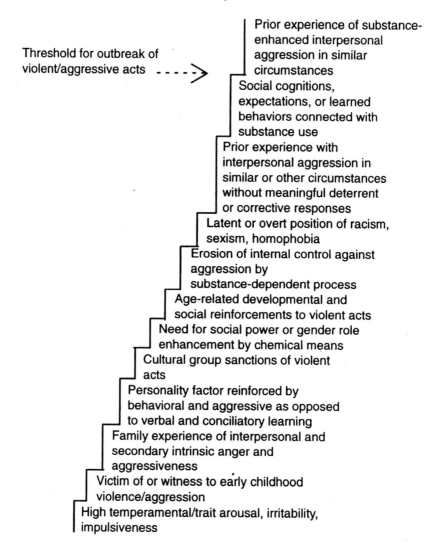

FIGURE 2. Present, Proximal, and State-Related Factors

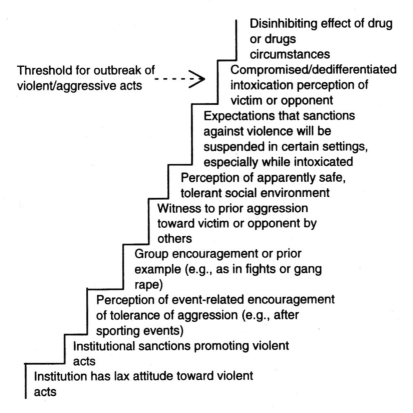

Threshold for outbreak of violent/aggressive acts - - - >

Disinhibiting effect of drug or drugs circumstances

Compromised/dedifferentiated intoxication perception of victim or opponent

Expectations that sanctions against violence will be suspended in certain settings, especially while intoxicated

Perception of apparently safe, tolerant social environment

Witness to prior aggression toward victim or opponent by others

Group encouragement or prior example (e.g., as in fights or gang rape)

Perception of event-related encouragement of tolerance of aggression (e.g., after sporting events)

Institutional sanctions promoting violent acts

Institution has lax attitude toward violent acts

Young people who have been victims of or are witnesses to violence and aggressive acts are likely to perpetrate or be victims of aggression and abuse substances themselves in adolescence or adult life (Wurmser & Lebling, 1983; Gold, 1986; Hotaling et al., 1989; Widom, 1989; Rivinus et al., 1992). Data also suggest that family and early environmental experience of interpersonal aggression and anger raises the level of anger and aggressiveness in adults experiencing interpersonal threat, especially in close relationships (McCord, 1983, 1988). Cultural, group, and family norms that tolerate violent acts, and do not encourage and teach problem solving by nonviolent methods, are major contributors to interpersonal violence. These attitudes are often coupled with and reinforced by alcohol and other psychoactive substance use. Children often learn to combine substance use and the expression of anger through violence from their families and proximal social environment (Jessor and Jessor, 1977; Pihl, 1983; 1992).

Much of our understanding of the correlation of intoxicants (particularly alcohol) and aggression in the young comes, in fact, from research with college students (Fagan, 1990). Paradoxically, in early stages a substance may be used by a young person in an attempt to control anger and aggression. At later stages of intoxication or substance use disorder, the chemical itself may then facilitate violent and aggressive acts (Taylor, 1983). Considerable research demonstrates that intoxicating regular use of a psychoactive substance erodes internal controls opposing the acting out of aggression toward others or toward property (Pernanen, 1981, 1991). A growing body of data also shows that cultural factors and expectations reinforce violent acts when a young person is under the influence of an intoxicating substance (MacAndrew & Edgerton, 1969; Jessor & Jessor, 1977; Wechsler, 1979; Kandel, 1980). Prior experiences of aggression, violence against others, or destruction of property, particularly when uncountered or undeterred by meaningful corrective responses, further promote aggressive acts in college students (MacAndrew & Edgerton, 1969; Reinarman & Leigh, 1987). Group encouragement and the modeling of aggression (such as in gang fights or rape) are proximal precursors of violent interpersonal events (Jessor & Jessor, 1977). The perceived threat of seduction by opponent or victim are also risk factors in the production of a violent outcome (Miczek & Thompson, 1983).

Institutional Factors

Institutions with lax sanctions against violent acts and substance-related incidents promote interpersonal aggression. Tolerance or encouragement of aggression, such as after a sporting event or in a fraternity, is an institutional green light to interpersonal violence (Bowker, 1983). Expectations of a "time-out" from administrative and legal sanctions that limit substance use is an encouragement to interpersonal violence or destructive acts (Collins, 1981; Beschner & Friedman, 1986).

A SYSTEMS MODEL RELATING
TO SUBSTANCE USE AND AGGRESSION

Systems models of the relationship between substance abuse and aggression offer a comprehensive view of the relationships among intoxication, substance use, and aggression (Collins, 1981; Gottheil et al., 1983; Goldstein, 1985; Fagan, 1990; Pernanen, 1991). Figure 3 illustrates how multiple sets of factors including psychoactive substance use interact simultaneously to produce a violent outcome.

Drug Factors

Psychoactive substances vary considerably in the type of intoxication they produce. Their stimulating or sedating properties, potency, the route by which they were used, and speed of their effects may differ. Today the availability of innumerable substances, the high potency of many drugs (such as cocaine, hallucinogens, and designer drugs), and the fact that young people sometimes use extraordinary quantities of a substance (or substances) while experimenting (Wechsler, 1979, 1992) magnify the potential outcomes of even so-called recreational or experimental substance use.

Set, Setting, Perceived Threat, and Victim Factors

Interactional models also account for the factors of the *set* and *setting* in which substances are used. *Set* is defined as the body of expectations and beliefs that an individual brings to the experience of intoxication. *Setting* is the interpersonal and environmental ambiance in which substance use occurs (Zinberg, 1984). A perceived threat by an opponent, or the perception of nonthreat by the victim (or opponent), are examples of *set*. An adverse *setting* might be a fraternity which routinely attempts to protect a violent intoxicated student from the negative consequences of aggression. Victim-related factors, include victim intoxication, or dedifferentiation (i.e., the perceived compromised position of the victim), a victim's history of risk taking, a victim's perception of *being* a victim, and the victim's expectation of violent outcome are also factors in outcomes contributing to an outcome of interpersonal violence (Green & Berkowitz, 1966; Zimbardo, 1970; Tannenbaum, 1972). Group factors such as the

FIGURE 3. Systems Model of Violent Interpersonal Event Where Drugs Are Used

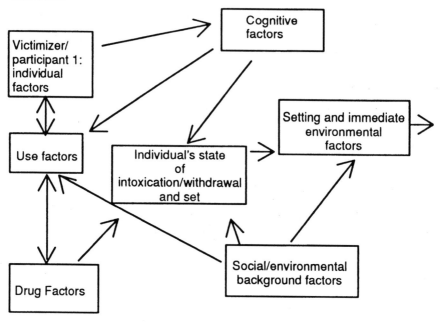

presence or absence of interventions and deterrents to violent outcome may be mediators or modulators of aggressive acts and substance use. Unprotected persons or property left as an open invitation to destruction should also be thought of as a potentially mediating setting fostering aggressive or destructive acts.

EXPECTATIONS, INTOXICATION, SEXUALITY, AGGRESSION, AND DEVIANCE DISAVOWAL

Violence and aggression are strongly reinforced in American family life and culture (Brown, 1969; Frantz, 1969). The "right" to drink, drug, and be aggressive–like the right to bear arms–has been vigorously defended and perpetuated. The media and advertising industries regularly, but without clarification, associate and equate the misuse of substances with aggression, violence, and sexuality (Belson, 1978; DeFoe & Breed, 1979; National Institute of Mental

FIGURE 3 (continued)

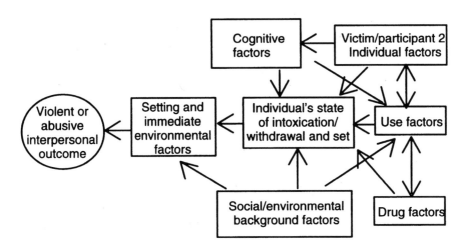

Health, 1982; Liebert & Sprafkin, 1988; Ryan & Mosher, 1991). Sexuality during adolescence is associated with aggressive acts (Kinsey et al., 1953; Ford and Beach, 1963). Maslow, Rand, and Newman (1973) note that most sexual behavior during adolescence is not what it appears to be: it is actually "pseudosexual"–a combination of aggression, dominance, power, and impulse satisfaction. Adolescent pseudosexuality may be part of the development of true sexual or relationship intimacy; but, its healthy development requires modeling, shaping and "corrective" experiences. Expectations of certain kinds of behavior while under the influence of psychoactive substances strongly predict acting out, loss of control, and physical and sexual aggression in interpersonal contexts (MacAndrew & Edgerton, 1969; Pernanen, 1976, 1981, 1991). These expectations follow cultural and institutional norms (Heath, 1983).

Studies of college undergraduates' drinking styles have shown that younger males commonly binge drink and that binge drinking is commonly associated with aggressive physical and sexual assault (Jessor & Jessor, 1973, 1977; Cahalan & Cisin, 1976; Blane & Hewitt, 1977; Wechsler, 1979, 1992). Use of intoxicating psychoactive substances is also commonly associated with gang or group violence (Fagan, 1990). Wechsler (1979, 1992) showed that New England College males had ten times the expectation that they would commit and be forgiven for a violent act when drunk than when sober.

Research has consistently demonstrated the phenomenon of a moratorium of sanctions against violent acts committed during periods of intoxication. "Time-out," "deviance disavowal," "relaxed standards of accountability," or "excuse function," as this phenomenon has been variously called (Reinarman & Leigh, 1987; Collins & Schlenger, 1988), relocates the blame for deviant behavior from the intoxicated *individual* onto the intoxicant itself and the substance-using situation. "Time-out" is culturally embedded and college subcultures commonly promote its continuance. Colleges have traditionally had particularly high tolerance for intoxicant-related fraternity, sport, or post-sports aggression. Institutional policies that refuse to tolerate substance-related aggression may, conversely, reduce violent interactions associated with intoxication (MacAndrew & Edgerton, 1969; Levinson, 1983; Heath, 1983; Zinberg, 1984).

CLINICAL STATES OF SUBSTANCE USE

Intoxication–the sought-after effects of euphoriant and abused chemicals–occurs when blood and central nervous system (CNS) levels of intoxicant(s) are rising. *Withdrawal* occurs when the blood and CNS levels of the substance are falling or have left the body. Intoxication and withdrawal can have different effects on the human nervous system in terms of thinking, mood, behavior and its consequences. For example, *during intoxication* stimulants are likely to result in an aggressive outcome as their effects stimulate the fight-flight (adrenergic and dopaminergic) areas of brain and sympathetic nervous system. *During withdrawal* from stimulants adrenergic and dopaminergic depletion causes a nervous and psychological depression associated with the dampening of aggressive impulses. *Protracted withdrawal syndrome* (PWS) is a stage of withdrawal lasting weeks or months after the drug has exited the body. PWS from stimulants is commonly associated with irritability, hair-trigger cue-responsiveness, drug-seeking behavior, and aggressive acts (Gawin & Kleber, 1986).

Pathological intoxication (PI) is the idiosyncratic reaction to a drug occurring at blood levels usually not associated with intoxicating or dementing effects (Maletsky, 1976; Pihl, 1993). PI is usually associated with set and setting factors such as fatigue, situational anger, jealousy, previous history of abuse or abusiveness, and the stress of the substance dependence process itself (Bean-Bayog, 1986; Pihl, 1993).

Substages of intoxication, withdrawal, or PWS may also be relevant to the potential for aggressive responses. For example, at low blood levels alcohol may repress aggression. Rapidly rising blood alcohol levels (BALs), during binge drinking for instance commonly stimulate aggression. On the other hand, very high BALs cause sedation and diminution of aggressive impulses (Taylor & Gammon, 1975). The stages of various substance use and their associations with aggression are summarized in Table 3.

TABLE 3. Substance Use Related Clinical States Associated with Aggressive Acts in College Students

    I. Intoxication

    II. Pathological intoxication (i.e., low dose or idiosyncratic intoxication)

    III. Substance-induced paranoid or psychotic states

        1. Paranoid reactions

        2. Pathological jealousy

        3. Psychotic rage

    IV. Substance-induced dementia

        1. Acute delirium

        2. Chronic dementia

    V. Withdrawal states

        1. Acute withdrawal

        2. Protracted withdrawal syndrome (PWS)

    VI. Dependence-driven, drug-seeking, antisocial behavior

THE PSYCHOACTIVE SUBSTANCES THEMSELVES

Alcohol is the substance most commonly associated with disinhibition, aggression, and violence in the college student (Koss, 1990; Wechsler, 1992). Alcohol-using behavior (acute intoxication or chronic alcoholism), associated with aggressive behavior has a long-documented history. Aristotle spoke of alcohol's disinhibiting effects (and of the individual's responsibility for them) stating that "men make themselves responsible for being unjust or self-indulgent . . . by spending their time in drinking bouts and the like" (Nicomacean Ethics, III, 5, 1958). The temperance, teetotal, and prohibition movements in 19th and early 20th centuries based their politics on what seemed to be an obvious relationship of alcohol intoxication and alcoholism to family violence, homicide and "moral degeneracy" (Sournia, 1990).

Studies in recent decades show with increasing precision a consistent association of alcohol intoxication, problem alcohol use, and aggressive acts (Taylor & Gammon, 1975; Taylor, 1983). Criminal violence and homicide are associated with intoxication by aggressor and victim in 60-70% of documented cases (Kittrie, 1971; Miller-Madsen et al., 1986; Goodman et al., 1986; Collins & Schlenger, 1988; Pernanen, 1991). Rape, courtship, and sexual aggression have been consistently associated with alcohol use (Amir, 1967; Rada, 1975; Johnston et al., 1978; Gerson & Preston, 1979; Cate et al., 1982; Koss et al., 1987; Koss & Dinero, 1989; Muelenhard & Linton, 1987; Rodenas et al., 1989). Studies of sexual violence on campuses estimate that 75% of victims *and* victimizers had been using alcohol at the time of the rape or rape attempt. Seventy-five percent of victimizers attribute their victim's "seductive" behavior to alcohol use (Koss, 1990).

Although still far from complete, research on alcohol and alcohol-related aggression gives us important information about the mediators and moderators of alcohol's (and other drug) effects. First, alcohol intoxication can directly disinhibit the human nervous system and increase the likelihood of aggressive "acting-out" (Moyer, 1983; Taylor & Leonard, 1983; Pihl, 1993). Second, alcohol decreases the pain (emotional and physical) sensitivity increasing the likelihood of violent responsiveness (Pihl and Ross, 1987;

Pihl, 1993). Third, alcohol reduces the anxiety related to the expectation of punishment for a violent act (Pihl, 1993). Fourth, alcohol significantly lowers frustration tolerance to non-reward and perceived threat (Mayfield et al., 1976; Lang and Sibrel, 1989; Murdoch et al., 1990; Peterson et al., 1990). Fifth, alcohol use decreases flexibility to deal with new or threatening situations (Peterson et al., 1990). Sixth, cultural and environmentally-related factors often strongly reinforce alcohol use with aggressive disinhibition (Collins, 1981; Gottheil et al., 1983; Zinberg, 1984; Brain, 1986; Bushman and Cooper, 1992; Fagan, 1990). Seventh, social learning, especially prior alcohol-related aggression experienced or witnessed in family members and peers, plays a major role in the connection between alcohol use and violent acts (Heath, 1983; Wurmser & Liebling, 1983; Coleman & Straus, 1989; Fagan, 1990). Eighth, *pathological intoxication* (the unexpected effects of normally subintoxicating levels of alcohol) and the effects of the dependence (addiction) process can lower the thresholds of control and increase the likelihood of aggressive and violent acts (Maletsky, 1976; Cohen, 1985; Pihl and Ross, 1987; Miller & Potter-Efron, 1990). Ninth, alcohol induced hypoglycemia may also play a role in the expected violent reactions (Gotheil, 1983; Pihl and Ross, 1987). Tenth, alcohol abuse biologically promotes *denial*. One study showed that those alcohol users who committed aggressive, violent, or destructive acts commonly had little or no memory of their aggressive acts (Tamerin et al., 1970)–a finding that has been replicated by Tarter et al. (1984). Alcohol use easily can be detected and measured by prompt use of a breathalizer.

Sedatives and Anti-Anxiety Drugs

Fortunately, the barbiturates and related compounds are now rarely used. Their dependent use was notorious for associated violent reaction (Levinson, 1983; Spotts & Shantz, 1984). Presently the *benzodiazipines*, including: diazepam (Valium), alprazolam (Xanax), clonazepam (Klonopin), lorazepam (Ativan), and temazepam (Halcion) are widely and promiscuously prescribed by physicians for anxiety and insomnia (Lion et al., 1975; American Psychiatric Association, 1990). They are associated with violent reactions and are sometimes abused by college students. Benzodiazepine use with alcohol dramatically increases disinhibition, loss of control, aggression, depression and suicidality (DiMascio et al., 1969; Lion et al., 1975). The benzodiazipines are commonly measured in blood and urine tests for intoxicants and other sedatives.

Stimulants

It is important to consider stimulants as a class, although today, much attention is directed specifically to cocaine–the stimulant most likely to be used by college students. Other stimulants, particularly amphetamines (e.g., Dexedrine), are sometimes used by students to enhance performance in exams, "cramming," paper writing, and in sport. Amphetamines increase aggression during intoxication and PWS (Ellinwood, 1971; Mayfield, 1983). Irritability, paranoia, and psychosis are common reactions to the short- and long-term use of amphetamines (Grinspoon & Backalar, 1985; Miczek & Tidley, 1989). The more commonly abused illegal stimulant methamphetamine ("ice" or "crystal meth") is notorious for inducing aggression. Methylphenidate (Ritalin) is a drug used in the treatment of attention deficit disorder (ADD) in children, adolescents, and adults (residual ADD). Ritalin is rarely abused by college students for whom it is therapeutically prescribed but can produce psychosis and aggressive behaviors if abused in high doses (Radcliffe & Rush, 1988).

Cocaine can trigger psychosis, bipolar-like episodes, and violence. Its use has been associated with domestic violence, rape, and murder (Post & Kompanda, 1976; Washton, 1984). Increased irritability and paranoia was noted in 99% of cocaine-using subjects studied by Crowley (1987). Honer and associates (1987) note that chronic low-dose intranasal cocaine use may increase paranoia and the likelihood of defensive flight reaction, showed that higher doses of smoked "crack" (or IV cocaine) is sometimes associated with violence. Aggression is rare during the early depressive phase (1-2 days) of cocaine withdrawal. After this depression cocaine users exhibit drug-seeking aggression, irritability and aggression often associated with efforts to get more (money for) cocaine. Observers also note the high association of chronic personality problems and aggression with regular cocaine use (Washton et al., 1984; Spotts & Shantz, 1984; Goldstein, 1985). Cocaine and the amphetamines can be detected on routine drug urine screens for 1-2 days after their last use.

Nicotine and caffeine are stimulants but are rarely associated with aggression and, in fact, appear to reduce aggression.

Phencyclidine (PCP) is often found as an adulterant of various ingested, smoked or inhaled compounds and may be present in compounds that students purchase in the belief that they are pure cocaine, marijuana, or an hallucinogen. It is rarely used in pure form by college students who have usually heard of its potentially disastrous effects. PCP is an anesthetic that induces aggressive and psychotic states. Because the victim/aggressor literally "feels no pain," he or she may become aggressive without regard to painful consequences (Simonds & Kashani, 1979, 1980; Baldridge & Bessen, 1990). PCP can be screened for (by urine or blood analysis) in students who have had aggressive episodes or a "bad trip."

Anabolic steroids. College student athletes are sometimes users of anabolic steroids. Students, usually males, who wish to increase their muscle mass, size, and appearance may also abuse steroids (Perry et al., 1990). Steroids are procured illegally or legally from "script docs"–doctors who prescribe them for a fee. "Roid rage" is now a well-known clinical phenomenon noted among steroid users (Cansacher & Workman, 1989; Perry et al., 1990). Steroid use has been associated with violent crime, including homicide (Pope & Katz, 1990). Steroids also induce physical and psychological dependence (Gianinni et al., 1987; Schuckit, 1988; Brower, 1990). Routine drug urine toxicity screens do not assess anabolic steroid use. Their use should, nevertheless, be suspected in cases of aggressive acts by college students and urine tests for their presence should be specifically requested.

Inhalants. Regular inhalant use is rare among college students. Inhalants vary widely in their effects. Nitrous oxide usually produces rapid sedation and danger of lethal overdose. Nitrous oxide and other inhalants such as solvents occasionally produce idiosyncratic dissociative and violent episodes that are strongly modulated by factors of set and setting (Radcliffe & Rush, 1988). Because they are rapidly metabolized and excreted, inhalants are difficult to detect, and their use is usually determined by direct evidence or by history.

Opiate/Opioid intoxication has been associated with dampening of aggression in users both with and without other drugs (Miczek & Thompson, 1983) which may be a reason for its preference by some intrinsically "angry" users (Khantzian, 1985). The reduction of hostility in long-term users of opioids is thought to be due to long-term reduction of testosterone levels (Mendelson et al., 1975). Opioids are rarely used by college students in injectable form. The availability of moderately priced heroin has risen however, and is sometimes used intranasally ("snorted") by students. The opioids commonly prescribed as analgesics (Percocet, Vicodin) are sometimes abused by students who obtain them both legally and illegally. During withdrawal from opiates/opioids, hostility may increase in proportion to craving (Woody et al., 1983). Opiate/Opioids use can be measured by blood and urine analysis.

Marijuana: Smoked or (rarely) ingested marijuana (cannabis or its resin hashish–or "hash") is common on college campuses. Like the opiate/opioids cannabis appears to suppress hostility during intoxication. Withdrawal from marijuana, however, is associated with depression, irritability, and hostility (Miczek & Thompson, 1983; Taylor & Leonard, 1983). Urine tests detect cannabis for 3-5 days or more (even weeks in the heavy user) after its last use.

POLYSUBSTANCE USE

Polysubstance use–in the 1990s, among the young, and college and university students–is the rule. Large-scale polysubstance use is a relatively recent phenomenon and the behavior associated with it has been difficult to research vigorously for obvious reasons. Clinical information derived from patient experience leads to a number of conclusions: (1) Cross-reactivity among substances and *synergistic* reactions are common. *Synergy* occurs when the effects of one drug are explosively exacerbated by the use of a similar or cross-reactive substance. If substances with somewhat opposing effects are used (such as a stimulant with a sedative), users commonly ingest greater amounts of both substances, increasing the likelihood of adverse reactions, including violence, suicide attempts, and other forms of loss of control. (2) Studies also indicate that combinations of intoxicating euphoriant psychoactive substances lead rapidly to habituation, abuse, and dependence. Polysubstance *use* is, in fact, a frequent and early symptom of problem substance abuse or dependence. (3) Polysubstance abuse and dependence impairs the abilities of the dependent individual to master and maintain higher levels of ego development, self-care, and respect for the rights and integrity of others. (4) Polysubstance-abusing individuals are also recognized for their higher levels of aggression and antisocial personality traits and disorder (Meyer, 1986; Cloninger, 1987). Multiple substances can be detected on routine drug urine screenings.

In summary, a review of the literature suggests a high association of violent and aggressive acts with substance intoxication and withdrawal (see Table 4). These reactions are further increased by the use of polysubstances. Exceptions to this rule are the aggression-reducing effects of cannabis and the opioids, the effects of which are reversed during withdrawal. In general, substance use can lower the threshold for acting out aggressive impulses by various mechanisms and pathways, including a direct stimulating effect on aggressive outbursts (Gottheil et al., 1983; Brain, 1986; Bushman and Cooper, 1990; Pihl, 1993).

SUBSTANCE USE AND AN EXPANDED DEFINITION OF VIOLENCE

The association of alcohol and other substance use, intoxication, abuse, and dependence with high-risk behavior of all types impels one to widen the general definition of violence. The current practices of fraternity hazing acts of vandalism and demonstrations of assertive "free speech" or other verbal aggression attacks occur can and should be defined as violent acts. The associations of these events with substance use is common.

Recently a college student was defended by his lawyer and by some of his peers under the principle of the exercise of "free speech" after he had stood, for a considerable period, in the middle of a college quadrangle shouting racial slurs at African-American and other "minority" students while intoxicated. In the review process that ensued, the president of the university and the college disciplinary committee ruled that

neither alcohol intoxication nor the rights of free speech protected the student's open prejudice, violent language, and public intoxication. The student was expelled from the university
for breech of the rules concerning the use of alcohol and other
substances and the codes of conduct of the university.

Driving under the influence (DUI) of alcohol and other drugs
among college students, for example, can and should be considered
a violent act since it threatens the health and well-being of others. If
passengers are aware of the driver's intoxication or are intoxicated
themselves, they should be seen as accomplices to as well as potential victims of a violent act.

There is a high association between alcohol and other substance
use, forcible and unprotected sexual encounters (Bloch & Ungerleider, 1986; Warshaw 1988; Tanzman, 1992). Unprotected sex and
sexual acts without birth control should also be classified as violent
acts, because they contribute to the risk and spread of sexually transmitted disease, particularly the lethal human immunodeficiency virus
(HIV or AIDS) infection, unplanned and unwanted pregnancy (Reinarman & Leigh, 1987; Simon, 1988, Simon, in press).

WOMEN AND SEXUAL VIOLENCE

All too often, campus women are the targets of young men's
aggression. As many as 15% to 30% of college women have experienced rape or attempted rape (Kanin, 1985; Koss et al., 1987;
Miller & Marshall, 1987). When other unwanted sexual contact is
considered, the prevalence rates are much higher, suggesting that
better than half the female college population has experienced some
form of sexual aggression (Koss et al., 1987). In the vast majority of
cases, the perpetrator is known to the victim, and indeed usually the
perpetrator is the victim's date (Koss et al., 1987). Women who
have experienced this type of sexual aggression by a trusted other
often experience serious life consequences, ranging from insomnia,
depression, disrupted relationships, academic failure, and suicidal
tendencies (Koss, 1990).

Alcohol's role in acquaintance rape has only recently been investigated, particularly from the victim's perspective (Pirog & Stets,

TABLE 4. Covariance of Substances of Use/Abuse and Violent/Aggressive Acts

	Intoxication	Withdrawal	Idiosyncratic paradoxical or Reactions	Paranoid States (Acute & Chronic)	Drug-seeking/ procurement Aggression or violence
Alcohol	XXX	XXX	XX	XX	X
Benzodiazipines (BZ)	X	XXX	XX	XX	
Barbituates and Barbituate-like substances		XXX	XX	XX	X
Opiods					XXX
Cocaine	XXX			XXX	XX
Phencyclidine (PCP)	XXX	X		XXX	XX
Amphetamines	XXX	X		XXX	XXX
Marijuana		X	XX	XX	
Hallucinogens	X	X	XX	XX	
Inhalants	X	X	XX		
Alcohol and Other Sedatives	XXX	XXX	XXX	X	
Alcohol and Stimulants (cocaine)	XXX	XXX	XXX	X	
Polystimulants	XXX	XXX	XXX	XXX	X
Stimulants and hallucinogens	XXX	XXX	XXX	XXX	XX
Polysubstances other combinations	XX	XX	XX	XX	X

1989; Abbey, 1991). Given that most college students drink at least occasionally (Berkowitz & Perkins, 1987), it is perhaps not surprising that alcohol and other drugs are frequently involved in acquaintance rape situations. Abbey (1991) noted three direct links between perpetrator violence and alcohol use and four direct links between victim status and alcohol use and the high co-occurrence of alcohol use in college student victims and victimizers. Studies indicate 40% to 60% of rape victims are under the influence of alcohol or other drugs at the time of the rape (Koss et al., 1987; Miller & Marshall, 1987; Muelenhard & Linton, 1987). More troubling is the finding that the victim's consumption of alcohol or other drugs is one of the four strongest predictors of rape (Koss & Dinero, 1989). In fact, one study of a national sample of college men and women (Koss et al., 1987) found that 27% of women in the sample had experienced rape or attempted rape *after being given alcohol or other drugs by the rapist.*

It appears, then, that consuming alcohol and, probably, other intoxicants puts women at risk for being victims of sexual aggression. The legal definition of rape in most states includes sexual intercourse when the victim is *unable* to give consent due to intoxication or other reasons (Sanday, 1990; Abbey, 1991). Therefore, any sexual intercourse with an intoxicated or unconscious woman must be assumed to be without her consent, regardless of whether she has given consent on previous occasions.

ALCOHOL, BLAME, AND RESPONSIBILITY FOR RAPE

Although the definition of rape includes sex with individuals deemed to be *unable* to give consent, society appears to continue to view intoxicated victims as responsible for their own victimization (Koss, 1990; Sanday, 1990; Abbey, 1991). As with other environmental risk factors for rape, the use of alcohol and other drugs is typically under the voluntary control of the victim, at least initially. This leads many individuals to believe that women who choose to drink and drug "get what they deserve" when they are raped. Discussions of ways to minimize risks are often used as proof that a woman "chose" to be raped because she walked alone after dark, went to a friend's room, drank alcohol, or got "high" with him. In fact, women deserve the same rights as men to make choices without having those choices used against them. Women do need to be aware of the possible consequences of their choices–particularly those involving alcohol and other drug use–so that they can take steps to minimize their risk, but this in no way implies that women are responsible for men's aggressive actions.

Unfortunately, the myth that the drinking woman is "asking for trouble" appears to be well established on college campuses as well as in courtrooms throughout our country. Several recent studies have investigated allocation of blame and responsibility for acquaintance rape when either or both have been drinking (Richardson & Campbell, 1982; Norris & Cubbins, 1992). In the Richardson and Campbell study, men were seen as more blameworthy overall than women for the rape, suggesting recent educational efforts about rape are succeeding to some extent. However, when allocating responsibility for the rape, men were seen as *less* responsible when they had been drinking; conversely, women were seen as *more* responsible when they had been drinking. In addition, although men's alcohol consumption appeared to have no effect on judgments of their character, the drinking woman in this study was judged to be less likable and less "moral" than nondrinking women and *all* men. In Norris and Cubbin's (1992) study, when both partners had been drinking the rape was more likely to be labeled as consensual sex by subjects, even when descriptions of the incident clearly included the use of force.

Not only do these stereotypes affect the way others view acquaintance rape situations, but they affect the way victims view the events surrounding the rape and their likelihood of reporting the rape. Many women who have been raped or otherwise aggressed against after drinking are reluctant to report the incident and may not even label what has happened as rape (Koss et al., 1987; Abbey, 1991). They may feel they were at fault for placing themselves in a risky situation, or that it will be "their word against his" and that their use of alcohol and/or other intoxicants will diminish their credibility. This assumption of their own responsibility for the rape is particularly damaging to rape victims and also helps perpetuate the myth that a drunken woman "gets what she deserves" (Sanday, 1990). The intoxicated woman, although not responsible for rape (or other aggressive acts) against her, is responsible for her intoxication. College women need to be proactively taught the social realities of female intoxication and should be given support and treatment, including focus on substance abuse, whenever they have been victimized.

ALCOHOL AND WOMEN'S SEXUALITY: PRECURSORS TO RAPE?

Not only does alcohol appear to play a role in allocations of responsibility for rape, but it also appears to play a role in women's sexuality, which may set the stage for rape to occur. Alcohol's role in women's sexuality comes not only from women's perceptions of alcohol as a disinhibitor, but also from men's perceptions of alcohol's effects on women's sexuality, as well as from cultural stereotypes regarding women's sexuality. Several studies suggest that, in general, men more frequently perceive certain cues as indicating a woman's interest in sex than do women. In controlled studies, events such as a woman going to a man's room, wearing revealing clothing, or even agreeing to lesser activities such as kissing or petting are more likely to be judged by men than women as consent to sexual intercourse (Abbey et al., 1987). Two surveys of men and women college students found that women were more likely than men to have had experiences in which they were misperceived as being interested in a sexual relationship, whereas men were more likely to report having misperceived that a woman was interested in them (Abbey et al., 1987; George et al., 1988). Both men and women tend to view the consumption of alcohol by a woman as evidence of openness to a sexual encounter, a conclusion repeatedly reinforced by most alcohol advertising in magazines and on posters and billboards, particularly those ads directed toward adolescents and college students. When presented with vignettes depicting a man and woman on a date, varying as to whether the woman consumed alcohol or cola, subjects in one study (George et al., 1988) rated the woman drinking as more sexually available and more likely to engage in foreplay and sex than the cola drinker. Therefore, the drinking woman, dressed for a date, who agrees to accompany a man to his home or dorm room may be automatically viewed as fair game for forced sexual intercourse if she rejects a man's advances.

Men and women expect alcohol to decrease sexual inhibitions and increase sexual enjoyment (Leigh, 1987). Interestingly, when rating alcohol's expected effects on others (George et al., 1988), both men and women reported alcohol would affect women's sexuality more than men's, and this finding was particularly true when women rated other women. Leigh (1990) found that the effects of alcohol-related expectancies about sex were most strong in predicting drinking behavior in sexual situations for individuals with negative attitudes toward sex generally. Given that women in this culture are valued and devalued for behaving in a sexual manner, it may be that the use of alcohol enables women to be sexual when they would otherwise be too inhibited. Unfortunately, using alcohol in this manner places women in an inherently vulnerable position, greatly reducing their control over the sexual encounter and increasing their risk for rape (Koss & Dinero, 1989).

ALCOHOL INTERFERES
WITH EFFECTIVE RAPE PREVENTION

Aside from the impact of expectations about the effects of alcohol, its pharmacological properties affect both physical and cognitive abilities necessary for rape prevention. Alcohol's effects on cognitive functioning, although not completely understood, are far-reaching. Intoxicated individuals evidence impaired decision-making capabilities, poor judgment, poor planning, and decreased awareness of both ongoing events and of their own level of impairment (Brain, 1986; Lang and Sibrel, 1989; Bushman and Cooper, 1990; Steel and Josephs, 1990; Pernanen, 1991). These effects contribute to women's victimization in complex ways. These cognitive effects of alcohol also appear to play a role in perpetration of sexually aggressive acts.

For women, alcohol's effects on decision making may delay or inhibit explicit communication regarding sexual limits. Women in a potentially sexual situation may themselves be initially unclear about their intentions to engage or not engage in intercourse, or may be unaware of their failure effectively to communicate these intentions. Given women's culturally defined role as the "gate-keeper" in sexual situations, failure to communicate effectively any limits may be perceived as an invitation, especially by a male whose decision-making abilities are also clouded by substance use. Regardless of whether women explicitly state their intentions early in the game or not, a "No" at any point must be assumed to mean "No" and not, "Maybe"; however, clear communication about sexual intercourse enhances intimacy and decreases the risk of rape.

Alcohol and other drug use interferes with this communication, which produces a type of *myopia*, or nearsightedness, that can interfere with the awareness of cues associated with danger of violence or sexual aggression (Steele & Josephs, 1990). In particular, alcohol appears to narrow the individual's focus to those cues that are most immediate in the situation while attenuating the individual's awareness of more subtle or more distal information. This myopic view may lead individuals to engage in actions while intoxicated that would be inhibited if the person were able to attend to the entire complexity of the situation. In the case of acquaintance rape, the woman may attend to the cues that signal romance (the kissing, the dancing, the laughter, etc.) while ignoring the cues that signal danger (being alone in his room, not knowing him very well, his intoxication, his insistence on further intimacy, etc.). Similarly, from the perpetrator's perspective, alcohol and other intoxicant use may lead to a focus on the cues that signal sex, while ignoring or undervaluing either her negative response or the potential consequences of continuing the aggressive behavior in the face of her negative response.

Finally, the use of alcohol and other substances interferes with the most effective physical forms of rape prevention. Studies indicate that rape avoiders are more likely than completed rape victims to have taken physical action to avoid the rape, such as running away, screaming, or otherwise physically resisting, and that certain cognitive responses (reasoning, etc.) also appear to be somewhat effective in preventing an attempted rape from being completed (Levine-MacCoombie & Koss, 1986). Intoxication clearly interferes with women's abilities to engage in either of these types of responses to attempted rape. Helping new college women know these realities in advance may provide yet further protection against rape.

TREATMENT OF THE INTOXICATED
ACQUAINTANCE RAPE SURVIVOR

The treatment of the rape victim is beyond the scope of this chapter. But the essential elements emphasized by leading practitioners of rape trauma therapy (Burgess and Holmstrom, 1974; Herman, 1992) require re-emphasis in the context of the relationships of victim alcohol and other drug intoxication. The working through of a traumatic episode and the provision of safety in the context of alcohol and other substance use is crucial. If the use of alcohol and/or other substances by the victim is not reviewed and examined in the process of therapy the episode may not be accurately and comprehensively revisited and worked through. Further, an essential ingredient of safety would be overlooked. Alcohol and other substance use compromise the victim physically, psychologically, and socially–compromising her defenses, and her judgment, causing her to be seen both by herself and others as vulnerable.

T. Were you using alcohol or other drugs at the time?

P. Well we just used a little pot together after we had a couple of beers.

T. Do you think that made a difference?

P. Not really, why should it've?

T. Why not? Why wouldn't the fact that you two used drugs together not send off some signals as well as have affected your thinking?

P. I guess I never thought of it that way.

T. Well, let's say we think about it that way now, now that you've realized what pain you've been through. . . .

Following the lead of an alcohol and other drug use history as it relates to a student's conduct and experience of victimization allows for a vital "teachable moment" in the student's life in relation to her/his victimization and in the provision of future safety (Rivinus, 1991).

Given alcohol's role in promoting, excusing, and inhibiting prevention of rape, it is important for both men and women to be conscious of the use, as well as their expectations about the effects of substances and the meaning of substance use as it relates to sexual availability. Women and men must examine their personal myths about alcohol and other drugs as facilitators of social interaction and sexual intimacy, and challenge their assumptions regarding the drinking woman. They must also be aware of the role of intoxication in limiting decision making and judgment, and should moderate their consumption to avoid intoxication, or abstain from substance use altogether.

Although it is important to be aware of alcohol's role in women's victimization, it is again important to recognize that failure to protect oneself from harm is in no way equivalent to choosing to be harmed. Indeed, our society's propensity to blame the victim rather than the perpetrator, particularly if the perpetrator has been drinking, may be one reason that alcohol and other drug use is so prevalent in acquaintance rape situations. Rather, it is the role of the college and university to assist and encourage men and women to learn to communicate effectively about sexual intimacy, without the daze of substance intoxication, to respect one another's right to say no, and build consensus regarding the universal unacceptability of sexual aggression, or any sexual contact in the absence of clear consent.

THE MALE ROLE

Male gender roles are often highly and unambivalently associated with substance use and aggression in our culture. Military service strongly emphasizes the interrelatedness of masculinity and aggression. During the college years ROTC training is supported by scholarship aid from the federal government (Arkin & DeBrofsky, 1978). Military training sanctions violence in the name of national "defense" (i.e., readiness for aggression). The military has in the past allowed for high deviance tolerance and "time-out" for intoxication-related aggressive acts by men (Cavern, 1966; MacAndrew and Edgerton,1969; the recent "Tail Hook" Incident).

Heavy drinking and acting out of sexual impulses is highly reinforced in American society at large. A commentator writing about

Playboy magazine notes, "The explicit sexuality of *Playboy* magazine is intended to confirm a manly status which implicitly legitimizes the childish indulgences so proudly pronounced in the name [of the magazine] itself" (Raphael, 1988, pp. 216-217). The strong emphasis on the need to "score" in college youth is no different now than in the past. Lionel Tiger noted in his pioneering work *Men in Groups* (1970, 1984) that the sexual initiation of an unwilling partner to whom a male is not attached is often part of the unwritten "initiation rites" of college and university students (see also Toch, 1972). Strong need for power is a primary motivator for excessive drinking and sexual "acting out" (McClelland et al., 1972). One commentator (Storr, 1991) noted, "young men . . . seem to need opportunities for aggressive display and rivalry which Western civilization does not easily provide." When such opportunities occur, they are usually not thoughtfully planned as to their consequences or implications. Many current college rituals prime males to commit sex-related or other types of violence, and substance use (and abuse) is often part of the permissive and destructive initiation formula.

THE MALE VICTIMIZER

Male college student victimizers are often regular or intermittent heavy users or abusers of psychoactive substance(s). They are usually unaware of, and would stoutly deny, their abuse but have distorted values of the rights of others, particularly women, minorities, and homosexuals. These distortions are heightened by intoxication and stress. Male perpetrators have few prohibitions against interpersonal injury and the destruction of property. They are often inexperienced in interpersonal communication and negotiation. They seek out women who are submissive or risk-taking. They are intolerant and hostile and avoid others who disagree with them. They have high degrees of intrinsic lability and anger, and they deny, project, or rationalize their aggressive behavior. They are preoccupied with fantasy and power. They often drink and use other psychoactive substances. They have themselves frequently been victims of abuse or witnesses to physical, sexual, or psychological abuse. Some are children of substance abusing parents (Greedlinger & Bryner, 1987; McClelland, 1975; May, 1980; Theweleit, 1989).

If this group of men is to be reached, they must be identified as high-risk on entry to college or after the occurrence of acts of aggression while in college. Most identified victimizers need to be suspended or expelled from college so that they may receive much needed intervention and treatment. Identified students retained in or returned to college or university will require ongoing monitoring and treatment.

EXCERPTS FROM AN INITIAL INTERVIEW WITH A DATE RAPE PERPETRATOR

T   What happened? Do you remember the details?

S   Well everybody's heard *her* story so you might as well hear mine, as I remember it. I asked her up to the room. We'd had a lot to drink at the "Home Cummer" [(sic)–a fraternity party on Home Coming Weekend]. She'd been X's lover before I dated her. So now that they'd broken up I figured it would be AOK with her . . . All the other guys were hustling *their* dates.

T   So then what happened?

S   I don't remember for sure but when she kind of woke up to it she started yelling, "Get off. . . . Get off me you ____."

T   And then what happened?

S   I guess I pushed her too far and that's when the trouble started. She really freaked out and started screaming. And that's when she called security . . .

T   Was it your first sexual experience?

S   No, not really, I wasn't a pro or anything. But I figured if we'd had enough to drink it would be no big thing if we got it on for a one-nighter. I mean how do you "score" anyway? How does anybody else get any sexual experience in college? This is the way it happens a lot. She and the deans just blew the whistle on me. But this kind of thing happens a lot, I know. *I* just got caught . . . I bet it happened in *your* day, too.

T   Certainly it did. But that doesn't make it right, or something we all can't improve upon. . . . How do you feel about the whole thing now?

S   Well, I wouldn't want to repeat it. If I'd only known more about how much trouble you can get into just trying to have sex. And I was really blasted, I drank a lot, I don't even know how much I had; and I smoked a couple of joints, too, that night. I don't know whether they were laced with something.

T   They sometimes are, but you'll still be held responsible for what you do no matter what you used.

S   Yeh, I guess so.

This young man was suspended for two years and underwent alcohol and other drug rehabilitation treatment and intensive individual and family therapy. He returned to college and went on to complete two more years of therapy in the college counselling service including attendance at campus and outside AA meetings. In therapy and in AA he repeatedly acknowledged personal and family alcohol abuse, physical abuse, and troubled, interpersonal relationships. A long and difficult revision of self-concept and attitudes toward women in particular, and relationships in general, in his therapy allowed him to complete college without the recurrence of similar behavior.

COLLEGE AND UNIVERSITY SPORTS, ALCOHOL, AND OTHER DRUGS

Substance use by athletes before events to increase performance (particularly amphetamines, and anabolic steroids) and after games for celebratory purposes is common (Russell, 1981; Butt, 1987).

Coaches and faculty members often protect athletes from the consequences of intoxication–from minor misdemeanors (e.g., vandalization) to gang rape (Michener, 1976, pp. 470-471). Thirty-eight percent of those involved in gang rape in one study, for example were athletes under the influence of alcohol and/or other drugs (O'Sullivan, 1991). Many gang rapes occur, in fact, during after-game functions and celebrations.

In college where there is so much emphasis placed on substance use as a masculine value, the heavy emphasis on sport and drinking or drugging also affects the attitudes of those who do not participate. At sporting events drinking and drugging becomes, then, not a choice but a compulsion (Brenton, 1966, p. 65).

Athletes' and coaches' examples strongly determine whether substance abuse and sports aggression (or post-sports aggression) co-occur. Decades of reports of harassment and assault of women by members of college and professional teams and the recent nationally publicized, successfully adjudicated case of rape by champion boxer Michael Tyson emphasize the points made here. It is also no coincidence that the widespread promotion of sports by alcohol merchandisers is a common phenomenon in this country. Most American children between the ages of 2 and 18 watch two to four hours of television per day and see more than 100,000 beer commercials, more than 90% of which are associated with an athletic event (Johnson, 1988, p. 70), cause for serious moral concern.

A CALL FOR HEALTHY INITIATION RITES

Male rituals are sorely needed in our college culture that exclude the random and often abusive rituals that take place presently under the rubric of partying, victimization of women (and others), sports-related events, war or violent demonstrations. These rituals will need to be designed by peers in the company of adult mentors, and they should exclude the use of psychoactive substances (Kimmel, 1987). Males (*and females*) are looking for empowerment and for role definition in college, and colleges and universities need to assist students to find responsible identities, and roles and rituals which are substance-free (Raphael, 1988; Rivinus, 1992).

THE INGREDIENTS OF EFFECTIVE INTERVENTION

1. *Accurate data:* Essential to any intervention into alcohol and other drug related violent acts is the availability of accurate data. Perpetrators, victims, and witnesses should be patiently and non-punitively encouraged to share the details of drinking, drug use, and the violent act. Accurate and timely measurement of blood alcohol levels (BALs) by blood analysis or breathalyzer and drug urine analysis are essential in making a clear and objective intervention. It is our recommendation that all college and university health services and security department have these technologies available and use them promptly. All cases of violence victims or perpetrators referred to community agencies such as hospitals or police should be administered these tests. Hiding or confiscating substance use as the mediator of an aggressive act only serves to perpetuate substance related violence (Hodgkins, 1993).

2. *Direct prompt focus on the problem:* Clarity and problem definition are essential ingredients of effective remediation (Olweus, 1993). Clarity about the role of intoxication, substance use, abuse and its treatment are also essential to any intervention (Johnson, 1987). Clarity of policies and legal procedures governing responses to aggressive and violent acts assures rapid triage of the problem once defined. No exception should be allowed to the enforcement of policy, administrative action, and treatment once accurate data has been collected. Substance use, intoxication, or other abuse should not be permitted to serve as an "excuse function" for the violent act. Intervention and treatment of substance abuse and related behavior should, however, be built into the institutional response (Lamb, 1992; Margolis, 1992).

3. *Institutional readiness:* The institution should have clear policies, lines of responsibility, and personnel responsible to handle alcohol and other drug-related violence or criminal acts. This implies collaboration between administrators and peers in disciplinary committees. Health, mental health, legal personnel and parents and peers should work together implementing help for victim(s) and perpetrator(s) alike.

4. *Systems involvement:* A systems response requires focus on the environment as well as the individual. A systems response implies

collaborative meetings among peers, staff, health personnel and families in response to a violent episode. It also implies similar collaborations for pro-active educational preventive purposes (Office for Substance Abuse Prevention, 1991).

5. *Authoritative approaches with emphasis on behavior change:* Punitive or permissive responses are usually counterproductive. Effective intervention requires a warm, firm, and authoritative approach with corresponding sanctions and follow-through (Lamb, 1992; Olweus, 1993). Effective treatment always anticipates potential relapse.

RECOMMENDATIONS

If human beings are to survive . . . committing acts of violence may eventually have to become as embarrassing as urinating or defecating in public.

–Miedzian, 1991, p. 43

Many factors lead to and contribute to violent acts. In our culture psychoactive substances play a crucial direct role by lowering the threshold of central nervous system control and management of impulse and aggression. Many people in our society accept the association of intoxication with expectations of, and reduced sanctions against, aggression. We can expect that substance use, abuse, and dependence in students will be associated with a higher frequency of aggressive and antisocial acts. *Any concerted effort to reduce campus interpersonal violence or crimes against property must address the use and abuse of psychoactive substances.*

We recommend that colleges and universities give special preventive and supportive attention to three high-risk groups:

1. *Students who have committed an act of aggression while intoxicated* should be confronted with a firm set of university policies. Treatment should be offered only within the context of strong sanctions against aggression and misuse of psychoactive substances. (The majority of euphoriant psychoactive substances, with the exception of nicotine, and caffeine in this culture are illegal under the age of 21 in most states.) By not enforcing these laws of state and land we enable psychoactive substance abuse and related aggressive acts.

2. *Students who come to college with psychoactive substance use disorders or develop psychoactive substance use disorder while in college* may have to deal with these disorders throughout life. Conversely, they may be passing through a transitional stage of problem substance use to the stage of moderate psychoactive substance use (Kandel et al., 1988). In either case, there is a considerable degree of impairment in substance-using group including: reduced self-esteem, developmental arrest, and impairment of impulse control.

3. *Students from dysfunctional backgrounds* are commonly at risk because they may have substance use disorder before entering college or family dysfunction, including physical, sexual, or psychological abuse. Parental psychoactive substance use disorder also needs early identification and student support.

PREVENTION

Substance abuse in college is frequently the equivalent of permission to be violent. Colleges need to teach safety, moderation in, or when necessary, abstinence from intoxicant use. They should give instruction in nonviolent and safe interpersonal, physical, and sexual encounters (Ehrart, 1985; Fischer, 1987; Pritchard, 1988; Rivinus, 1988; Prothrow-Stith, 1991; McMillan, 1992) as part of normal required course work. Courses could include classic and contemporary works to teach about modern problems including the associations of violent or aggressive interpersonal acts and substance use (Rivinus, 1992). For example, a course given at Brown University examines works of public policy and literature (such as the history of American Prohibition and the plays *Long Day's Journey into Night* and *Who's Afraid of Virginia Woolf?*) with an eye to teaching the relationships between the effects of intoxicating substances and prosocial or antisocial behavior (Lewis, 1991). Many other creative prevention strategies for colleges are discussed in a recent publication from the U.S. Office of Substance Abuse Prevention (1991).

CONCLUSION

Pathways to violence related to substance use can be divided into various subgroups for purposes of clarity. Table 5 indicates mecha-

TABLE 5. Pathways of Drugs and Violence

I.Drug pathways to violence

1. Disinhibition occurs under intoxication.
2. Disinhibition occurs during withdrawal.
3. Disinhibition occurs during drug-seeking behavior.
4. Preexisting values are eroded by intoxication or the addiction process.
5. Pathological intoxication occurs.
6. Cultural and psychological expectations associate drug using and antisocial behavior generally.

II.Psychological pathways to violence

1. Substances provide easy access to repetition compulsion of previous traumatic experience.
2. Substances promote stereotypic behavior patterns.
3. Substances promote fight/flight mechanisms.
4. Substances reduce perceived pain and the messages of pain.
5. Substances reduce perceived consequences of antisocial acts.
6. Intoxication and substance use can increase an individual's sense of depression, helplessness, hopelessness, and worthlessness and promote recourse to violent behavior.

III. Biological pathways to violence

1. Substances trigger brain dysfunction in susceptible individuals.
2. Substances increase trait predispositions and genetic predispositions toward aggressive acting out.

IV. Social mediators of violence

1. Substances are used in the company of others who also act out aggressive impulses.
2. Substance use is associated with pathological expectations by perpetrator and victim.

nisms of the alcohol drug-aggression relationship. These associations can and should be brought to the awareness of all college students before they embark on (further) illicit or illegal experimentation with psychoactive chemicals. The consequences of substance abuse for the student and any behavior associated with it should be unambivalently adjudicated and treated.

Colleges and universities prepare the leaders of the next generation. When so many young people arrive at the threshold of adulthood with the burden of increasing levels of family and individual dysfunction and high availability of psychoactive substances, the role of colleges as guides and mentors cannot be avoided. Colleges and universities need well-articulated social policies with regard to risk behavior, use of intoxicants, and involvement in aggressive interpersonal acts.

REFERENCES

Abbey, A. (1991) Acquaintance rape and alcohol consumption on college campuses: How are they linked? *Journal of American College Health* 39 (4): 165-169.

Abbey, A., Cozzarelli C., McLaughlin, K., & Hamish, R.J. (1987) The effects of clothing and dyad sex composition on perceptions of clothing and dyad sex composition on perceptions of sexual intent: Do women and men evaluate these cues differently? *Journal of Applied Social Psychology* 17: 108-126.

American Psychiatric Association, (1990) *A Task Force Report: Benzodiazipine Dependence, Toxicity, and Abuse*. Washington, DC: Author.

Amir, M. (1967) Alcohol and forcible rape. *British Journal of Addictions* 62: 219-232.

Arendt, H. (1969) *On Violence*. San Diego: Harcourt Brace Jovanovich Inc.

Aristotle. (1958) *The Pocket Aristotle*. J.D. Kaplan & W.D. Ross, eds. and trans. New York: Washington Square Press, p. 207.

Arkin, W., & Dobrofsky, L.R. (1978) Military socialization and masculinity. *Journal of Social Issues* 34 (1): 155-166.

Baldridge, E.B., & Bessen, H.A. (1990) Phencyclidine. *Emergency Medicine Clinics of North America* 8 (3): 541-550.

Bausell, R.B., Bausell, C.R., & Siegel, D.G. (1991) *The Links among Alcohol, Drugs and Crime on American College Campuses: A National Followup Study*. Towson, MD: Towson State University.

Bean-Bayog, M. (1986) Psychopathology produced by alcoholism. In *Psychopathology and Addictive Disorders*, R.E. Meyer, ed. New York: The Guilford Press.

Belson, W.A. (1978) *Television Violence and the Adolescent Boy*. Lexington, MA: Lexington Books.

Berkowitz, A.D., & Perkins, H.W. (1987) Recent research on gender differences in collegiate alcohol use. *Journal of American College Health* 36: 123-129.

Beschner, G.M., & Friedman, A. (1986) *Teen Drug Use*. Lexington MA: Heath.

Blane, H.T., & Hewitt, L.E. (1977) Alcohol and youth: An analysis of the literature, 1960-75. Final report prepared for the National Institute on Alcohol Abuse and Alcoholism. Rockville, MD: U.S. Public Health Service.

Bloch, S.A., & Ungerleider, S. (1986) *Brown University Chemical Dependency Project*. Eugene, OR: Integrated Research Services.

Bowker, L. (1983) *Beating Wife Beating*. Lexington, MA: Heath.

Brain, P.E., (1986) *Alcohol and Aggression*, London: Croom Helm.

Brenton, M. (1966) *The American Male*. New York: Coward-McGann.

Brower, K.J., Eliopolos, G.A. et al. (1990) Evidence for physical and psychological dependence on anabolic-androgenic steroids in eight weightlifters. *American Journal of Psychiatry* 147: 510-512.

Brown, R.M. (1969) Historical patterns of violence in America. In *The History of Violence in America*, H.D. Graham & T.R. Gurr, eds. New York: Bantam Books, pp. 45-84.

Burgess, A. and Holmstrom, L., (1974) *Rape: Victims of Crisis*, Bowie, Maryland: Brady Company.

Bushman, R.J. and Cooper, H. M., (1990) Effects of alcohol on human aggression: An integrative research review in *Psychological Bulletin*, 107, pp. 341-354.

Butt, D.S. (1987) *Psychology of Sport: The Behavior, Motivation, Personality and Performance of Athletes*. New York: Van Nostrand Reinhold Co., Inc.

Cahalan, D., & Cisin, I. (1976) Drinking behavior and drinking problems in the United States. In *The Biology of Alcoholism: Social Aspects of Alcoholism*, vol. 4. B. Kissin & H. Begleiter, eds. New York: Plenum Publishing Corp.

Canacher, G.N., & Workman, B.G. (1989) Violent crime possibly associated with anabolic steroid use. *American Journal of Psychiatry* 40: 679.

Cate, R.M., Henton, J.M., Koval, J.E., Christopher, F.S., & Lloyd, S.A. (1982) Premarital violence: A social psychology perspective. *Journal of Family Issues* 3: 79-90.

Cavan, S. (1966) *Liquor License: An Ethnography of Bar Behavior*. Chicago: Aldine.

Cherek, D.R. (1981) Effects of smoking different doses of nicotine on human aggressive behavior in *Psychopharmacology*, 7, pp. 339-345.

Cherek, D.R., Steinberg, J.L. and Brauchi, J.T., (1983) Effects of caffeine on human aggressive behavior in *Psychiatry Research*, 8, pp. 137-145.

Cherek, D.R., Steinberg, J.L. and Brauchi, J.T., (1984) Regular or decaffeinated coffee and subsequent human aggressive behavior in *Psychiatry Research*, 11, pp. 251-258.

Cloninger, D.R. (1987) Neurogenetic adaptive mechanisms in alcoholism. *Science* 236 (Apr.): 410-416.

Cohen, S. Aggression: (1985) The Role of Drugs. In *The Substance Abuse Problems*, vol. 2. New York: The Haworth Press, Inc.

Coleman, D.H., & Straus, M.A. (1983) Alcohol abuse and family violence. In *Alcohol, Drug Abuse and Aggression*. E. Gottheil et al. eds. Springfield, IL: Thomas, pp. 104-124.

Collins, J.J., Jr., ed. (1981) *Drinking and Crime: Perspectives on the Relationship between Alcohol Consumption and Criminal Behavior*. New York: The Guilford Press.

Collins, J.J., Jr., & Schlenger, W.E., (1988) Acute and chronic effects of alcohol use on violence. *Journal of Studies on Alcohol* 49 (6): 516-521.

Crowley, T. (1987) Clinical issues in cocaine abuse. In *Cocaine: Clinical Behavioral Aspects*, S. Fisher, A. Raskin, & E.H. Ulenhuth. New York: Oxford Univ. Press.

DeFoe, J.R., & Breed, W. (1979) The problem of alcohol advertisements in college newspapers. *Journal of American College Health* 27: 197-199.

DiMascio A., Shader, R.I., & Harmatz, J. (1969) Psychotropic drugs and induced hostility. *Psychosomatics* 10: 46-47.

Ehrart, J., & Sandler, B. (1985) *Campus Gang Rape: Party Games?* A Publication of the Project on the Status and Education of Women, Association of American Colleges, 1-20.

Eigen, L., (1991) *Alcohol Practices, Policies, and Potentials of American Colleges and Universities*, An OSAP White Paper, U.S. Dept. of Health and Human Services, Office for Substance Prevention, Rockville, MD.

Ellinwood, E.H. (1971) Assault and homicide associated with amphetamine abuse. *American Journal of Psychiatry* 127: 1170-1175.

Fagan, J. (1990) Intoxication and aggression. In *Drugs and Crime*, M. Tonry & J.Q. Wilson, eds. Chicago: Univ. of Chicago Press, pp. 241-320.

Fischer, G.J. (1987) College student attitudes toward forcible date rape: Changes after taking a human sexuality course. *Journal of Sex Education and Therapy* 12 (1): 42-46.

Ford, C.S., & Beach, F.A. (1965) *Patterns of Sexual Behavior*. London: Methuen.

Frantz, J.B. (1969) The frontier tradition: An invitation to violence. *The History of Violence in America*, H.D. Graham & T.R. Gurr, eds. New York: Bantam Books, pp. 127-154.

Gawin, F.H., & Kleber, H.D. (1986) Abstinence symptomatology and psychiatric diagnosis in cocaine abusers. *Archives of General Psychiatry* 43: 107-113.

George, W.H., Gournic, S.L., & McAfee, M.P. (1988) Perceptions of post drinking female sexuality: Effects of gender, beverage choice, and drink payment. *Journal of Applied Social Psychology* 18: 1295-1317.

Gerson, L.W., & Preston, A.D. (1979) Alcohol consumption and the incidence of violent crime. *Journal of Studies on Alcohol* 40: 307-312.

Gold, E. (1986) Long-term effects of sexual victimization in childhood: An attributional approach. *Journal of Consulting and Clinical Psychology* 54: 471-475.

Goldstein, P.J. (1985) The drugs-violence nexus: A tripartite conceptual framework. *Journal of Drug Issues* 15: 493-506.

Goodman, R.A., Mercy, J.A., Loya, F. et al. (1986) Alcohol use and interpersonal violence: Alcohol detected in homicide victims. *American Journal of Public Health* 76 (2): 146-149.

Gottheil, E., Druley, K.A., Skoloda, T.E., & Waxman, H.M. (1983) Aggression and addiction: Summary and overview. In *Alcohol, Drug Abuse and Aggression*, E. Gottheil, K.A. Druley, T.E. Skoloda, & H.M. Waxman, eds. Springfield, IL: Thomas, pp. 333-356.

Graham, K., (1980) Theories of intoxicated aggression, *Canadian Journal of Behavioral Science*, 12, pp. 141-158.

Green, R., & Berkowitz, L. (1966) Name-mediated aggressive cue properties. *Journal of Personality* 34: 456-465.

Greendlinger, V., & Byrne, D. (1987) Coercive sexual fantasies of college men as predictors of self-reported likelihood to rape and overt sexual aggression. *Journal of Sex Research* 23 (1): 1-11.

Grinspoon, L., & Backalar, J. (1980) Drug dependence: Non-narcotic agents. In *Comprehensive Textbook of Psychiatry*, 3d ed. H.I. Kaplan, A.M. Freedman, & B.J. Sadock. Baltimore: Williams & Wilkins, pp. 1614-1629.

Gustafson, R., (1986) Threat as a determinant of alcohol-related aggression in *Psychological Reports*, 58, pp. 287-297.

Hare, R., and Hart, S., (1993) Psychopathy, mental disorder and crime in *Mental Disorder and Crime*, Sheilagh Hodgins, Ed., Newbury Park, CA: Sage, pp. 104-115.

Heath, D.B. (1983) Alcohol and aggression: A "missing link" in worldwide perspective. In *Alcohol, Drug Abuse and Aggression*, E. Gottheil et al., eds. Springfield, IL: Thomas, 1983, pp. 89-103.

Hogkins, Sheilagh, ed. (1993) Introduction: *Mental Disorder and Crime*, Newbury Park, CA: Sage, pp. 9-17.

Honer, W., Gewirtz, G., & Turey, M. (1987) Psychosis and violence in cocaine smokers. *The Lancet* (Aug 27): 451.

Hotaling, G.T., Straus, M.A., & Lincoln, A.J. (1989) Intrafamily violence, and crime and violence outside the family. In *Family Violence*, L. Ohlin & M. Tonry, eds. Chicago: Univ. of Chicago Press.

Jessor, R., & Jessor, S.L. (1973) *Problem Drinking in Youth: Personality, Social and Behavioral Antecedents and Correlates*. Publication No. 144. Boulder: Univ. of Colorado, Institute of Behavioral Sciences.

Jessor, R., & Jessor, S.L. (1977) *Problem Behavior and Psychosocial Development: A Longitudinal Study of Youth*. New York: Academic Press.

Johnson, W.O. (1988) Sports and suds: The beer business and the sports world have brewed up a potent partnership. *Sports Illustrated* (Aug. 8): 70.

Johnston, L.D., O'Malley, P.M., & Eveland, L.K. (1978) Drugs and delinquency: A search for causal connections. In *Longitudinal Research on Drug Use*, D. Kandel, ed. New York: Wiley.

Kagan, J. (1984) *The Nature of the Child*. New York: Basic Books Inc.

Kandel, D. (1980) Drug and drinking behavior among youth. In *Annual Review of Sociology*, vol. 6, A. Inkeles, N.J. Smelser, & R.H. Turner, eds. Palo Alto, CA: Annual Reviews.

Kandel, D., Simcha-Fagan, R., & Davies, M. (1988) Risk factors for delinquency and illicit drug use from adolescence to young adulthood. *Journal of Drug Issues*, 16: 67-90.

Kanin, E.J. Male aggression in dating courtship relations. (1957) *American Journal of Sociology* 63: 197-204.

Kanin, E.J. (1985) Date rapists. *Archives of Sexual Behavior* 14: 219-231.

Khantzian, E.J. (1987) The self-medication hypothesis of addictive disorders. *American Journal of Psychiatry* 142: 1259-1264, 1985.

Kimmel, M.S. *Changing Men: New Directions in Research on Men and Masculinity*. Newbury Park, CA: Sage Publications Inc.

Kinsey, A.C., Pomeroy, W.B., Martin, C.E., & Gebhard, P.H. (1953) *Sexual Behavior in the Human Female*. Philadelphia: Saunders.

Kirkpatrick, C., & Kanin, E. (1957) Male sex aggression on a university campus. *American Sociological Review* 22: 52-58.

Koss, M.P. (1990) The women's mental health research agenda: Violence against women. *American Psychologist* 45 (3): 374-380.

Koss, M.P., & Dinero, T.E. (1989) A discriminant analysis of risk factors for rape among a national sample of college women. *Journal of Consulting and Clinical Psychology* 57: 242-250.

Koss, M.P., Gidycz, C.A., & Wisniewski, N. (1987) The scope of rape: Incidence and prevalence of sexual aggression and victimization in a national sample of higher education students. *Journal of Consulting and Clinical Psychology* 55 (2): 162-170.

Lamb, C. Sue, (1992) Managing Disruptive Students: The Mental Health Practitioner as a Consultant for Faculty and Staff, *Journal of College Student Psychotherapy*, 7 (1): 23-40.

Lang, A.R. and Sibrel, P. (1989) Psychological perspectives on alcohol consumption and interpersonal aggression in *Criminal Justice and Behavior*, 16, pp. 289-324.

Leigh, B.C. (1987) Beliefs about the effects of alcohol on self and others. *Journal of Studies on Alcohol* 48: 467-475.

Leigh, B.C. (1990) The relationship of sex-related alcohol expectancies to alcohol consumption and sexual behavior. *British Journal of Addiction* 85: 919-928.

Levine-MacCoombie, J., & Koss, M.P. (1986) Acquaintance rape: Effective avoidance strategies. *Psychology of Women Quarterly* 10: 311-320.

Levinson, D. (1983) Alcohol use and aggression in American subcultures. In *Alcohol and Disinhibition: Nature and Meaning of the Link*, R. Room & G. Collins, eds. Research Monograph no. 12.

National Institute on Alcohol Abuse and Alcoholism, Washington, DC, U.S. Department of Health and Human Services, U.S. Public Health Service.

Lewis, D. (1991) Drug and alcohol addiction in the American consciousness. Brown University Catalogue. Brown University, Providence, R.I. p. 458.

Lewis, D.O. et al. (1982) Psychomotor epilepsy and violence in a group of incarcerated adolescent boys. *American Journal of Psychiatry* 139 (July): 882-887.

Liebert, R.M., & Sprafkin, J., (1988) *The Early Window: Effects of Television on Children*. New York: Pergamon Press Inc.

Lion, J.R., Azcarte, C.L., & Koepke, H.H. (1975) Paradoxical rage reactions during psychotropic medication. *Diseases of the Nervous System* 36: 537-558.

MacAndrew, C., & Edgerton, R.B. (1969) *Drunken Comportment: A Social Explanation.* Chicago: Aldine.

Maccoby, E., & Jacklin, C.N. (1974) *The Psychology of Sex Differences.* Stanford: Stanford Univ. Press.

McClelland, D.C. (1975) *Power: The Inner Experience.* New York: Irvington.

McClelland, D.C., Davis, W.N., Kalin, R., & Wanner, E., eds. (1972) *The Drinking Man,* New York: The Free Press.

McCord, J.F. (1983) Alcohol in the service of aggression. In *Alcohol, Drug Abuse and Aggression.* E. Gottheil et al., eds. Springfield, IL: Thomas pp. 270-279.

McCord, J.F. (1988) Parental aggressiveness and physical punishment in long-term perspective. In *Family Abuse and Its Consequences: New Directions in Research,* G.T. Hotaling, D. Finkelhor, J.T. Kirkpatrick, & M.A. Straus, eds. Newbury Park, CA: Sage Publications Inc.

McMillan, M.L. (1992) *Peer Education Training Manual,* Office of Health Education, Brown University, Providence, RI.

Makepeace, J.M. (1981) Courtship violence among college students. *Family Relations* 30: 97-102.

Maletsky, B.M. (1976) The diagnosis of pathological intoxication. *Journal of Studies on Alcohol* 37: 1215-1228.

Margolis, G. (1992) Earlier Intervention: Confronting the Idea and Practice of Drinking to Drunkenness on College Campuses: A Next Step, *Journal of College Student Psychotherapy.* 7 (1): 15-22.

Maslow, A.H., Rand, H., & Newman, S. (1973) Some parallels between sexual dominance behavior of intrahuman and the fantasies of patients in psychotherapy. In *The Farther Reaches of Human Nature,* A.H. Maslow, ed. Baltimore: Penguin, pp. 369-386.

Matthews, A. (1993) The campus crime wave: The ivory becomes an armed camp. *New York Times Magazine,* March 7, 1993; Section 6: 38-42, 47.

May, R. (1980) *Sex and Fantasy: Patterns of Male and Female Development.* New York: W.W. Norton & Co., Inc.

Mayfield, D. (1983) Substance abuse and aggression: A psychopharmacological perspective. *Alcohol, Drug Abuse and Aggression.* E. Gottheil et al., eds. Springfield, IL: Thomas, pp. 139-149.

Mayfield, D. (1976) Alcoholism, alcohol intoxication, and assaultive behaviour in *Diseases of the Nervous System,* 37, pp. 288-291.

Mendelson, J.H., Meyer, R.E., Ellingboe, J., Mirin, S., & McDougle, M. (1975) Effects of heroin and methadone in plasma cortisol and testosterone. *Journal of Pharmacological Experimental Therapy* 195: 296-302.

Meyer, R.E., ed. (1986) *Psychopathology and Addictive Disorders,* New York: The Guilford Press.

Michener, J.A. (1976) *Sports in America.* Greenwich, CT: Fawcett Publications.

Miczek, K.A., & Thompson, M.L. (1983) Drugs of abuse and aggression: An ethopharmacological analysis. In *Alcohol, Drug Abuse and Aggression*. E. Gottheil et al., eds. Springfield, IL: Thomas, pp. 164-188.

Miczek, K.A., & Tidley, J.W. (1989) Amphetamines: Aggressive and social behavior. *Pharmacology and Toxicology of Amphetamine and Related Designer Drugs*. NIDA Monograph No. 94, Washington, DC: U.S. Government Printing Office, pp. 68-100.

Miedzian, M. (1991) *Boys Will Be Boys: Breaking the Link Between Masculinity and Violence*. New York: Doubleday & Co. Inc.

Miller, B., & Marshall, J.C. (1987) Coercive sex on the university campus. *Journal of College Student Personnel* (Jan): 38-47.

Miller, M.M., & Potter-Efron, R.T. (1990) Aggression and violence associated with substance abuse. In *Aggression, Family Violence and Chemical Dependency*, R.T. Potter-Efron & P.S. Potter-Efron, eds. Binghamton, NY: The Haworth Press, Inc., pp. 1-36.

Miller-Madsen, B., Dalgaard, J.B., Charles, A.V. et al. (1986) Alcohol involvement in violence: A study from a Danish community. *Zeitschrift fur Rechtsmedizin (Journal of Legal Medicine)* 97 (2): 141-146.

Moyer, K.E. (1983) A psychobiological model of aggressive behavior: Substance abuse implications. In *Alcohol, Drug Abuse and Aggression*. E. Gottheil et al., eds., Springfield, IL: Thomas, pp. 189-202.

Muelenhard, C.L., & Linton, M.A. (1987) Date rape and sexual aggression in dating situations: Incidence and risk factors. *Journal of Counseling Psychology* 34 (2): 186-196.

Murdoch, D. Pihl, R.O. and Ross, D. (1990) Alcohol and crimes of violence: Present issues in *The International Journal of the Addictions*, 25, pp. 1065-1081.

National Institute of Mental Health (1982) *Television and Behavior: Ten Years of Scientific Progress and Implications for the Eighties*. Rockville, MD: Author.

Norris, J., & Cubbins, L. (1992) Dating, drinking, and rape: Effects of victim's and assailant's alcohol consumption on judgments of their behavior and traits. *Psychology of Women Quarterly* 16: 179-191.

Office for Substance Abuse (1991) Strategies for Preventing Alcohol and Other Drug Problems. *Program Administrator's Handbook, Strategies for Preventing Alcohol and Other Drug Problems*, U.S. Dept. of Health and Human Services, Rockville, MD.

Olweus, D. (1993) Bully/victim problems among schoolchildren: Long-term consequences and an effective intervention program in *Mental Disorder and Crime*, Sheilagh Hodgins, Ed., Newbury Park, CA: Sage Publications Inc., pp. 317-349.

O'Sullivan, C. (1991) Acquaintance gang rape on campus. In *Hidden Rape: Sexual Assault among Acquaintances, Friends and Intimates*. A. Parrot & L. Bechhofer, eds. New York: John Wiley& Sons.

O'Sullivan, C. (1992) Navy resembles a fraternity in its sexism. *New York Times*, letter to the editor, August 10, 1992.

Pernanen, K. (1976) Alcohol and crimes of violence. In *The Biology of Alcohol-*

ism: Social Aspects of Alcoholism, vol. 4. B. Kissin & H. Begleiter, eds. New York: Plenum Publishing Corp.

Pernanen, K. (1981) Theoretical aspects of the relationship between alcohol use and crime. In *Drinking and Crime: Perspectives on the Relationship between Alcohol Consumption and Criminal Behavior*, J.J. Collins, Jr., ed. New York: The Guilford Press.

Pernanen, K. (1991) *Alcohol in Human Violence: Findings and Explanatory Frameworks*. New York: The Guilford Press.

Perry, P.J., Yates, B.R., & Andersen, K.H. (1990) Psychiatric effects of anabolic steroids: Controlled retrospective study. *Am. Clin. Psychiatry* 2: 11-17.

Peterson, J.B., Rothfleisch, J., Zelazo, P.D. and Pihl, R.O., (1990) Acute alcohol intoxication and cognitive functioning in *Journal of Studies on Alcohol*, 51, pp. 114-122.

Pihl, R.O. (1983) Alcohol and aggression: A psychological perspective. In *Alcohol, Drug Abuse and Aggression*, E. Gottheil et al., eds. Springfield, IL: Thomas, pp. 292-313.

Pihl, R.O. and Ross, D., (1987) Research on alcohol-related aggression: A review, and implications for understanding aggression in *Drugs & Society*, 1:105-126.

Pihl, R.O. and Peterson, J., (1993) Alcohol/drug use and aggressive behavior in *Mental Disorder and Crime*, Sheilagh Hodgins, Ed., Newbury Park, CA: Sage Publications Inc, pp. 263-283.

Pirog, Maureen A., & Stets, Jan E. (1989) *Violence in Dating Relationships, Emerging Social Issues*. New York: Praeger.

Pope, H.G., & Katz, D.L. (1990) Homicide and near-homicide by anabolic steroid users. *Journal of Clinical Psychiatry* 51: 28-31.

Post, R.M., & Kopanda, R.T. (1976) Cocaine, kindling, and psychosis. *American Journal of Psychiatry* 133: 627-637.

Pritchard, C. (1988) *Avoiding Rape On and Off Campus*, 2d ed. Winona, L: Winona State College Publishing Co.

Prothrow-Stith, D. (1991) *Deadly Consequences: How Violence Is Destroying Our Teenage Population and A Plan to Begin Solving the Problem*. New York: Harper Collins.

Rabow, J., Neuman, C.A., Watts, R.K., & Hernandez, A.C. (1987) Alcohol-related hazardous behavior among college students. *Recent Developments in Alcoholism* 5: 439-50.

Rada, R.T. (1975) Alcoholism and forcible rape. *American Journal of Psychiatry* 132: 444-456.

Radcliffe, A.B, & Rush, P.A. (1988) Physical effects and consequences of mind altering drugs used by college students. In *Alcoholism/Chemical Dependency and the College Student*, T.M. Rivinus, ed. New York: The Haworth Press, Inc.

Raphael, R. (1988) *The Men from the Boys: Rites of Passage in Male America*. Lincoln: Univ. of Nebraska Press.

Reinarman, C., & Leigh, B.C. (1987) Culture, cognition and disinhibition: Notes on sexuality and alcohol in the age of AIDS. *Contemporary Drug Problems* 14: 435-460.

Richardson, D., & Campbell, J.L. (1982) Alcohol and rape: The effect of alcohol on attributions of blame for rape. *Personality and Social Psychology Bulletin* 8 (3): 468-476.

Rivinus, T.M. (ed.) (1988) *Alcoholism/Chemical Dependency and the College Student.* New York: The Haworth Press, Inc.

Rivinus, T.M. College age student substance abuse as a developmental arrest. *Journal of College Student Psychotherapy* 6 (3/4): 141-166.

Rivinus, T.M., Levoy, D., & Matzko, M. (1992) Hospitalized children of substance-abusing parents and physically and sexually abused children: A comparison. *Journal of the American Academy of Child and Adolescent Psychiatry* 31 (6): 1019-1023.

Robins, L., (1993) Childhood conduct problems, adult psychopathology, and crime in *Mental Disorder and Crime*, Sheilagh Hodgins, Ed., Newbury Park, CA: Sage Publiccations Inc., pp. 173-193.

Rodenas, J.M., Osuna, E., & Luna, A. (1989) Alcohol and drug use by rapists and their victims. *Medical Law* 8 (2): 157-164.

Russell, G.W. (1981) Aggression in sport. In *Multidisciplinary Approaches to Aggression Research*, P.F. Brain & D. Benton, eds. Elsevier: North Holland Biomedical.

Ryan, B.E., & Mosher, J.F. (1991) *Progress Report: Alcohol Promotion on Campus.* San Rafael, CA: Marin Institute for the Prevention of Alcohol and Other Drug Problems.

Sanday, P.R. (1990) *Fraternity Gang Rape: Sex, Brotherhood, and Privilege on Campus.* New York: New York Univ. Press.

Schalling, Daisy, (1993) Neurochemical correlates of personality, impulsivity, and disinhibitory suicidality in *Mental Disorder and Crime*, Sheilagh Hodgins, Ed., Newbury Park, CA: Sage Publications Inc., pp. 208-226.

Schuckit, M.A., (1988) Weightlifters folly: The abuse of anabolic steroids. *Drug Abuse and Alcoholism Newsletter* 17(8): 1-7.

Simon, T. (1988) *Annual Report, 1987-88.* Providence, RI: Office of Health Education, Brown University.

Simon, T., & Harris, C. *Sex without Consent: Peer Education Training for Colleges.* Holmes Beach, FL: Learning Publications, in press.

Simonds, J.F., & Kashani, J. (1979) Phencyclidine (PCP) use in males committed to training school. *Adolescence* 14: 721-725.

Simonds, J.F., & Kashani, J. (1980) Specific drug use and violence among delinquent boys. *American Journal of Drug and Alcohol Abuse* 7: 305-322.

Slaby, R.G., & Roedell, W.C. (1982) The development and regulation of aggression in young children. In *Psychological Development in the Elementary Years*, J. Worell, ed. New York: Academic Press.

Sournia, J.C. (1990) *A History of Alcoholism.* Oxford: Basil Blackwell.

Spotts, J., & Shantz, F. (1984) Drug-induced ego states. I. Cocaine: Phenomenology and implications. *International Journal of the Addictions* 19 (2): 119-151.

Steele, C.M., & Josephs, R.A. (1990) Alcohol myopia: Its prized and dangerous effects. *American Psychologist* 45: 921-933.

Stone, M.H. (1990) *The Fate of Borderline Patients.* New York: The Guilford Press.

Storr, A. (1991) *Human Destructiveness.* New York: Ballantine.

Straus, R., & Bacon, S.D. (1953/1971) *Drinking In College.* New Haven, CT: Yale Univ. Press, Reprint. Westport, CT: Greenwood.

Tamerin, J.S., Weiner, S., & Mendelson, J.H. (1970) Alcoholics' expectancies and recall of experiences during intoxication. *American Journal of Psychiatry* 126: 1697-1704.

Tannenbaum, P.H. (1972) Studies in film and television mediated arousal and aggression. In *Television and Social Behavior,* vol. 5. G.A. Comstock, E.A. Rubenstein, & J.P. Murray, eds. Washington, DC: U.S. Government Printing Office.

Tanzman, E.S. (1992) Unwanted sexual activity: The prevalence in college women. *College Health* 40 (Jan): 167.

Tarter, R.E., Jones, B.M., Simpson, C.D., & Vega, A. (1971) Effects of task complexity and practice on performance during acute alcohol intoxication. *Perceptual and Motor Skills* 33: 307-318.

Tartt, D. (1992) *The Secret History.* New York: Viking.

Taylor, S.P. (1983) Alcohol and human physical aggression. In *Alcohol, Drug Abuse and Aggression,* E. Gottheil et al., eds. Springfield, IL: Thomas, pp. 280-291.

Taylor, S.P., & Gammon, C.B. (1975) Effects of type and dose of alcohol on human physical aggression. *Journal of Personality and Social Psychology* 2: 169-75.

Taylor, S.P., & Leonard, K.E. (1983) Alcohol and human physical aggression. In *Aggression: Theoretical and Empirical Reviews,* vol. 2. R.G. Green & E.I. Donnerstein, eds. New York: Academic Press, pp. 77-102.

Theweleit, K. (1989) *Male Fantasies,* vols. 1 and 2. Minneapolis: Univ. of Minnesota Press.

Tiger, L. (1972) *Men in Groups.* New York: Marion Boyars, 1970, 1984.

Toch, H. *Violent Men: An Inquiry into The Psychology of Violence,* Harmondsworth: Penguin.

Treadwell, D. (1987) Influences on masculinity. In *The Making of Masculinities,* H. Brod, ed. Boston: Allen & Unwin, pp. 259-285.

Warshaw, R. (1988) *I Never Called It Rape: The Ms. Report on Recognizing, Fighting and Surviving Date and Acquaintance Rape.* New York: Harper & Row Pub., Inc.

Washton, A., Gold, M., & Pottash, A.L.C. (1984) Survey of 500 callers to a national cocaine hotline. *Psychosomatics* 25 (10): 771-775.

Wechsler, H. (1979) Patterns of alcohol consumption among the young: High school, college and general population studies. In *Youth, Alcohol and Social Policy,* H.T. Blane & M.E. Chafetz, eds. New York: Plenum Publishing Corp.

Wechsler, H., & Isaac, N. (1992) 'Binge' drinkers at Massachusetts colleges. *Journal of the American Medical Association* 267 (21): 2929-2931.

Widom, C.S. (1989) The intergenerational transmission of violence. In *Pathways* to *Criminal Violence*, N.A. Weiner & M.E. Wolfgang, eds. Newbury Park, CA: Sage Publiccations Inc.

Woody, G.E. et al. (1983) Psychoendocrine correlates of hostility and anxiety in addicts. In *Alcohol, Drug Abuse and Aggression*, E. Gottheil et al., eds. Springfield, IL: Thomas, pp. 227-244.

Wurmser, L., & Lebling, C. (1983) Substance abuse and aggression: A psychoanalytic view. In *Alcohol, Drug Abuse and Aggression*, E. Gottheil et al., eds. Springfield, IL: Thomas, pp. 257-269.

Zimbardo, P.G. (1970) The Human Choice: Individuation, reason, and order versus deindividuation, impulse, and chaos. *Nebraska Symposium on Motivation*, W.J. Arnold & D. Levine, eds. Lincoln: Univ. of Nebraska Press.

Zinberg, N.E. (1984) *Drug, Set, and Setting: The Social Bases of Controlled Drug Use*. New Haven, CT: Yale Univ. Press.

Chapter 5

The Role of the Mental Health Consultant in Dealing with Disruptive College Students

Gerald Amada

SUMMARY. Ordinarily, the primary purpose of a college mental health program is to provide direct psychological services to students who are in crisis, usually on a short-term basis. During the course of providing such services, the staff of the program will also be called upon to provide consultation to various employees of the college regarding students who are, allegedly, disruptive. This article will describe the role of the mental health consultant, highlighting the specific ways in which the consultant can contribute to the resolution of disruptive crises as well as describing some of the misunderstandings and disjunctions that may arise between complainants and the consultant.

Ordinarily, the mainstay of an on-campus psychological service is the provision of direct assistance to students who are in some form of emotional crisis. As well, the mental health program inevitably will be called upon by college staff to assist them in their efforts to deal with disruptive students. In those instances in which the disruptive student is deemed acutely psychotic or a danger to

Gerald Amada, PhD, is Co-Director, Mental Health Program, City College of San Francisco, 50 Phelan Avenue, San Francisco, CA 94112.

[Haworth co-indexing entry note]: "The Role of the Mental Health Consultant in Dealing with Disruptive College Students." Amada, Gerald. Co-published simultaneously in *Journal of College Student Psychotherapy* (The Haworth Press, Inc.) Vol. 8, No. 1/2, 1993, pp. 121-137: and: *Campus Violence: Kinds, Causes, and Cures* (ed: Leighton C. Whitaker and Jeffrey W. Pollard) The Haworth Press, Inc., 1993, pp. 121-137. Multiple copies of this article/chapter may be purchased from The Haworth Document Delivery Center [1-800-3-HAWORTH; 9:00 a.m. - 5:00 p.m. (EST)].

121

himself or others, the mental health team can facilitate the psychiatric hospitalization of the student in a timely, humane and efficient manner, albeit an often quite formidable procedure when the student is uncooperative.

When the disruptive student is not at the same time a person who is experiencing a psychiatric emergency that requires direct crisis intervention and, possibly, arrangements for hospitalization, the college psychotherapist can then appropriately serve in the alternative role of consultant to those staff who report complaints about student disruptiveness. This article will describe my own model for carrying out the role of a college mental health consultant in dealing with student disruptiveness, drawing particular attention to the unique value of this role as well as noting some of the occasional snags, misunderstandings and disjunctions that occur between complainants and the consultant.

Before proceeding further, I wish to point out that my use of the masculine pronoun throughout this article reflects only the fact that most of the students who have been reported to me as disruptive are male.

College staff who are confronted by highly disruptive students are frequently frightened, diffident and unclear about their rights and prerogatives. Thus, the consultant can be helpful by offering vital emotional support and empathy to complainants throughout the crises such students cause. The alarming nature of many disruptive incidents may paralyze some college staff to the extent that they become inert, ineffectual and dangerously permissive in dealing with these crises. Other college staff, out of fear, anger or desperation, react with disproportionate severity and punitiveness toward the disruptive student. The consultant can intervene in such cases by pointing out some of the pitfalls and adverse consequences that could conceivably result from an inappropriate handling of the crisis, suggest alternative and more constructive modes of response, and empathize with the feelings of apprehension, doubt, and anger that often accompany encounters with highly disruptive students.

GUIDELINES FOR REPORTING DISRUPTIVE INCIDENTS

It appears that instructors, more than any other college employees, have the most direct contact with disruptive students and therefore most often appeal to the mental health consultant for help. For a wide variety of reasons–including fear of legal or physical reprisals from the disruptive student or, perhaps, dread over the possibility that an administrator who learns of the incident will hold the instructor/complainant to blame for its occurrence–it is common for faculty to display a reluctance to report incidents of disruption.

Prerogatives. The mental health consultant is in an excellent position to ferret out some of the reasons for this reluctance, and then to help the complainants overcome their aversion to reporting acts of student disruptiveness, assuming, of course, that the complainant appears to have legitimate reasons for filing a complaint against a student. An initial step in this process is for the consultant to point out to instructors that they have two highly essential prerogatives (Amada, 1992). The first, and most obvious, is to establish and implement academic standards. The second is to establish and enforce in each class behavioral standards, the latter taking into consideration: (1) minor disruptions (such as students who only occasionally and briefly chatter during lectures) should be tolerated as well as possible while major disruptions (such as students who have verbally or physically threatened an instructor) should immediately be reported and investigated; (2) behavioral standards may vary according to the particular expectations and sensibilities of the instructor, the nature of the course itself, and the physical ambience in which the course is taught. To suggest one obvious example of such variations, it is likely that an instructor of physical education would tolerate a greater degree of physical activity and horseplay in a gymnasium than the instructor of history who lectures in a conventional classroom situation. In any case, it is normally very reassuring to faculty to be reminded that they do have rights to insist upon general conformity to reasonable codes of conduct.

Dangerousness. Considering the ubiquity of violence in contemporary America, it is not surprising that many faculty initiate their discussions with the consultant by raising questions about the disruptive student's potential dangerousness. If, after hearing the facts, the consultant believes that the student is not likely to behave in a retaliatory or dangerous manner, it is probably appropriate to share that opinion. However, no matter how innocuous a disruptive student may appear, it is usually unwise and even risky for the consultant to state with absolute certainty that the instructor is completely safe from harm. Many well-documented studies (see esp. Monahan, 1981) have demonstrated that mental health professionals' ability to predict dangerous or violent behavior is quite limited. Therefore, it is ordinarily best for the consultant to advise the instructor to take whatever precautions are necessary to avoid the possibility of being endangered. One example of such a precaution would be to meet with the disruptive student only in the company of other staff. In California, an education code permits community college instructors to unilaterally (that is, without administrative approval) remove disruptive students from two consecutive classes. As a consultant to the faculty, I have very often recommended this handy intervention in cases that involved highly disruptive and potentially dangerous students. Its value is twofold: it buys time that can be used for a thorough administrative investigation and resolution of the crisis, and it can immediately defuse a volatile, imperiling situation.

When instructors describe disruptive students who clearly pose no physical danger but are simply a chronic distraction and nuisance, the consultant may take a different tack. Many such students are, for one reason or another, incapable of controlling their behavior. No matter how many times they are warned or reminded about the need to curb their disruptiveness, they somehow cannot stop being disorderly. Quite commonly, the chronically disruptive student, who is evidently manifesting poor overall adjustment to his role as a student, is also having severe scholastic difficulties and may be failing the very course in which he is misbehaving. In any case, when the consultant has determined that the instructor and the student have reached an unfortunate, insoluble impasse that can only become worse, it might be necessary to advise the instructor to tell the student that it is in his best interest immediately to withdraw from the class without penalty. Coupled with this advice could be a warning that if the student remains in the class and persists in behaving disruptively, he will be reported and a request for disciplinary measures will ensue. To avoid the stigma and pain of undergoing a disciplinary procedure, many such students, in my experience, opt to withdraw. If they do not, and the disruptive behavior continues, the instructor, obviously, must follow through on his earlier threat.

Documentation. The consultant can play an important role in assisting faculty and other college staff in developing the requisite technical skills for documenting cases of disruptive student behavior. These skills are not especially complicated and are therefore easily teachable (Amada, 1986). Instructors are advised to accompany their oral reports with written documentation of their observations, which should be devoid of psychological jargon or speculation. In other words, the instructor is advised not to speculate in writing about the disruptive student's putative mental condition. Then, with as little editorializing as possible, the instructor should provide information that is concise, specific, concrete and chronological, emphasizing only the *behavior* of the disruptive student. Finally, if the instructor holds any particular preferences regarding the ultimate disposition of his complaints, he should state those preferences in the report. Upon completion, the documentation should be accurately dated and transmitted to the appropriate administrative officer for investigation and resolution. When a disruptive incident has already spiraled dangerously out of control, the instructor can be advised to report the matter both to an administrator and to the campus or city police.

NONINSTRUCTIONAL STAFF

In addition to instructors, the mental health consultant will receive requests from a great many other college employees for assistance with disruptive students. Counselors, support staff who work as secretaries, custodians, librarians, and managers of college book stores will, from time to time, seek help in resolving disruptive incidents. Therefore, it is essential that the consultant help these individuals determine whether the student is violating the code of student conduct in their specific workplace and then to advise them about their own prerogatives to initiate disciplinary proceedings. Although they may not have the right to bar students from their work area on a unilateral basis, they certainly are entitled to report disruptive students to their supervisors and to expect that action will be taken to protect themselves from harassment and interference with their work assignments. As I have often stated to support staff, it is in no one's job description to suffer abuse. No one should put

up with intimidation, bullying or violence. The mental health consultant can be very helpful in meeting with support staff and their
supervisors in order to discuss these matters and to develop specific
strategies for reporting and resolving incidents of student disruptiveness.

MENTAL HEALTH REFERRALS

It is quite common for those who report a disruptive student to
question immediately whether the mental health consultant already
knows the student as a client of the college's psychological services. Underlying the complainant's question is usually an assumption that, if the student is already known to the mental health service
as a client, the mental health consultant will be in an advantageous
position to understand and resolve the crisis. Another, often unspo-
ken, reason for this query is the complainant's wish to know if the
disruptive student is a dangerous person. The complainant, therefore, hopes and expects that if a student is receiving psychological
services at the college and is truly dangerous, the mental health staff
will not only note that fact, but will duly report it to the proper
administrative and law enforcement authorities in order to protect
the college community from any known dangers posed by the student.

Unless a student is demonstrably a danger to himself or others,
the information regarding students' use of psychological services
ordinarily is confidential. How, then, should the consultant respond
to queries about whether the allegedly disruptive student has already seen a college psychotherapist? My own tack has been
respectfully to point out the fact that such information is confidential, but that I, in my role as a consultant, will nevertheless be able
to help the complainant in a variety of effective ways—including a
review of disciplinary procedures, the code of student conduct and
the need for documentation—without having to disclose whether or
not the student has ever utilized the college's psychological services. It has been my experience that most complainants are quickly
reassured by the offer of help and do not unreasonably persist in
seeking confidential information. As May (1986) has cogently
stated, in our consultation, as in our psychotherapeutic practice, our

work is to help others explore and contain their anxieties rather than simply and inappropriately accede to their initial requests.

Quite frequently, when a complainant reports a disruptive student, the report is accompanied by a request that the student be seen for psychotherapy, perhaps involuntarily, by the consultant or another member of the mental health staff. Such requests are often motivated by the notion that disruptive students have obviously never before received psychotherapeutic help and should now, for the first time, avail themselves of the golden opportunity afforded them by a free and convenient psychological service on the campus. Oftentimes, this assumption is made because the complainant–who thinks of psychotherapy as a treatment with a permanently civilizing effect–finds it impossible to believe that a student who has behaved in an outrageous manner could have ever been a recipient of a course of psychotherapy. Yet, quite often, I have discovered that many of the students who have been reported by complainants for being disruptive had actually been clients of the college mental health program and, as well, were prior long-term patients of other psychiatric agencies in the community. Thus, it seems advisable to alert complainants, who are urging disruptive students to enter therapy, to the possibility that these students may already have their own therapist or, in some instances, have had a long skein of unsuccessful therapeutic experiences which may cause them to regard the prospect of additional therapy with a good degree of fear and skepticism.

Complainants frequently favor psychotherapy over the imposition of discipline for disruptive students because they consider it to be the kinder, more humane, intervention with which to deal with disruptive behavior. This viewpoint is, at best, arguable. As I have pointed out elsewhere (Amada, 1992), discipline is not inherently immoral or cruel. On the other hand, psychotherapy, as clients and therapists know full well, is not a painless or uncomplicated process. And, in some instances, to attain even moderate success, the therapy must continue for many weeks, months, or years.

I have known many students who would much prefer to receive a one-time form of just and proportionate punishment than to sit with a therapist week after week, undergoing the painful process of self-disclosure, however salutary the results might be in the end. In any case, the mental health consultant may find it advisable to point out to complainants that the choice between psychotherapy and discipline for disruptive students is not as clear-cut as it might appear at first glance, and that there often are decided advantages in disciplining rather than psychotherapeutically treating the disruptive student.

It is a common practice at many colleges and universities to require students who are disruptive to enter psychotherapy on an involuntary basis. Sometimes this practice is employed quite openly and explicitly, with little remorse or reservation regarding its potential dangers or drawbacks. At some colleges, where this practice is correctly recognized as coercive and authoritarian, it is conducted, to a degree, on a *sub rosa* basis, in hopes that it will not be generally discovered or legally challenged by students or their families.

Except in those cases that involve students who are a clear and imminent danger to themselves or others, there are cogent reasons for abolishing the use of mandatory psychotherapy as a form of, or a substitute for, discipline. Whenever a complainant, whether it is an administrator, instructor or a member of the college's support staff, requests that I, as the mental health consultant, countenance the use of mandatory psychotherapy in order to deal with a disruptive student, I strenuously object, while spelling out the following rationales for my qualms.

1. Requiring disruptive students to receive psychotherapy distorts and undermines the basis for corrective disciplinary action. The focus and impetus for disciplinary action is the disruptive behavior of the student, not the student's putative mental illness or disorder. When college administrators require the disruptive student to undertake psychotherapy, they are perforce making a *psychiatric* judgment using *psychiatric* criteria. Even if they were doing this with the benefit of having first consulted a mental health professional, the requirement is being carried out by means of the administrator's authority and, therefore, it is the administrator who is making the psychiatric determination that the student requires therapy. College administrators generally do not possess the legal right or expertise to make psychiatric evaluations and determinations of this nature. On the other hand, they most certainly do have the legal right and prerogative to determine what is and is not acceptable

student behavior on their respective campuses and to carry out nonpsychiatric discipline in cases of student misconduct.

2. The requirement of psychotherapy for the disruptive student is often motivated by fanciful and naive notions about psychotherapy itself. One such notion, for example, is the belief that once students receive psychotherapy, their disruptive behavior will abate or cease. Although this is sometimes true, it is also true that many persons who receive psychotherapy remain socially disruptive and at times actually become violent, despite their psychiatric treatment.

3. Requiring a disruptive student to receive psychotherapy is unequivocally a coercive measure that serves to instill in the student resentment toward the therapist and therapy itself. If such students comply with this requirement, and on many campuses they do, they will agree to see a therapist, but frequently will make no personal investment in the treatment process itself. As a consequence, such students typically derive little from the therapy other than the impression that psychotherapy is a form of punishment that must be stoically endured.

4. For psychotherapy to work effectively, it must ordinarily be conducted on a confidential basis. Requiring a disruptive student to receive psychotherapy often removes this cornerstone of therapy because someone, either the student or the therapist, will eventually be expected to report to the college administration that the student is, indeed, receiving psychotherapeutic services.

Several safeguards can generally serve to protect confidentiality in such cases: (a) therapists may refuse to transmit substantive reports about students who have not given their voluntary, written consent to this procedure; (b) students who have been referred for psychotherapy may willingly, and in writing, authorize their therapists to transmit certain information about them to specified college officials; (c) students who are referred to therapists may be permitted explicitly to refuse, for whatever reason, the disclosure of therapists' reports about them to college officials without the threat of duress, penalty, or reprisal on the part of the college. In this regard, it is probably worth mentioning that there are significant differences of opinion among both mental health professionals and college administrators regarding what constitutes "substantive" disclosures that violate the confidentiality of students who receive psychotherapy.

In my own view, the simple fact that a student has entered psychotherapy is intrinsically substantive (and potentially inflammatory) information that should not be disclosed without the express voluntary and written consent of the student himself or herself. Although the disclosure of such limited information may seem quite innocuous, it can be used by the college, with or without intention, to embarrass, stigmatize, or manipulate students. I believe, therefore, that the student's decision to enter therapy should be given the same protections of confidentiality as are accorded the personal self-disclosures that later follow during the psychotherapy sessions themselves.

5. The administrative requirement of psychotherapy tends to transfer the responsibility and authority for administering discipline from where it rightfully belongs–the office of the designated administrator–to where it does not belong–the offices of counselors and therapists. Thus an institutional anomaly is created: Therapists and counselors (whose job it is to guide and heal) are asked or required, under administrative pressure, to assume quasi-disciplinary functions and responsibilities; and administrators (whose job, among others, is to administer discipline) are, instead, counseling disruptive students about their need for mental health services. This anomaly is especially apparent when the evident purpose and expectation of the administrative referral are to have the therapist or counselor, by hook or crook, "stop" the student from being disruptive. Although there may be nothing wrong with an administrator's recommending psychotherapy to a student, it is ordinarily inappropriate and counterproductive to use such recommendations as a handy substitute for appropriate disciplinary action.

6. The requirement that disruptive students receive psychotherapy as a condition of continued enrollment is essentially predicated upon a policy that can exclude them because of their alleged mental or psychiatric disability. This is probably in violation of Section 504 of the Rehabilitation Act of 1973, which reads, in part: "No otherwise qualified handicapped individual shall, solely by reasons of his handicap, be excluded from participation in, be denied the benefits of, or be subjected to discrimination under any program or activity

receiving Federal financial assistance." As Pavela (1985) has pointed out, Section 504 expressly prohibits discrimination against individuals suffering from a mental disorder and every relevant interpretation of Section 504 distinguishes between a simple diagnosis of a mental disorder and the behavior resulting from such a disorder. In other words, the antiquated practice of *requiring* disruptive students to receive psychological evaluations and/or psychotherapy on the basis of their putative mental illness is perhaps illegal and, in my view, definitely unethical.

When complainants seek to have the mental health consultant arrange for the involuntary psychotherapy of the disruptive student, it is essential that the consultant carefully and respectfully explain the many drawbacks to such an arrangement before denying such requests. In my experience, most complainants are completely satisfied with such explanations since they help them to recognize the greater efficacy of using a sound judicial/disciplinary procedure than of using the ethically questionable intervention of involuntary psychotherapy to deal with disruptive students.

AVERSIONS TO THE ADMINISTRATION OF DISCIPLINE

It is common to find that college instructors and administrators are averse to meting out discipline, even well-deserved discipline, to disruptive students. For this reason, many acts of serious disruption are trivialized and remain unreported, in some instances, even when they have reached truly dangerous proportions. Therefore, one of the most valuable services the mental health consultant can render to the college is to help those who must contend with disruptive students identify their own resistances to reporting disruptive crises.

Many faculty are reluctant to report a disruptive student because they one-sidedly believe that discipline has no positive value. They view disciplinary measures as necessarily punitive, harsh and harmful to students. When the consultant recognizes that it is this set of beliefs and viewpoints that has discouraged a prospective complainant from reporting a disruptive student, it may be helpful for him to point out that discipline, if applied in an even-handed and proportionate way, can have enormous positive value. If necessary, examples can be provided to illustrate this point. For example, discipline can instill a sense of responsibility and accountability to others. It can serve as a reminder that no member of the college community possesses a license to abuse or interfere with the rights of others. In short, the prospective complainant is helped to understand that reporting a disruptive student is not an act of betrayal and usually does not have serious deleterious effects upon that student.

If, however, there is some likelihood that the disruptive student will be adversely affected by a certain disciplinary measure (e.g., expulsion), the consultant can help the prospective complainant understand that the rights of many individuals must be acknowledged and protected in dealing with disruptive incidents. If, as so often occurs, the disruptive student is not reported and continues to behave disruptively with impunity, it is likely that other students as well as the instructor will suffer adverse consequences. The instructor is then encouraged to consider the larger context of the problem, weighing the interests and rights of all those individuals who are in regular contact with and adversely affected by the disruptive student. Such considerations quite often are decisive in activating a prospective complainant to report disruptive behavior.

Some college staff are reluctant to report disruptive students because they anticipate that the resultant discipline will serve only to exacerbate and escalate an already inflamed conflict. Although this expectation should not be dismissed out of hand, it must be carefully scrutinized by the consultant for its potential flaws. For example, many disruptive crises have resulted from the fact that the instructor has passively and protractedly tolerated unacceptable behavior. Often, when instructors are questioned about the consequences of their inaction, they readily admit that their passivity has had, alas, a paradoxical effect.

Rather than being appreciated by the disruptive student as a gesture of goodwill and kindness, the disruptive student has viewed the instructor's passivity as emblematic of a weakness in the instructor's character and as an official passport to behave disruptively in the future. Therefore, when discussing with reluctant complainants the unwisdom of their passive posture, the consultant can point out that, apparently, it is their ongoing inaction that has inadvertently contributed to an escalation of the disruptiveness and that it is, therefore, high time to assert their institutionally conferred right to report student disruptiveness.

Of course, it is possible that a disruptive student who is reported to the college administration will react by behaving more uncontrollably and more offensively. Therefore, in recommending that the instructor report the disruptive student, the mental health consultant can point out that this intervention may, at least initially, cause an escalation of the student's disruptiveness. The consultant can then advise the complainant about how to proceed in the event that the initial use of discipline is ineffectual. For example, the instructor can then petition the college administration to remove and bar the student from the classroom immediately until a judicial hearing can be held in order to determine a proper course of action.

Another concern of prospective complainants is the potential litigiousness of the disruptive student. Stated plainly, the complainant fears that the disruptive student will sue him and/or the college if disciplinary action is taken against the student. Obviously, no college employee is immune from lawsuits at the hands of disruptive students, but there are times when such apprehensions are rather groundless. Many disruptive students are guilty of egregious misconduct and, being aware of their own culpability, would hardly consider suing the college for exercising its institutional right to enforce a reasonable code of student conduct. Furthermore, even if a given disruptive student does threaten a lawsuit, the college should not be held hostage to such threats. If, in the view of the college–represented by the complainant, the designated administrator, the mental health consultant, the college attorney and the judicial advisor–the student has repeatedly or grossly violated the code of student conduct, it should by all means enforce its disciplinary prerogatives and let the legal chips fall where they may. The college that eschews this essential responsibility is guilty of moral cravenness and, as a kind of self-fulfillment of everyone's worst fears, invites legal retribution from disruptive students, who are often quick to detect a college's vulnerabilities, at the "drop of a hat." In any case, the prospective complainant who fears legal reprisals from the disruptive student can be advised by the mental health consultant to consult a private attorney or the college's attorney in order to determine the legal advisability of filing a complaint.

A quite prevalent concern of faculty who report disruptive incidents relates to the potential dangerousness of the disruptive student. Although this concern is sometimes disproportionate and groundless, it should never be dismissed out of hand. After all, many disruptive students are bigger, younger, and more vigorous than the instructor, and may, in extreme cases, have little compunction about using a weapon. When it appears there is a definite and imminent risk of physical harm to the complainant, the mental health consultant should recommend that the complainant report the student at once to the designated administrator and to the campus police. If the campus does not have a law enforcement unit, the assistance of the city police or sheriff's office may be enlisted. In such cases, an administrative investigation and assessment should be undertaken immediately to determine the advisability of allowing the student to remain in the instructor's class.

Another fear of prospective complainants that dampens their desire to report disruptive students is their worry that a disciplinary measure, no matter how mild and warranted, will be excessively harmful to the disruptive student, who is seen as too fragile psychologically to withstand any added pressure in his life. Therefore, it is usually very reassuring for complainants to learn from the mental health consultant that those disruptive students who are also apparently "mentally ill" quite often benefit and even flourish when rules and regulations are well defined and reasonably enforced. Conversely, those mentally ill persons with poor inner controls frequently languish and founder when they discover that their disruptive behavior is ignored or tolerated.

In short, it usually does disturbed students no favor to regard their disruptive behavior as simply pitiful, entirely uncontrollable acts committed by pitiable people. Defining and enforcing reasonable codes of conduct for all students, including the mentally ill, is one of the college's principal vehicles for expressing its dignified concern for the rights of all members of the college community. In my view, to hold mentally ill students to a less dignified standard of conduct conveys, not genuine compassion, but a form of contempt toward their personal capabilities. In any case, complainants who fear that they will irreparably harm the disruptive mentally ill student through the use of discipline can be told by the mental health consultant that in many cases it is precisely the use of external controls, via disciplinary interventions, that will aid the student to restore his sense of inner equilibrium and behavioral control.

Obviously, colleges should attempt to make reasonable accommodations to the mentally and physically disabled student. For this reason, the mental health consultant can recommend to the staff that they adhere to the following guidelines: When a student requests special accommodations on the basis of a disability, the college may, if it wishes, request that the student substantiate the disability by providing to the college psychiatric or medical records that attest to that disability. Then, if the college is satisfied that the request for special accommodations is both reasonable and practicable, it probably should be granted. If the disabled student, whose request for special accommodations has already been granted, is also a disruptive student, and his disruptive behavior continues after he has received special accommodations, the college has a clear right to initiate disciplinary proceedings against the student. If, for whatever reason, the college deems the disabled student's petition for special accommodations to be unacceptable at the outset, it must show good cause before denying such a request. If the request is ultimately denied *with good cause* and the disabled student subsequently behaves in a disruptive manner, the student is subject to the same disciplinary procedures and sanctions as are all other disruptive students.

Finally, the mental health consultant obviously should not presuppose that a complainant's allegations against a supposedly disruptive student are either accurate or valid. There are college employees who, for whatever reasons, develop an unwavering animus for particular students and use their complaints against them to carry out personal vendettas. Sadistic and mendacious college personnel may deliberately lie and distort the facts when submitting complaints against students. Other college employees–racists, ageists, sexists, homophobes–may use their xenophobic prejudices to denounce and punish students who are different from themselves. Therefore, when dealing with complainants whose testimonies seem dubious, the consultant may wish to either temporize or, if necessary, recommend that no disciplinary action be taken. If this recommendation serves only to engender in the complainant more resentment and vindictiveness toward the student, the consultant might find it necessary to recommend that the complainant and the student part ways immediately and completely without, hopefully, causing the student to incur any penalty whatsoever as a result.

The Role of Mediator. Because complainants and administrators sometimes have widely different and conflicting viewpoints regarding the causes and the degree of the seriousness of disruptive crises, they may tend to favor and pursue disparate courses of action to resolve these crises. The mental health consultant can assist them by identifying areas of disagreement and, as a mediator for the contending principals, offer recommendations about how their differences and the disruptive crisis, itself, can best be resolved. The role of mediator between sometimes contentious principals is often a problematic and delicate assignment. In my own experience, it is quite easy for one or the other principal, in the heat of trying to resolve an acute crisis, to attempt to enlist the consultant as a loyal ally. The consultant must take particular care to point out that he is doing his best to evaluate the situation on its own merits, has no vested interest in favoring one position or person over the other, and has formulated his recommendations according to the information he has received from all available sources.

Despite the best of intentions and the most eloquent attestations of neutrality and disinterestedness, the mental health consultant, who often will be placed in the rancorous crossfire between acrimonious adversaries, will probably find himself alternately accused of being "anti-administration" or "anti-faculty" from time to time. It has been the former charge that has sometimes been levelled at me. I've taken it with a large grain of salt because I know it is untrue. Frequently, one's personal integrity requires one to take bold and unpopular positions that may rankle those who do not understand or agree with those positions. That is, for better or worse, the ineluctable onus of the person who chooses to serve as a college mental health consultant.

The Mental Health Consultant and the Law. Obviously, the mental health consultant, unless he or she happens to be an attorney, should not dispense legal advice to college personnel who are coping with disruptive students. Nevertheless, it behooves each consultant to learn as much as possible about those federal, state and municipal laws and education codes that govern and shape college life. The consultant should become especially conversant with the rather specialized field of university and college law, not only to ensure that his advice and recommendations fall within the parameters of the law, but also to be able to inform his consultees about the various laws and education codes that may affect the outcome of judicial and disciplinary proceedings that are undertaken to deal with the disruptive students they have reported.

Finally, and most importantly, the mental health consultant should use his knowledge of the law to ensure that both he and his consultees fulfill the requirements of procedural due process–the legal principles requiring that the student be given oral or written notice of the charges against him and, if he denies them, an explanation of the evidence the school authorities have and an opportunity to present his side of the story.

REFERENCES

Amada, G. "Coping with the Disruptive College Student: A Practical Model." *Journal of American College Health*, 1992, March; Vol. 40.

May, R. "Boundaries and Voices in College Psychotherapy." *Journal of College Student Psychotherapy*, 1986, Winter; Vol. 1, No. 2.

Monahan, J. *Predicting Violent Behavior.* Beverly Hills: Sage Publications Inc., 1981.

Pavela, G. *The Dismissal of Students with Mental Disorders.* Asheville, N.C.: College Administration Publications, Inc., 1985.

Chapter 6

Keeping Their Antennas Up:
Violence and the Urban College Student

Paul Grayson

SUMMARY. Because urban areas have a deserved reputation for violence, it makes sense to consider the impact of violence on the urban campus. Surprisingly, urban colleges and universities may not be unusually violent, for a combination of reasons. Urban students do risk more *types* of violent threats, however, than their peers at rural and suburban schools. Two groups of students–victims of violence and city phobics–have strong negative reactions to the city and urban violence. For most students, though, urban violence has more subtle effects. While students lead relatively normal college existences, they do learn to be on their guard.

When we think of violence, big cities come readily to mind. Images appear of teenagers packing handguns, rioters on the loose, muggers springing out from dark alleys and subway tunnels. It is therefore appropriate in a volume on campus violence to consider

Paul Grayson, PhD, is Director of University Counseling Service at New York University, 3 Washington Square Village Suite 1M, New York, NY 10012.

The author wishes to thank the following NYU administrators for sharing their insights into campus violence: Sara Arthur, Assistant Vice President for Student Affairs; Marijo Rusell-O'Grady, Director of Residence Life Resource Center; and Michael Russo, Assistant Director of Protection Services.

[Haworth co-indexing entry note]: "Keeping Their Antennas Up: Violence and the Urban College Student." Grayson, Paul. Co-published simultaneously in *Journal of College Student Psychotherapy* (The Haworth Press, Inc.) Vol. 8, No. 1/2, 1993, pp. 139-150: and: *Campus Violence: Kinds, Causes, and Cures* (ed: Leighton C. Whitaker and Jeffrey W. Pollard) The Haworth Press, Inc., 1993, pp. 139-150. Multiple copies of this article/chapter may be purchased from The Haworth Document Delivery Center [1-800-3-HAWORTH; 9:00 a.m. - 5:00 p.m. (EST)].

139

the special case of the urban campus. Specifically, how dangerous are city colleges and universities? In what ways are their dangers distinctive? Above all, what is it like for college students to study near or in the midst of a high-crime area? What are the psychological costs, if any, of attending school in the asphalt jungle rather than a remote, picturesque college town?

THE INCIDENCE OF URBAN VIOLENCE

It would help to have hard data on the extent of urban campus violence. Unfortunately, the few studies that have compared crime on urban and nonurban campuses either did not specifically study *violent* crime or else yielded conflicting answers. One study found higher overall crime rates on urban campuses than more rural campuses, but did not directly speak to the issue of violence (McPheters, 1978). Another study found no difference in overall crime rates but did find a "somewhat higher" rate of violent crimes on urban than rural campuses (Fox & Hellman, 1985). Still a third study found no significant relationship between rates of violent crime and the population of the surrounding community (Stephens, 1991). Findings like these discourage sweeping generalizations.

Meanwhile, experts agree that campus crime statistics have to be interpreted with skepticism anyway. Many colleges and universities did not report crime rates prior to the Campus Security Act of 1990, and most reports that were filed understated the problem. Campus crimes have been "largely hidden and denied" (Roark, 1987). Reviewing the field, Smith (1988) concludes that there is a "dearth of information."

In the absence of empirical verification, can we simply fall back on common sense and *assume* urban campuses to be especially violent? After all, we do know that large cities are much more violent than small towns; homicide rates are six times higher, robbery rates 15-25 times higher (Smith, 1988). Doesn't the level of violence of the surrounding community correlate with the level of violence on campus?

Not necessarily. For one thing, it is well known that most violent acts are committed close to home. Relatives attack relatives and neighbors attack neighbors more often than one stranger attacks another stranger from a different part of town. Therefore the campus boundaries to some extent serve as a barrier, even without walls and gates. Violence does not fully spread to colleges and universities from the surrounding community because violent outsiders don't live on campus and usually don't have personal relationships with campus residents.

Further, while violent outsiders are to some extent kept at bay, violent insiders, one would think, are a comparable problem on all campuses. It is estimated that students commit from 30% to 90% of campus violence (Stephens, 1991), while campus employees commit additional violent acts. Date and acquaintance rape, assaults on roommates or RA's, so-called courtship violence, hate crimes, alcohol induced aggression, and sexual harassment: All these are largely internal matters, not the doing of the surrounding community. Presumably college students, faculty and staff are no more violent at city institutions than country institutions. To the extent then that campus violence is an in-house problem, not an infusion from the outside, city colleges and universities should be as safe, or unsafe, as anyplace else.

Still another reason violence may not be higher on urban campuses is because urban campuses concentrate on preventing it. Security is stressed at city colleges and universities; it has to be if only to attract and retain students. At New York University, for example, residential students attend a monthly Safety in the City Program to learn safe and unsafe areas to walk, ways to avoid drug dealers, and tips on being "street smart." To reinforce the message, safety fliers and brochures blanket the campus. One brochure has by my count 98 safety tips covering every aspect of urban crime. These educational messages teach students to steer clear of danger areas.

In addition to educational efforts, NYU takes many other security measures. Neighborhood merchants volunteer their stores as 24-hour "green light buildings," places students can go for safety. Emergency telephones are conspicuously placed throughout the neighborhood. An escort van transports students from designated buildings to residence halls. Uniformed security officers, 200 strong, patrol the streets day and night on foot and in patrol cars. An officer is posted in many campus buildings and every student residence. No one is allowed entrance to any residence hall or many academic buildings without a university I.D. or a guest pass. Parties in the student center only admit people who are on the guest list.

Nonurban institutions stress safety too. Yet if New York University is at all representative, city colleges and universities pay particular attention to the threat of violence. The danger in the streets is matched by the security campaign on-campus, and for this reason too there may be less violence on urban campuses than one would think.

TYPES OF URBAN VIOLENCE

Danger in the city assumes protean forms. It also can come from literally almost any direction. Up ahead one may spot a mentally ill person cursing at invisible enemies, from the side a fellow built like a fullback may suddenly appear demanding "Spare any change?", and from the rear a Chinese takeout deliverer may narrowly whiz by on his bicycle. Down below isn't too safe either, what with open trapdoors and breaks in the pavement and the contributions of man's best friend. Only from above is harm unlikely, which helps explain why nobody looks up in the city except for tourists admiring the tall buildings.

For the urban college student, the potential for threats from any direction is a fact of life. Whether or not city students suffer more violence than other students, they certainly risk more *types* of violence, more sources of danger. Not only must they guard against the typical collegiate threats such as date rape and alcohol influenced assaults (which, because they are typical, will not be discussed here [see Rivinus et al., this issue]), but they also must beware of perils lurking in the streets and the subways, the parks and the clubs.

A glance at the New York University brochure, "NYU–Keeping You Safe" (NYU Office of Student Life, no date), gives some idea of the variety of urban threats. Included are many standard safety tips as appropriate for the hinterlands as for the metropolis: "Do not leave wallets, money, or jewelry exposed on desks or drawers." "Keep your purse on your lap in restaurants." "Set clear limits for sexual behavior." In addition, however, dangers are covered that are rare or unknown in rural America.

For example, there is a 9-item section on subway safety. Students are advised to ride in the center car during non-rush hours and told not to talk to strangers. They should stand away from the edge of the platform, too. Otherwise some nut might push them onto the tracks.

The brochure also warns about false job advertisements. Students, it states, should be wary of suspicious criteria for positions, especially if the employment is in a home or apartment, and should always go with a friend when responding to ads.

Another section, on car safety, doesn't contain the usual admonitions to stop for flashing school buses and to turn on headlights in foul weather. No, the advice here, which would sound paranoid in rural America, is geared toward peculiar urban dangers. Students should drive with car doors locked and windows mostly closed. They should check the front and back seats of their cars before entering. If someone in a car asks a question, they should stay a good distance away when responding.

The brochure also counsels about con artists, explaining that college students "are not exempt from their wiles." Con games are so sophisticated, in fact, that they merit their own brochure. A New York City police department pamphlet describes eight ingenious schemes, including handkerchief switch, the fortune teller and gypsy burglary; one can see why students get sucked in.

While the brochure effectively suggests the diversity of urban crime, its sober, practical advice does not convey, nor is it meant to, how frightful some urban crimes are. Certain acts of violence, particularly violent assaults by strangers, are nothing short of brutal. When parents and students worry about safety in the city, these are the crimes they most fear.

A well-publicized recent case at Yale University chillingly fit this description. The victim was Christian Prince, a fourth-generation Yale student, whose studiousness, blond good looks, athleticism and social consciousness seemed, according to a reporter, "almost too good to be true" (Nordheimer, 1992). By contrast, his black teenage assailant from New Haven's crime infested inner city, James Fleming, seemed all too familiar with his spotty high school record, police record, and sense of alienation. The two dwelt only a few miles apart but lived in separate worlds; it was only by blind chance that their paths crossed. According to police statements, on

February 17, 1991 about 1 a.m. Fleming and three friends, wanting money to attend a rap concert, borrowed handguns and set off by car to "stick up a cracker"–a derogatory street term for whites. Meanwhile Prince was returning from an on-campus party to his apartment three blocks away. When Fleming and his friends saw the Yale student, they reportedly stopped the car and demanded Prince's wallet, and then Fleming pistol-whipped him across the forehead. Shortly afterward, Prince was killed when a bullet pierced his heart. Across the street police later found his abandoned wallet still containing $46 and credit cards. His attackers hadn't bothered to keep his money (Nordheimer, 1992).

The case was newsworthy on many levels: the senselessness of the crime; the racial, class and educational contrasts; the dual tragedies of one promising life meaninglessly snuffed out and another life never allowed to have promise. But for those of us at city colleges and universities, another inescapable point was the vulnerability of the urban campus. The academic community is no sanctuary, this murder reminded us. The violence raging in the surrounding streets, however remote it seems, can indeed trespass college borders.

Two more classes of urban threats deserving of mention are impulsive violence and accidental violence. City living by its very nature can be hazardous to health, even apart from calculated crime. Consider that the urban populace speaks different languages, holds different values, combines the rambunctious young with the vulnerable elderly. What's more, city residents generally don't know each other, not even on their own blocks. Most of the time everyone peacefully coexists, but it's not surprising when tempers flare up. If say, a Korean youth and a Latino youth accidently bump into each other, or a black and a Hasidic Jew, one can't assume an exchange of smiles and apologies. The communal bonds aren't strong enough to ensure a harmonious outcome.

Meanwhile the city's crowdedness and pace of life also jeopardize safety. People are pressed together at street corners and on rush hour buses and subway platforms and cars. They struggle to pass each other on the hectic sidewalks without being tripped by dog leashes or rollerbladers. Drivers, blasting their horns in fury, play chicken in the streets. At intersections, it's not at all clear who has the right of way, an inherently chaotic system made even crazier by the cars and taxis that run through red lights and the many pedestrians who ignore "Don't Walk" signs. Practically everywhere one looks, it seems, is a free-for-all, with the potential for someone to get hurt.

The volatility of urban living was most horribly borne out at New York University last April 23rd. In the middle of that afternoon thousands had entered Washington Square Park, which adjoins the main campus buildings, to enjoy the warmest day of the spring. Suddenly an Oldsmobile driven by a 74-year-old woman bolted out of control, either from mechanical failure or the driver's panic. The car took off from a block away and then barrelled into the park's walkway at 60 mph. For those strolling or sitting on benches in its path, there was no hope of escape. Twenty-seven people were seriously injured, and four others were killed. Ten of the injured and one of the dead were NYU students.

The accident was a freakish event, of course. In no sense can the city be held accountable for the mechanical or human error that caused the crash. And automobile accidents happen everywhere, on country lanes as surely as city streets. Yet the scale of the disaster could only have taken place in the city. In another setting a handful of people might have been hurt; here 31 were casualties. People were packed together, allowing the greatest possibility for destruction.

For city college students, then, muggers and con artists are not the only hazards. In the heterogeneous, densely packed, fast-paced city, risk factors are all around.

VICTIMS OF VIOLENCE

Students are drawn to city colleges and universities because of the excitement, and that includes a hint of danger. The same Washington Square Park where the automobile tragedy occurred is also a lure for students searching for stimulation. One can find there owners walking pet iguanas and ferrets, carrying huge snakes coiled around their shoulders–even taking a nap on a tiger. (Or was I hallucinating one morning?) Flame tossing jugglers and obscene comedians come there looking for audiences, while skateboarders flash by and leap over trashcans. Among the throng are tattooed bikers, inner city kids wearing "X" baseball caps, drug dealers whispering "Smoke?", and an assortment of shaved heads and dreadlocks and spiky hairstyles and bright blue or orange coiffures. For a college student from suburban Connecticut or rural Nebraska, it is all a little bit scary and very thrilling.

It is important therefore not to exaggerate the psychological costs of urban violence. Many students thrive in the urban environment, feel liberated by it, despite or even partly because of the danger. Most others at least do not seem thrown by the city. For this unconcerned majority the city is in the background, a relatively minor concern provided basic precautions are taken. When these students go into counseling, the topic of urban violence rarely comes up.

Yet the dangers of urban life do trouble two groups of students. One category, those actually victimized by violence, react as one might expect in the wake of a traumatic event. According to an NYU administrator in the residence life office, students who are held up or beaten tend to blame themselves for having taken unnecessary risks. Some have a strong need to talk about what happened, to revisit the experience and get support. Others refuse to discuss it, either because they feel ashamed or want to bury the episode. Very often, victims' studies and sleep are impaired. Although generally they elect to stay in school, usually they become more cautious afterward, venturing outside only with a friend.

For example, one female Asian student, a commuter, was molested by a man on the way to class. At first this rather naive young woman had willingly chatted with the friendly stranger, but then she became frightened when his talk turned sexually aggressive, especially when he followed her for several blocks. She was not actually touched or physically harmed, but the event had a traumatic impact. A year later she still looked around for the man on the streets, not feeling at peace until she safely entered her classroom building.

In a way, witnesses of the Washington Square Park accident were also victims of violence, since they were injured too by what they saw. Some were on the scene as bodies were smashed and hurled in the air, while others were drawn to the commotion and came upon the dead and the maimed. For a full week after the disaster these shaken students found their way to the Counseling Service. Common reactions to the trauma were anxiety, agoraphobic symptoms, flashbacks, troubling dreams and memories, disturbed sleep and concentration, and unfocused rage. Many expressed guilt ("Why didn't I do something to help out?" "Why am I alive when José is dead?") and philosophical reflections ("This makes me realize life can end just like that.")

The accident disturbed witnesses on a personal level too, exposing old traumas and unresolved issues. A woman said that the deaths made her feel guilty about having an abortion three weeks earlier. A Chinese student was painfully reminded of being present in 1989 at the Tiananmen Square massacre. A male student who was feeling out of control was found to be reliving the helplessness and chaos of growing up with a schizophrenic mother. For other witnesses as well, the violence of the accident brought to the surface something violent in their own backgrounds.

But reactions to the accident turned out to be as short-lived as they were intense. One week after the disaster came the Rodney King verdict and the Los Angeles riots, and New York University closed two hours early that Friday afternoon as a precautionary measure. From that point on, and with final exams looming on the horizon, the park accident was scarcely mentioned in counseling sessions, whether by witnesses or by other students. It seemed as if the average student had a short attention span, while witnesses, with the resilience of youth, had quickly recovered from the shock.

CITY PHOBICS

In addition to victims, a second category profoundly disturbed by urban violence are city phobics. These are students, few in number, who develop an abnormal dread of the city. City phobics' fears transcend reasonable reactions to danger. So afraid and unhappy are these students that they lead narrowed lives and can't fully concentrate on their studies.

For example, a 30-year-old married graduate student from the midwest came to the Counseling Service because of anxiety attacks. Though unpredictable, her attacks were especially likely outside her apartment, which made her reluctant to leave home. The woman had been treated for anxiety problems before, but her symptoms had worsened shortly after coming to NYU and New York City. She said she hated the city and was terrified walking the streets, imagining someone about to pounce on her.

Such extreme fear, of course, is a symptom of underlying concerns. Watchfulness is normal in the city, but city phobia points to other problems. For this married graduate student, anxiety could be traced to fear of abandonment by her new husband, fear of her own angry impulses, and fears about academic and financial disaster. She had mentally converted the many amorphous threats in her life into the tangible threat of a menacing stranger. When these other issues were explored in therapy, her fear of the city subsided.

For younger students, city phobia tends to be an expression of homesickness and separation fears. Not feeling ready to leave the family, these students fear and loathe their new locale, the city. Again, exploration of these underlying themes can lessen the symptomatic fear of the city.

VIOLENCE AND THE CAMPUS CLIMATE

Victims of violence and city phobics together make up only a small fraction of urban college students. The typical city student does not tremble at shadows or flinch when strangers come near. Still, the threat of violence does insidiously influence the metropolitan campus. Students in the city don't feel completely free to go and do as they please. They live, if not in a climate of fear, then certainly in an atmosphere of watchfulness. In the words of NYU's Assistant Vice President for Student Life, "Antennas are up here."

These effects are subtle. By most outward signs, urban college students behave normally. Like college students everywhere, they go out for pizzas and movies. They have their favorite hangouts and clubs, and toss frisbees and footballs. On a nice day they stroll around campus and take a walk in the neighborhood. If they want to go to the library or to a party across campus, or to a museum or concert across town, they go there.

But in small ways city students feel restricted. They do go to the destinations they want, but they must avoid certain streets and sections along the way. They go out late at night, but for many this requires traveling together. On the way back it's common to pay for a taxi, because public transportation, though cheaper, is more risky, and walking is riskier still.

Psychologically, city students maintain a state of preconscious alertness. They acquire the sixth sense for danger that all urban residents possess. This state of mind can be compared to driving an automobile. Experienced drivers cruise along as if unthinkingly, mind on the radio or the day's events, but on some level of awareness they make sure to check the side and rearview mirrors, the cars ahead, and the upcoming side streets. At the first hint of trouble, they bring their full attention to bear on the problem. In the same way, experienced city residents may be engrossed in their thoughts or their Walkman as they travel through town, but never to the exclusion of sensing what's going on around them. They keep a lookout for danger, just in case.

As an example of this sense of awareness, I can cite my own experience. After nearly twenty years in sleepier settings, I moved back to New York City three years ago. In the first few months I carelessly walked the streets, safe, I assumed, because I'm a tall male, not a likely victim. In my naivete I made a rookie mistake one evening and tried to brush past four loud adolescents standing on the corner. The smallest one rammed me with his shoulder, not very hard actually, and then tauntingly laughed for the benefit of his companions. Shaken but unhurt, I continued on my way.

That moment marked my awakening. I realized that I am a potential victim too; my size is no protection against greater numbers, nor against weapons. Since then I still go wherever I please, day and night. I still love the city despite its indignities and believe it offers riches for college students. But I have regained my sensitivity to city dangers. When something threatening comes, I notice it now and routinely cross the street. I watch my way and take precautions like a true New Yorker.

Sooner or later, all city students learn the same lesson. They become wiser, warier, less trusting than when they arrived in the city. They learn about the subways and the alleys, the drug dealers and the con men. They learn not to smile at fellow pedestrians and to be wary when a stranger asks a question. However naive they were originally, they learn to become street smart.

In one sense, this knowledge of violence is not undesirable. Since the real world is plagued by violence, not to mention poverty, homelessness, drug addiction, racial hatred and AIDS, perhaps it's just as well that students observe these problems firsthand. They receive for their tuition money a laboratory in urban ills as well as instruction in the classroom. Exposure to the city's problems can spark interests and shape career decisions. For example, students may feel motivated to volunteer making sandwiches at homeless shelters or tutoring illiterate adults, and may set their sights on careers in community service such as teaching, nursing, or social work. A common reaction to the city is, "With all that's wrong out there, I want to do something to help." All in all, there is arguably less of an ivory tower mentality at big city institutions, less myopia about the real world and its problems.

Still, on balance one wishes these young persons could be spared their cognizance of danger. Ideally, college students should learn and care about society, but shouldn't have to keep an eye out for muggers. College is stressful enough in a tranquil setting. The stress is even more intense when antennas have to be kept up.

REFERENCES

Fox, J.A. & Hellman, P.A. (1985). Location and other correlates of campus crime. *Journal of Criminal Justice*. 429.

McPheters, L.R. (1978). Economic analysis of factors influencing crime on campus. *Journal of Criminal Justice*. 6. 47.

Nordheimer, J. (1992). Son of privilege, son of pain: Random death at Yale's gate. *The New York Times*, June 28. 23, 30.

NYU Office of Student Life. (no date). NYU: Keeping you safe. New York: New York University Public Affairs Department.

Rivinus, T. & Larimer, M.D.(1993) Substance use and destructive behavior. *Journal of College Student Psychotherapy*, Vol. 8(1/2).

Roark, M.L. (1987). Preventing violence on college campuses. *Journal of Counseling and Development*. 65. 367-71.

Smith, M.C. (1988). *Coping with crime on campus*. New York: American Council on Education and Macmillan.

Stephens, G. (1991). *Crime on campus*. Unpublished doctoral dissertation.

Chapter 7

Race Relations
and Polycultural Sensitivity Training
on College Campuses

Linda Berg-Cross
B. James Starr
Lloyd R. Sloan

SUMMARY. The major factors contributing to racial strife on college campuses are discussed and different conceptualizations of appropriate race relations goals are reviewed. A number of widely used and/or exciting, new race relations training interventions are presented for use with students, faculty and administrators. Institutional policies and faculty activities that would enhance poly-culturalism are also presented.

Consider the problems posed by the following incidents:

* Tenured Black professors are booed in their classrooms and declared incompetent (Vontress, 1992).

Linda Berg-Cross, PhD, ABPP, is Director of the Clinical Psychology Training Program, Department of Psychology, Howard University, Washington, DC 20059. B. James Starr, PhD, is Associate Professor, Department of Psychology, Howard University, Washington, DC 20059. Lloyd R. Sloan, PhD, is Associate Professor, Department of Psychology, Howard University, Washington, DC 20059.

Correspondence may be addressed to: Linda Berg-Cross, PhD, Director of Clinical Psychology, 525 Bryant Street, C.B. Powell Building, P.O. Box 1097, Department of Psychology, Washington, DC, 20059.

[Haworth co-indexing entry note]: "Race Relations and Polycultural Sensitivity Training on College Campuses." Berg-Cross, Linda, B. James Starr, and Lloyd R. Sloan. Co-published simultaneously in *Journal of College Student Psychotherapy* (The Haworth Press, Inc.) Vol. 8, No. 1/2, 1993, pp. 151-175; and: *Campus Violence: Kinds, Causes, and Cures* (ed: Leighton C. Whitaker and Jeffrey W. Pollard) The Haworth Press, Inc., 1993, pp. 151-175. Multiple copies of this article/chapter may be purchased from The Haworth Document Delivery Center [1-800-3-HAWORTH; 9:00 a.m. - 5:00 p.m. (EST)].

- At faculty Senate meetings, white faculty members are perceived as making derogatory racial assertions without being challenged by their colleagues (Vontress, 1992).
- A Black Harvard University Medical School student is accused of striking a white student who came to a party in blackface (Barnes, 1992).
- A white student denied admission to Duke University initiates a racial discrimination suit because an African American student with lower standardized scores was accepted (Collison, 1992).
- A Georgetown law student causes an uproar by publishing a report that African American students had lower LSAT scores than White students.

All of these incidents are examples of how multicultural relations on college campuses have become associated with hostile and violent behavior. This is not surprising when one considers that prejudice, intergroup conflict and aggression share multiple common roots including cultural-social learning, a high "we" vs. "they" identity, real and perceived intergroup competition, frustration-aggression, authoritarianism, and a host of consequent cognitive mechanisms. All of these phenomena distort perceptions and confirm biases. It is a small wonder then that in our increasingly multicultural society, violence arising from intergroup conflict is becoming a major concern on college campuses.

Indeed, both public opinion and data suggest that the late 1980s were a time of increasing intergroup conflict on college campuses. Between 1986 and 1990, there were 250 racial incidents reported to the National Institute Against Violence and Prejudice (Shenk, 1990). Between 1985 and 1988 the Anti-Defamation League of B'nai B'rith reported a sixfold increase in anti-Semitic episodes (Shenk, 1990). In 1986, the National Institute Against Prejudice and Violence reported that one in five minority students experience harassment, prejudice or bigotry every year. Since then, there have been more than 15 studies that indicate that we are now experiencing more incidents of campus bigotry motivated violence than in 1986. For example, two recent studies at Rutgers and SUNY-Cortland indicate that at least 25%, and possibly as high as 30% of all minority students are victims of campus bigotry motivated violence (Abadu, 1991). In 1991, 36% of all post secondary schools reported incidents of bigotry that received official handling and 74% of all doctorate granting institutions reported such incidents (Cox, 1991).

There is every reason to believe that the 1990s will be a time of unprecedented divisiveness on college campuses. Interventions need to be focused on helping students learn new, adaptive skills for relating to different groups. These skills must give cognizance to the key factors that promote bias related incidents.

Jon Dalton (1991) has isolated and listed seven factors that have promoted racial intolerance: white students' lack of knowledge and experience with people of color and their cultures, peer group influence, increased competition and stress, use of alcohol, protection of turf and territory, influence of off campus groups, perception of unfair treatment, coverage of people of color in the campus media, and treatment of minorities by campus and community law enforcement agencies.

Some of these factors are best addressed by peer interventions. For example, lack of knowledge, experience with other groups and peer group influences are best addressed by residence life personnel. Faculty need to take the initiative in dealing with perceptions of unfair treatment, by providing intellectually and culturally relevant classes, and mentoring experiences. The administration must ultimately take leadership in addressing systemic issues such as the use of alcohol, training of campus and community law enforcement, the increased competition and stress for scarce financial and academic resources, and how space is allocated and used on campus.

It is both interesting and symptomatic of the polarization in our society that minority and nonminority students often have diametrically opposite evaluations of the usefulness of Dalton's list. On the one hand, some nonminority students feel that the list implies that racial intolerance is primarily a problem among white students and staff. They feel that it minimizes the fact that many minority students also have little experience with members of other ethnic and racial groups. They argue that media coverage helps everyone to develop a picture of members of a myriad of minority groups as well as the majority white culture. These students feel the factors of racial intolerance which Dalton mentions are not the unique province of any single group.

On the other hand, some minority students believe that Dalton's list correctly suggests that nonminorities do experience greater racial intolerance and that they do bear a greater responsibility for initiating changes in attitude and behavior because of their oppressor status. This feeling is often a significant one among minority students and is the source of much reactivity among nonminorities. Mura (1991) summarizes this position quite well when he says, "Whites must see the problem of race as one of giving up power. They have to acknowledge that our economic, political and cultural systems have been designed, in part, for the benefit of whites, and that they, as whites, are less likely to acknowledge or understand the injustice of these systems than are people of color. Whites have to admit that their understanding of the lives of people of color is limited, and that limited knowledge has allowed them to feel comfortable with the status quo."

This position has important historical merit and is highly accurate in describing many current situations. Yet, the meta message that places the primary burden of change on nonminority students generates antagonism among many of them. The chicken and egg parable teaches us the futility of searching for the "origin," instead of focusing on the cycle (searching for which group causes racial conflict instead of focusing on how to improve relationships). In the Middle East, in Eastern Europe, and in the United States, the road to intergroup harmony involves moving toward here and now solutions that change the cycle of current interactions and relinquishing the search to assign blame.

We believe that the "intellectually correct" campus of the 90s is no longer being perceived as promoting politically correct, chicken and egg searches (a perception that we feel was more myth than reality). However, now there is an active, open push for students to grapple with personal answers to the following types of interactional questions:

How can cultural relativism be a worthy moral and intellectual goal when many cultures support violence, oppression, sexism and racism? How can cultural relativism be a worthy moral and intellectual goal when I find my own culture in desperate need of criticism, revision, and growth? How does increasing my understanding of human kind increase my understanding of self and empower me to shape my own destiny? How much of our destiny is shaped by our culture and how much can the individual overcome influences within his/her culture?

The purpose of this paper is to review the innovative, nationwide efforts being made on campuses throughout the U.S. to reduce prejudice, increase racial harmony and, orient students towards intellectually correct modes of inquiry.

COMPETITION FOR SCARCE RESOURCES: THE PROVOCATIVE ROLE OF PERCEIVED INEQUALITY

Today, the two most powerful and divisive factors affecting race relations on campus seem to be the increased competition for scarce resources and the increase in voluntary separatism (a factor not mentioned by Dalton). Before discussing specific interventions that have been used to improve race relations on college campuses, these two potent factors must be discussed.

The Provocative Role of Perceived Inequality and Scarce Resources. Most often the arguments for and against minority focused programs on college campuses are based on conflicting political, social, economic, public policy, and personal values. While this situation reflects general societal conditions, it is polarized and energized by the fact that once in college, the "haves" (middle class white students) feel demoted to "have nots" (they are under enormous financial pressure and/or debt and feel that they were accepted into the college under more stringent admission standards). The original "have nots" (lower income minority students) are perceived by the white students as the "haves" (they assume minorities have increased financial support from the university and lower admission standards). The cataclysmic change in lifestyle experienced by most middle class white students is extremely frustrating and a strong precursor of overt and covert aggression against the "out group." But are these feelings in accord with reality?

The reality is that according to the Department of Education's latest study on the 1986-1987 school year (1988), the average full time, undergraduate received $3,813 in aid with ethnic breakdowns as follows: Asian ($4,374); American Indian ($4,201); African American ($4,126); Hispanic ($3,817); and White ($3,716). To look at some of the subgroups, the grants, with an overall average of $2,630, were distributed as follows: Asian ($3,280); American Indian ($3,299); African American ($2,827); Hispanic ($2,728); and White ($2,525). The overall average loan was for $2,456 and broke down as follows: Asian ($2,478); American Indian ($2,762); African American ($2,257); Hispanic ($2,439); and White ($2,484). Given the well known income discrepancy between minority and nonminority families, these figures reveal far more parity than many nonminority students would expect.

Admissions criteria vary widely from institution to institution and many unwritten rules of thumb may be used. Yet, when specific criteria vary for different ethnic groups, openly stating the precise criteria could be very helpful in giving all students greater feelings of efficacy.

While nonminorities feel displaced, minority students, particularly African Americans, Hispanics, and Native Americans feel they are continuing to be the real "have nots" at predominantly white institutions (PWIs) because they are perceived through a racist societal lens, stigmatized as not really academically motivated and/or able. Many African American students carry a racial vulnerability that equates academic success with something alien from their identity. Academic failures create a double jeopardy for some disadvantaged minorities–they experience the stigma associated with personal incompetence and the weighty confirmation of the broader, racial inferiority of which they are suspected. Asian students are ironically just as stigmatized when they are branded as providing "unfair" intellectual competition.

In order for students to identify with academic achievement and the institution, they must feel personally valued by their teachers; they must feel the challenge and promise of reaching inspired goals (instead of remedial measuring posts); they must be socially integrated into campus life; and they must experience the particulars of their life and culture within relevant curricula (Steele, 1992). Thus, for minorities to become included among the "haves" at PWIs they need to develop personal relationships with faculty, to have minority issues addressed in relevant courses, to be able to develop deep friendships with white students as well as minority students, and to be able to adhere to a uniform standard of high academic expectations. Perhaps, most important is for minority students to have a college climate that acknowledges that their ethnicity is a critical and valued aspect of their learning-about-self.

We have ended up with a situation wherein both minority and nonminority students feel that they are being differentially treated, short changed and in a duplicitious relationship with the university.

All students need to find a common and fair playing ground at the university. Where there are perceptions of favored children, there are jealousies and animosities.

PREVENTING PERCEIVED COMPETITION FROM PROMOTING VIOLENCE ON COLLEGE CAMPUSES: THE BASIC PSYCHOLOGICAL STRATEGY

The systemic question colleges ultimately struggle with is, "How can we reduce the amount of we-them competition that exists on campus?" Competition is the result of two or more groups wanting what is usually in short supply when only one group can have the desired item; separating the groups into haves and have nots. Surprisingly, groups can develop into a state of conflict at the simple expectation of competition. Groups seem uniquely given to conflict and even small groups are six to eight times more likely to choose competitive over cooperative responses in free choice situations (Blake and Mouton, 1986).

Threats, insults, attacks and punishment often are triggered by these competitive feelings on campus and can spiral into full intergroup conflict even though they initially are displayed by only a few members. Recall that in the famous Sherif et al. Robber's Cave experiment (cf. Streufert and Streufert, 1986) children at a summer camp who were segregated into arbitrary groups had conflict advance progressively from verbal abuse to self isolation to discrimination to physical violence. Clearly, we need to employ influence tactics to interrupt or break and reverse the spirals. Sherif et al. (1961) found that instituting more contact between self isolated groups wasn't effective at reducing conflict. This "contact" strategy is the most obvious intervention and has been implemented in schools, colleges and the communities throughout the country. It is painful that research and life experience demonstrates its ineffectiveness to enhance intergroup relationships. Instead, to reduce conflict a series of task demands with superordinate goals that require cooperation from all parties is necessary to break down intergroup hostility and competition. These types of tasks are difficult but not impossible to duplicate on a college campus among discordant ethnic/cultural groups. Rallying around an environmental problem on campus or creating a more streamlined registration process could feasibly unite disparate student groups if they were given the power to initiate common solutions. In the race relations training section a number of interventions are suggested that have cooperative superordinate goals.

VOLUNTARY SEPARATISM

Voluntary separatism is the social, economic, intellectual and/or territorial segregation of minorities due to their own choosing. Voluntary separatism on campuses has been supported by university practices and philosophies throughout the past decade. Nearly all schools of higher education have understood the appropriateness and positive benefits of recognizing, celebrating, and reinforcing activities that strengthen intragroup identifications.

The major force promoting strong intragroup identifications on college campuses is the universal need to validate our beliefs and attitudes through social comparisons with others who are similar to us on the dimension of our current concern (e.g., the worthiness of my identity can be validated on a racial/ethnic dimension by affiliating and comparing myself to others in my racial/ethnic group) (Goethals and Darley, 1987).

The strongest benefit of intragroup affiliations is the intense experience of cohesion such groups engender. Students with high intragroup affiliations feel more unity (we-ness); a positive sense of belonging; a perceived similarity of goals, qualities and beliefs; more stability or desire to remain at the university; greater satisfaction and enjoyment; positive self esteem, increased motivation to succeed, heightened security, reduced anxiety; and a friendly, supportive cooperative atmosphere.

However, the effects of intragroup solidarity are not merely unidirectional and self enhancing. Intragroup solidarity very often is coupled with strong intergroup hostilities. When there is an increasing spiral of perceived value differences, the attitudes and activities of the ingroup become highly valued while those of the outgroup are proportionately devalued and their members depersonalized.

Respecting voluntary separatism is at the heart of much politically correct behavior. Many campus intellectuals have been ambivalent about sending an explicit message that individualism may be as valued as ethnic/racial allegiances. Instead, strong intragroup support has been affirmed as critical for survival–and even more important for success. During the last decade, intragroup solidarity with intergroup tolerance and appreciation has become the primary social goal on many campuses.

Many are now concerned that an unbalanced support of ethnic intragroup solidarity has several serious academic, societal, and developmental goals. Academically, a most basic goal of the university is to prepare students for world citizenship. Societally, the university has historically been a model of social changes for the next generation. Rather than merely mirroring societal ills, the campus has evolved with the potential to bathe in ideologies of better tomorrows. Developmentally, the highest stage of racial development in most models is an integrative world view rather than a benign separatist view.

Consider the five stage model developed by Jackson and Hardiman (cited in Bidol, 1987), where the first stage, naivete, is thought to be experienced by children. All people are considered the same and no differences are seen as important. At the second or acceptance stage, an individual identifies with the prevailing societal values and tries various integrative strategies to overcome their status as "different." Resistance, the third stage, is defined by the embracing of group values and the awareness of oppression. The ensuing stage is termed redefinition. It represents an attempt to embrace the positive aspects of one's own group while developing a real picture of those in power in society. The fifth and final stage is "internalization" (multiculturalism), where individuals work authentically with one another to develop mutual empowerment. Clearly, the university is poised to help students develop the highest levels of reasoning.

In the early part of the twentieth century, we were content to describe ourselves as a "melting pot," blending together disparate cultures into a new American culture. After a time, many voiced dissatisfaction with this metaphor because it implied the eradication of the unique character of the combining racial/ethnic groups. The new metaphor became the "salad bowl," wherein the individual elements retained their character. The emerging resynthesis of the 90s may well be seeking to create a national "casserole"; distinct ingredients and yet the blended juices from continual interaction combine to make the dish more palatable. The menu for prejudice abatement would then contain a casserole of recognizable but intermingled and partly shared elements rather than stark, separate and unchanging elements of the over-simplified salad-bowl of intercultural existence.

Universities are now starting to promote poly-cultural self perceptions wherein students belong to an ethnic/racial in-group culture and also to a more inclusive superordinate in-group culture which reflects the greater society and the whole planet. Polyculturalism stresses that the similarities between us are overwhelming, unchanging, and uplifting. The differences between us are vital, dynamic, and rich in meaning. But our differences are best understood in the context of shared human experiences. Polyculturalism suggests that it is vital to use intragroup solidarity to learn about this shared human condition. From within the safety of our own group, if we are motivated and guided, we can reach out and explore the unknown (Gaertner et al., 1988, 1989).

In short, voluntary separatism on college campuses is part of a larger cultural movement for people to gain strength and direction from their historical roots. Colleges have been in the forefront, supporting and encouraging this movement. Inadvertently, the push for individualism has not been as glamorized or promoted. The nineties are assuredly bringing renewed emphasis on the individual. Academic articles are again discussing the importance of social evolutionists, such as Carl Jung and Joseph Campbell, who stressed the need of the social group to foster the development of individual potential. When the individual is living primarily to glorify and protect the group (nation, class, community), the members become increasingly hostile, belligerent, narrow minded and mean spirited to all designated "outsiders." The pendulum for race relations has begun to swing towards respecting, honoring and supporting the individual in his or her quest for existential meaningfulness and responsibility. Indeed, it has been well documented that the most insecure students, who have suffered personal failure (Cialdini and Richardson, 1980) or embarrassment (Meindl and Lernes, 1984) are the ones most likely to derogate an outgroup in order to benefit from the contrast of a yet, more inferior group than themselves.

In the quest to promote individualism within a vibrant multicultural society, it is as important to stress commonalities as to appreciate differences. For example, workshops and programs could be developed around the work of researchers such as Sampo Paunonen and Douglas Jackson (1992) who have established a cross cultural verbal personality inventory and a nonverbal personality questionnaire. Their research shows five universal personality factors: academic orientation, aesthetic-intellectual orientation, autonomy, aggression, and social control. Exploring how these traits are found within each racial/ethnic group would build strong people-to-people identifications across traditional racial/ethnic groups.

When the issues of scarce resources are honestly and openly addressed and the values of voluntary separatism are open for individual discussion, specific peer, faculty, and administrative interventions are likely to be positively received.

PEER INTERVENTIONS USED IN RACE RELATIONS TRAINING

The time limited, experiential, prejudice reduction workshop will continue to serve as the college student's first introduction to improved race relations on campus and as an ongoing consciousness raiser for students, faculty and administrators. The following activities are hopefully representative of the best of these efforts.

1. Prejudice Reduction Workshops

The National Coalition-Building Institute (NCBI) is typical of many nonprofit leadership training organizations that have led prejudice reduction workshops across a wide array of American campuses. The NCBI and other prejudice reduction workshops use an intense one day to one week format of integrated interactions between a diverse group of students.

Nearly all universities expose students to the values of tolerance and multiculturalism during freshman orientation which is very appropriate because it sets the tone of what is expected from students. Some programs, such as at the University of Texas, Austin, spark their dialogues with a stimulus film. For example, in the classic film, "A Class Divided," a group of third graders are divided into different privilege groups based on eye color. After viewing the film, students discuss the creation of stereotypes and issues of discrimination. Many colleges use more recent college oriented films. Some of the most popular films include "Bill Cosby on Prejudice" (distributed by Pyramid Productions, 1978), which focuses on the academic, financial, and social aspects of being African American on a predominantly White campus, and "Facing Differences: Living Together on Campus" (distributed by the Anti-Defamation League, 1990) which explores racial, religious, ethnic and sexual orientation diversities. Some universities, including Tufts and the University of Maryland, have their own student-produced films about campus policies, procedures and issues on stereotyping and prejudice. The added relevancy, interest and identification value of materials developed by and focused on the home institution are probably well worth the effort and cost of production. Many of the exercises discussed above are used during these freshman orientation sessions.

Structured experiential exercises form the core of the program and each exercise is designed to foster openness, communication and understanding. Typical of the exercises used by these groups are the following:

A. *First Thoughts Exercise.* Participants pick a partner whom they do not know. They then choose ethnic, gender, racial, or religious groups to which neither partner belongs. One partner mentions the group, and the second partner gives their first association. Then the roles are reversed. It quickly becomes apparent that most people have internalized negative images about a variety of groups different from their own (National Coalition-Building Institute (NCBI), Brown and Mazza, 1991).

B. Internalized Oppression and Pride Exercise. In this exercise, partners pair off and find fault with their own group identity. A woman might say, "What I can't stand about women is that they love to gossip." The partner would then find a fault with one of his/her group identities. Participants learn from this exercise that they have internalized negative stereotypes about their group from the larger society. After discussion of this phenomenon, the same pairs reunite and this time share something they are proud of with one of their group identities (NCBI, Brown and Mazza, 1991).

C. Caucus Reporting Exercise. Special interest groups are formed based on gender, race, sexual orientation, class, language, physical characteristics, etc., and each caucus prepares a report, responding to the question, "What do you never again want others to say, think or do toward your group?" Each report is presented to the whole group for discussion (NCBI, Brown and Mazza, 1991).

D. Speak Out Exercises. This is a very powerful exercise in which workshop participants volunteer to share painful experiences of discrimination. It should occur after group members have gotten to know each other by participating in some prior exercises (NCBI, Brown and Mazza, 1991).

E. Mixed Ethnic Groups. Groups of individuals unknown to one another are asked to interact in various ways in order to learn about each other. For example, participants can be asked to free associate to terms such as "my home," "this town," or "this university" in order to get at various perceptions. The group members can be asked to share their lists and indicate why they used the descriptors that they did. Additionally, they can be paired off into mixed ethnic groups and instructed to gather information so that they can "introduce" their partner to the group. The types of information gathered and the way they are filtered and presented can lead to useful discussions about group differences (adapted from Weeks, Pederson, and Brislin, 1979).

F. Fish Bowl. This exercise utilizes small groups, composed of students of the same ethnic and/or racial identification. The groups should be approximately of equal size. They are asked to discuss meaningful problems (e.g., feelings of isolation on campus; interracial friendships, covert sexism and racism, etc.). A different ethnic/racial group observes from the outside, each member focusing on a particular participant in the inner group. After a predetermined time, the outer group processes what they perceive as having happened "in the fish bowl." Various groups take turns in the fish bowl. The process can be used to learn about group values, decision making processes, and acceptable styles (adapted from Weeks et al., 1979).

G. Should the Child Be Taught. This exercise explores the cultural relativity of childrearing practices. Small groups discuss various questions with a view toward deciding what children should be taught. For example, they might be asked, "Should the child be taught to be independent or to respect and accept obligations from their parents" (see Pusch, 1979). Today, this exercise is useful in demonstrating the fallacy of stereotyping individual attitudes on the basis of race or ethnicity.

H. Role Playing Bigoted Remarks. Students repeat bigoted jokes, remarks or slurs that they have heard around campus, in front of the group. They begin by voicing their own negative reactions to the comment. Then they role play the situation and the remark, and effective interventions are discussed by the group. The National Coalition Building Institute (NCBI) makes three basic assumptions which guide the search for appropriate responses: there are no unreachable bigots; prejudicial remarks are a call for help, indicating that the speaker's self esteem is being threatened and he/she feels a need to be one up; and because prejudicial remarks can arouse enormous anger in listeners, they are often impulsive and inappropriate in their responses.

I. Person-in-Culture-Interview (PICI). The PICI is a structured interview-encounter, in which two participants from different groups meet privately to learn about one another. Participants are urged to mill around the room looking for a participant very different from themselves. By exploring universal themes, participants emotionally experience the extent to which their similarities outweigh their differences (Berg-Cross & Zoppetti, 1991).

J. White Racial Identity Programs. Katz (1978) has developed a program to allow whites to understand their own whiteness. The six themes addressed in these workshops include definitions of racism, confronting the reality of racism, dealing with feelings, cultural differences, cultural racism, and the meaning of whiteness. Many campuses have used Katz's program. At Pennsylvania State University, 85% of 1,100 participants showed positive attitude changes after being in the program (Katz, 1978).

A similar program has been developed by the University of Massachusetts. "White Allies Against Racism" is a six to eight week seminar in which whites examine their own attitude and beliefs and are encouraged to develop strategies for facilitating change.

K. Prediction and Perception. A mixed group of people unknown to one another is assembled and a member is chosen for an interview. The group may ask any five questions (i.e., a total of five for the entire group). Participants are then asked to indicate in writing at least three to five intuitive impressions in each of the following areas: the interviewee's personal background, his or her opinions of political or social issues, cultural preferences (for food, music, clothing, etc.), and action taken in certain situations. The exercise can be relatively structured or unstructured. The group can learn about bias and stereotypes by comparing their judgments to the interviewee's responses (Pusch, 1979).

L. Actor and Act. Culturally homogeneous groups are given one of two prepared newspaper stories about a victim and a perpetrator. After reading the story, students are asked to rate the behavior of the various actors in the story (e.g., How bad do you feel for the victim? How much harm has been done to the victim? How heinous is the crime of the perpetrator? What should the punishment be?). The ethnic or cultural group affiliations of the victim and the perpetrator appear in one order in half the stories and in the reverse order in the other half. Such presentation of the two stories, counterbalanced within the group, can lead to valuable experiential insights by the participants (Starr, 1992).

M. The Parable. This is a well known exercise in training circles which centers on a story regarding a young woman's desire to cross a river to be with her fiance. The story involves several characters, each of whom acts in ways that the group members are asked to judge. While there are many variants, the core story involves a man who will take the women across the river if she sleeps with him. She initially refuses and then changes her mind.

She sleeps with him and he takes her to her fiance the next day. The exercise helps participants become aware of the effect of culture and values.

2. Special Services for Minorities

Race relations are improved to the extent that minority students on predominantly White campuses feel at home and respected. To this end, universities and colleges have offered minority students a range of experiences including peer counselling, support groups, minority student organizations, cultural centers and events and heritage activities (Bourassa, 1991).

3. Cultural Assimilators as Education Tools

Culture assimilators are widely used and widely researched interactive computer programs that present students with a set of social situations which would normally lead to a culture specific interpretation. Trainees read a story about a different cultural group than their own and then choose among alternative interpretations of the event. After choosing, they get feedback as to whether or not their reactions to the situation are similar to how natives of that culture would react. The participants are encouraged to make choices until they make the best one. In the process of working through the set of critical incidents, the participant learns to make choices like those that the members of the culture would make. Gradually, student attributions become isomorphic to those of the culture bearers.

Assimilators have been used in racial settings both at universities and in the armed forces (see, e.g., Landis, Day, McGrew, Thomas and Miller, 1976; Landis, Hope and Day, 1984; Landis, Brislin, and Hulgus, 1985; Weldon, Carlston, Rissman, Slobodin & Triandis, 1975). A culture general assimilator has been developed (Brislin, Cushner, Cherrie, & Young, 1986) and two of the current authors (BJS & LRS) are currently working on a decentered culture assimilator (Starr, 1990) to be used with Jamaican and African American students at Howard.

EVALUATION OF RACE RELATIONS TRAINING PROGRAMS

The evaluation of race relations training is possible, but the broader the objectives of the training, the harder it is to evaluate. Thus, the first step for a cost effective, efficacious intervention is for campus committees to determine the goals of the race relations training: if a goal is to decrease the number of complaints about offensive comments, the training needs to focus on the causes of making offensive comments and how to deal with them when one hears them from others. If a goal is to increase the number of students from different groups who interact socially with one another, a very different type of training is called for—one that deals with societal prohibitions and risk taking.

Creating specific goals requires courage and minimizes double speak. Realistically, most institutions end up seeking "a climate of tolerance," or a "general attitude change." These types of goals are difficult to achieve, but programs have shown that, at least in the short run, a brief race relations training program can increase tolerance. One of the most common ways of measuring increases in group tolerance is by administering a pre-post assessment measure, such as the Measure of Social Distance (See Table I). This measure assesses how comfortable a person would be with individuals from other groups in a variety of social situations. It has been proven sensitive to changes in attitude.

Any race relations training program should have the following evaluation components: (1) A measure of adverse outcomes, both short term and long term. It is important to find out if the training boomeranged and engendered more hostility and intolerance among the students; (2) A measure of desirable outcomes, both short term and long term. Follow up evaluations that assess adverse and desirable outcomes and are sent to participants one month and one semester after training would give more informative feedback than end-of-the-session evaluations; (3) The planning group should have a clear rationale for why the expected interventions should have specific effects. Whether using packaged programs, consultants or internally designed interventions, activities need to be grounded in well understood, plainly described, psychological phenomena and mecha-

TABLE I. Measure of Social Distance and Social Attitudes

Using the following scale, please assign the whole number (1-7) that best describes the closest relationship you would be willing to have with each group below. The numbers form a continuous scale from the closest relationship (1 = marry) to the furthest relationship (7 = exclude). Make sure that your reactions are to each group as a whole, not to the best or worst members you may have known.

1. Would marry or allow family member to marry
2. Would have as a good friend
3. Would have as my neighbor
4. Would have in the same work group
5. Would have a speaking acquaintance only
6. Would have a visitor to my country only
7. Would exclude from my country

marry	friend	neighbor	co-worker	acquaintance	visitor	exclude
1	2	3	4	5	6	7

a. _____ Whites

b. _____ African Americans

c. _____ Hispanic Americans

d. _____ American Indians

e. _____ Internationals

f. _____ Orientals

g. _____ Arabs

h. _____ Africans

j. _____ Europeans

k. _____ Central Americans

l. _____ Russians

m. _____ Iranians

n. _____ South Africans (blacks)

o. _____ South Africans (whites)

p. _____ Nicaraguans

q. _____ Homosexuals

r. _____ Drug users

s. _____ Drinkers

t. _____ Nondrinkers

u. _____ Smokers

v. _____ Nonsmokers

w. _____ Christians

x. _____ Born again Christians

y. _____ Jews

z. _____ Muslims

aa. _____ Fraternity/sorority members

bb. _____ Students from rural areas

cc. _____ Students from large urban areas

dd. _____ Football players

ee. _____ Basketball players

ff. _____ Wrestlers

gg. _____ Swimmers

hh. _____ Gymnasts

ii. _____ Track/field athletes

jj. _____ Tennis players

Source: Quality of Life Survey. Department of Residence Life, Iowa State University (Robinson, 1987). Used with permission.

nisms of change; (4) Process measures are needed to assess whether the race relations training was implemented as planned. Were the leaders accepted and capable, was the space ample, was the time allotted too much or too little?

INSTITUTIONAL INTERVENTIONS
TO IMPROVE RACE RELATIONS

More and more, universities and colleges are reshaping the mission of the administrative offices on minority affairs. Student, faculty and administrative leaders are being trained as prejudice reduction workshop facilitators and minority office staff are spending less and less of their own time in direct service or conducting student programs. Peer led groups relieve administrators from these time consuming programs and make the workshops more accessible and palatable to students. We do not know how many colleges have their psychological services unit play a major role in the development, implementation, or evaluation of race relations training.

Minority office administrators have now begun concentrating on reducing racism and prejudice at a systemic level. They serve as consultants to campus organizations, departmental faculty, housing personnel and health services. Broad university-wide activities and policies that such offices implement to encourage positive race relations include:

a. *Development of Comprehensive Affirmative Action Programs.* Most programs are three pronged: recruitment efforts; development efforts; (in the form of seed money, travel funds, etc.) and retention.

b. *Providing Year Round Multicultural Enrichment Programs.* Many campuses have a yearly celebration of cultural differences that involves theater, foods, music, and sport. For example, the University of Wisconsin (1990) has established a COW (Celebrating Our World) committee whose mission is to promote anti oppressive activities, with a yearly week long celebration which includes programs on self esteem, international food tasting and entertainment, speakers forums, outreach to grade school children to discuss and promote diversity and a fund raiser for a "people problem" (e.g., AIDS). Often, one large event serves to mobilize and energize smaller events throughout the academic year.

c. *Creating Theme Communities.* Some campuses have developed multicultural, multiethnic communities where Whites and minorities learn about issues of race and racism. For example, at the University of Massachusetts, Amherst, white and minority students who choose to live in this community have parallel but distinct programs to learn about racism.

Integrated theme communities appear to be a much better mechanism for encouraging racial tolerance than specialized ethnic/racial housing programs. While segregated specialized housing allows strong intragroup support mechanisms, it clearly isolates students from working together interracially on various dorm living and recreational activities.

d. *Ongoing Campus Wide Groups on Racism and Prejudice.* Most campuses have a variety of groups working to increase cooperation and good will between all students. They run workshops which utilize the training exercises described above and respond to incidents of harassment when they are reported.

e. *Anti-Harassment Policies.* Campuses have to develop anti-harassment policies that do not violate or threaten to violate First Amendment Rights. The university community must condemn harassment of individuals based on such factors as their race, ethnicity, gender, national origin, sexual preference, religion or disability. However, intelligent differentiation among incidents is needed. Individual incidents, however noxious, should be approached as opportunities for education, insight, and personal change. Offending individuals should be approached as well-meaning people who inadvertently caused severe insult to another person and not as villainous characters who are out to commit intentional crimes against humanity.

Repeated acts of harassment, on the other hand, which serve as "fighting words" are recognized legally as criminal behavior and should be treated as such by the university.

The legal issues surrounding anti-harassment policies are complex and the subject of much debate within the legal community. On the one hand, restrictionists point to the 1942 U.S. Supreme Court case, Chaplinsky v. New Hampshire (315 U.S. 568), which limited free speech when the verbal expressions were "in a form that constitutes fighting words or their functional equivalent . . . [these were] face to face words plainly likely to cause a breach of peace by the addressee." Free speech advocates, on the other hand, point to cases such as Collin v. Smith, where a group of Nazis was allowed to hold a march because the Court refused to recognize that every Jew in the community was the target of the Nazis' prefigured anti-Semitic speech. Without being legal experts and knowing the many fine points being debated, it appears that speech that is clearly and directly intended to incite specific others can be restricted without violating First Amendment Rights. All other cases are subject to debate (Metz, 1990).

Some universities and colleges have been so upset by the increased level of harassment that they have argued that the First Amendment does not apply to their institutions. They argue that the primary mission of the university is to protect the integrity of the academic process. Punishing speech within the university should be allowed if it interferes with this primary mission despite the fact that such speech is protected outside the institution. A second argument is that universities have a responsibility to protect students from discrimination and harassment (Tatel, 1990).

Our own preference is to treat cases of harassment as a socialization/mental health issue and not as a crime. Students who harass other students may have a legal right to say what they say. Still, they may not be receiving the important benefits inherent in the college education mission: tolerance; broadening of outlook; and the resolution of conflicts through intellectual means. When students harass others, they need to be counselled. They cannot be forced to attend, but the social pressures within the institution can be such that recommendations to attend such counselling would be difficult to avoid.

f. *Partnership Programs.* Universities and colleges with a commitment to reducing race relation tensions need to implement partnership programs which extend further down the educational pipeline. These programs were highlighted in the State Higher Education Officers (SHEEO) 1991 report entitled, *Building Coalitions for Minority Success.* If minority and majority children have joint, positive exposures to local colleges throughout their school careers, they will enter the college with an emotional tie and acceptance that are critical for maximum interracial harmony.

FACULTY INTERVENTIONS
TO IMPROVE RACE RELATIONS

One of the areas where faculty can make the greatest difference is in the broadening of mentoring programs. As most mentoring programs exist today, minority students are placed as much as possible with minority faculty. This procedure is probably an excellent one for first year students who need appropriate and easy to relate to role models. After the first year, though, minority faculty should distribute some of their mentees to majority faculty based on perceived overlapping interests and compatible personalities, allowing minority students to identify and relate to university faculty on a more diversified ethnic continuum and encourage their integration (versus isolation) on the campus.

Faculty can encourage other positive racial interactions, both in and out of the classroom. First, faculty can arrange study and research groups that have diverse compositions. Second, faculty can plan course related assignments that deal with multicultural issues. Third, faculty can broaden their own levels of expertise to include the contributions of minorities (Bell, 1992). Fourth, faculty can invite informal, diverse groups of students to their homes.

Vasquez and Wainstain (1990) suggest that faculty match teaching styles to the learning styles of diverse students, employing more oral traditions, more inductive reasoning, more learning by doing, and using more affect. In addition, faculty should serve as problem solvers and offer an emotional, caring connection to students. Finally, faculty must maintain high expectations for every student and encourage achievement through cooperation. All of these goals can readily be operationalized and used to generate very specific action plans.

REFERENCES

Abadu, M. (1991, April 29). Current trends in diversity affecting American Higher Education. *Black Issues in Higher Education*. 8(13), pp. 46-55.

Anti-Defamation League (Producer). Facing difference: Living together on campus (Film) (1991). New York: Anti-Defamation League.

Barnes, E. (1992). No criminal charges for Black student accused of striking white students in blackface incident, district attorney's office says. *Black Issues in Higher Education*. 9 (6), 11.

Bell, E. (1992, April 23). Helping our students towards multicultural behavior. *Black Issues in Higher Education.* 9(4), p. 60.

Berg-Cross, L. and Zoppetti, L. (1991). Person-in-culture interview: Understanding culturally different students. *Journal of College Student Psychotherapy.* 5(4), 224-232.

Bidol, P. (1987). Actualizing synergistic multicultural training programs. In W.B. Reddy and C.C. Henderson, Jr., (Eds.). *Training, theory and practice.* San Diego: University Associates.

Blake, R.R., & Mouton, J.S. (1986). From theory to practice in interface problem solving. In S. Worchel & W.G. Austin (Eds.), *Psychology of intergroup relations* (2nd. ed., pp. 67-87). Chicago: Nelson-Hall.

Brislin, R.W., Cushner, K., Cherrie, C., and Young, M. (1986). *Intercultural interactions.* Newberry Park, CA: Sage Publications Inc.

Brown, C. and Mazza, G. (1991). Peer training strategies for welcoming diversity. in J. Dalton (Ed.) *Racism on campus: confronting racial bias through peer interventions.* (56, pp. 39-51). New York: Jossey-Bass, Inc., Publishers.

Brown, C. and Mazza, G. (1991). How white students and students of color organize and interact on campus. In J. Dalton (Ed.) *Racism on campus: confronting racial bias through peer interventions.* (pp. 39-53). New York: Jossey-Bass, Inc., Publishers.

Bourassa, D. (1991). How white students and students of color organize and interact on campus. In J. Dalton (Ed.) *Racism on campus: confronting racial bias through peer interventions.* New York: Jossey-Bass, Inc., Publishers. (pp. 13-25).

Cialdini, R.B., & Richardson, K.D. (1980). Two indirect tactics of image management: Basking and blasting. *Journal of Personality and Social Psychology, 39,* 406-514.

Collison, M. (1992). When a black applicant is accepted and a white is not: Case at Duke U. illustrates the use of race in admissions. *The Chronicle of Higher Education.* Feb. 5, 38(22), A38(2).

Cosby, B. (Producer and Director). (1978). Cosby on Prejudice (Film). New York: Pyramid Productions.

Cox, T. (1991, August 29). Study examines reasons for lack of campus diversity. *Black Issues in Higher Education.* 8 (13), p. 3.

Dalton, J. (1991). Racial and Ethnic Backlash in College Peer Culture. In J. Dalton (Ed). *Racism on campus: confronting racial bias through peer interventions.* New York: Jossey-Bass Inc., Publishers. (pp. 3-13).

Gaertner, S.L., Mann, J., Murrell, A., & Dovidio, J.F. (1989). Reducing intergroup violence: The benefits of recategorization. *Journal of Personality and Social Psychology.* 57, 239-249.

Gaertner, S.L., Mann, J., Murrell, A., Pomare, M. & Dovidio, J.F. (1988). How does cooperation reduce intergroup bias? Paper presented to the Eastern Psychological Association.

Goethals, G.R., & Darley, J.M. (1987). Social comparison theory: Self evaluation and group life. In B. Mullen & G.R. Goethals, (Eds.), *Theories of group behavior* (pp. 21-47). New York: Springer-Verlag New York Inc.

Healy, M., Cooper, D., and Fygetakis, E. (1991). Evaluating peer interactions. In J. Dalton (Ed.) *Racism on campus: Confronting racial bias through peer interventions.* New York: Jossey-Bass Inc. Publishers. 67-77.

Hively, R. (1990). *The lurking evil: Racial and ethnic conflict on the college campus.* American Association of State Colleges and Universities.

Katz, J.H. (1978). *White awareness: A handbook for anti-racism training.* Norman: University of Oklahoma Press.

Landis, D., & Boucher, J. (1987). Themes and models of conflict. In D. Landis, J. Boucher and K.A. Clark (Eds.). *Ethnic conflict.* Newbury Park, CA: Sage Publications Inc.

Landis, D., Brislin, R.W., and Hulgus, J.F. (1985). Attributional training versus contact in acculturative learning: A laboratory study. *Journal of Applied Social Psychology.* 15, 466-482.

Landis, D., Day, H.R., McGrew, P.L., Thomas, J.A., and Miller, A.B. (1976). Can a black "culture assimilator" increase racial understanding? *Journal of Social Issues*, 32, 169-183.

Landis, D., Hope, R.O., and Day, H.R. (1984). Training for desegregation in the military. In N. Miller and M.B. Brewer (Eds.), *Groups in contact: Psychological approaches to desegregation.* New York: Academic Press.

Meindl, J.R., & Lerner, M. J. (1984). Exacerbation of extreme responses to an out-group. *Journal of Personality and Social Psychology*, 47, 71-84.

Metz, H. (1990). Bad apples, evil deeds. *Student Lawyer.* February. 33-38.

Mura, D. (1991). *Turning Japanese: Memoirs of a Sansei.* New York, Anchor.

Paunonen, S., Jackson, D., Trzebinski, J., and Forsterling, F. 1992. Personality structure across cultures: A Multimethod evaluation. *Journal of Personality and Social Psychology*, 1992, 62(3), 447-456.

Pusch, M. (1979). *Multicultural education: A cross-cultural training approach.* Chicago: Intercultural Press.

Robinson, T. (1987). Quality of Life Survey. Department of Residence Life, Iowa State University.

Shenk, D. (1990). Young Hate. *CV: The College Magazine*, 2(1), 34-39.

Sherif, M., Harvey, O.J., White, B.J., Hood, W.R., & Sherif, C.W. (1961). *Intergroup conflict and cooperation. The Robbers Cave Experiment.* Norman, OK: Institute of Group Relations.

Steele, C. (1992). Race and the schooling of Black Americans. *The Atlantic*, 269(4), 68-78.

Starr, B.J. (1992, February). *Xenophobic attribution: An examination of ethnocentrism.* Paper presented at the meeting of the Society for Cross Cultural Research, Santa Fe, NM.

Starr, B.J. (1990, June). Evaluating and evolving culture assimilator technology with Jamaican sojourners. In M. Janssen-Mathes (Chair), Intercultural approach in education. Panel presentation at the 16th. Congress of the International Society for Intercultural Education, Training, and Research, Kilkenny, Ireland.

State Higher Education Officers (1991). *Building Coalitions for Minority Success.* Washington, D.C.

Streufert, S., & Streufert, S.C. (1986). The development of international conflict. In S. Worchel & W.G. Austin (Eds.) Psychology of intergroup relations (2nd ed., pp. 134-152). Chicago: Nelson-Hall.

Tatel, D. 1990. Suppression and Controls on American College campuses. (Ed.) Hively, R. *The lurking evil: Racial and ethnic conflict on the college campus.* American Association of State Colleges and Universities.

Undergraduate Financing of Post Secondary Education: 1986-87. (1988). National Center for Educational Statistics.

Vasquez, J. and Wainstein, N. (1990). Instructional Responsibilities of college faculty to minority students. *Journal of Negro Education.* 59(4), 599-610.

Vontress, C. (1992). Hard times and meanness. *Black Issues in Higher Education.* 8 (22), 80.

Weeks, W.H., Pederson, P.B., & Brislin, R.W. (1979). *A manual of structured experiences for cross-cultural learning.* Yarmouth, ME: Intercultural Press.

Weldon, D.E., Carlston, D.E., Rissman, A.K., Slobodin, L. and Triandis, H.C. (1975). A laboratory test of the effects of culture assimilator training. *Journal of Personality and Social Psychology,* 32, 300-310.

Chapter 8

Violence Against Lesbian
and Gay Male College Students

Barbara R. Slater

SUMMARY. Most of our colleges and universities are strongholds of homophobic discrimination and heterosexism which impact directly on lesbian and gay students, staff, and faculty, upon those exploring their orientation, and upon the entire campus community. The negative effects of external violence and of internalized homophobia include physical, sexual and emotional injury/damage, self-doubt, isolation, engaging in heterosexual attempts in order to survive, identifying with the aggressors and allowing further abuse, inability to function socially or academically, self-hatred, and engaging in serious self-destructive behaviors. Colleges and universities can establish policies and procedures to combat homophobia and heterosexism across the entire community and can develop a safe, supportive environment for all students, including those who are not heterosexual. Strong administrative support is needed to ensure the required strenuous, continuing efforts.

Barbara R. Slater, PhD, is Professor of Psychology at Towson State University, Baltimore, MD, and she maintains a small private practice working with children and women. Dr. Slater is a Fellow of the American Psychological Association and a former member of the APA Committee on Lesbian and Gay Concerns. She teaches undergraduate and graduate courses related to lesbian and gay issues, is conducting long-range research on lesbian development with a colleague, and has published and presented at national and regional conferences on lesbian and gay issues, particularly youths.

[Haworth co-indexing entry note]: "Violence Against Lesbian and Gay Male College Students." Slater, Barbara R. Co-published simultaneously in *Journal of College Student Psychotherapy* (The Haworth Press, Inc.) Vol. 8, No. 1/2, 1993, pp. 177-202: and: *Campus Violence: Kinds, Causes, and Cures* (ed: Leighton C. Whitaker and Jeffrey W. Pollard) The Haworth Press, Inc., 1993, pp. 177-202. Multiple copies of this article/chapter may be purchased from The Haworth Document Delivery Center [1-800-3-HAWORTH; 9:00 a.m. - 5:00 p.m. (EST)].

177

In order to understand the ramifications of violence against lesbian and gay youths during their college years, it is necessary to examine homophobic violence in general and violence against lesbian and gay young persons in particular. In this chapter youths are defined as individuals under the age of 23 years, because by age 23 most persons have completed undergraduate college or have entered the world of work. While it used to be common thinking that youth ended as early as age 18, society's perception of youth has changed, as illustrated by increasing legal ages of drinking in many states and by the large numbers of young persons now attending college while depending upon parental support (D'Augelli, 1989; Evans & Wall, 1991; Gonsiorek, 1988). Also, the mean age of undergraduate students is increasing as older and returning students become a common phenomenon.

An increase in the amount of social/emotional (including verbal), physical, and/or sexual violence directed against young lesbians and gay men over the past several years (Comstock, 1991; Freiberg, 1987; Herek, 1989; National Gay and Lesbian Task Force, 1990, 1991a; Schaecher, 1989; Whitlock, 1988) parallels the increase in violence reported by adult gay men and lesbians, as documented by researchers (Berrill, 1985, 1992; Herek, 1989; Herek & Glunt, 1988; National Gay and Lesbian Task Force, 1988, 1990, 1991a). For example, the National Gay and Lesbian Task Force (1991b) reported that of more than 2,000 lesbians and gay men surveyed nationwide in 1984, "19% reported having been 'punched, hit, kicked or beaten' at least once in their lives because of their sexual orientation. Forty-four percent (44%) had been threatened with physical violence and 94% experienced some type of victimization" (p. 1).

This author's premise is that violence impacting on lesbian and gay youths takes two major forms, external and internal, and falls into three categories, social/emotional, physical, and/or sexual. Homophobia, the hatred and/or fear of homosexuals and of homosexuality experienced by heterosexuals and by homosexuals (De Cecco, 1981; Slater, 1988) is a primary factor in violence against lesbian and gay adults and youths (Herek, 1986b). Herek (1992) described anti-gay violence as "a logical, albeit extreme, extension of the heterosexism that pervades American society" (p. 89).

Anxiety and fear associated with AIDS and a "moral majority" attitude that homosexuals have brought AIDS on themselves as punishment for their evil, has been escalating violence against gays and lesbians in general, including youths (Gross, 1988; Herek, 1989; Herek & Glunt, 1988; Slater, 1989). Governmental emphasis in the two administrations prior to 1993 on traditional family values, which excludes any alternative way of living, further increases the likelihood of violence by homophobic persons who take governmental policy and attitude as license to attack those outside the protection of the government. An example of the discrimination perpetrated by the government is the controversy accompanying the U.S. Department of Health and Human Services' *Report of the Secretary's Task Force on Youth Suicide*, published in 1989 (U.S. Department of Health and Human Services, 1989). A variety of resources have indicated that the government withheld distribution because three relatively small sections in this multi-volume work documented and discussed the increased risk of suicide for lesbian and gay youths, which may be up to three times that of heterosexual youths and which may include up to 30% of completed youth suicides. At one time it was indicated that the Secretary intended to remove the materials on lesbian and gay youths, reprint the report, and then distribute it. The rationale was that discussing homosexual persons in a government document did not uphold the administration's commitment to "traditional family values." Ultimately the document was released with a disclaimer that the presence of references to homosexuality did not represent government support. Clearly the United States government at that time was willing to allow the deaths of lesbian and gay youths from suicide in order to suppress information which might have been useful in alleviating such tragedies.

Only recently has society addressed the reality of gay and lesbian youths, for the most part having preferred to reject research and to believe, mythically, that homosexuality is an adult condition which cannot exist in youths (Coleman & Remafedi, 1989; D'Augelli, 1991; Rofes, 1983; Vergara, 1984), and that lesbians and gay men typically seek to recruit young persons into their way of life through seduction (Gonsiorek, 1988; Herek, 1991). These myths have led to condemnation of lesbians and gay men working with youths, for fear that they might corrupt or seduce "innocent youths" away from heterosexuality, thus depriving many coming-out youths (youths exploring lesbian or gay orientations) of healthful role models needed for the development of positive self-concepts (Berzon, 1979 a & b; Coleman, 1982; Gonsiorek, 1988). These ideas are, as noted, not supported by research and theory which indicate that sexual orientation most likely has both biological and social/personality components (Cass, 1985; Herek, 1991; Hoult, 1985; Money, 1988; Ruse, 1981; Saghir & Robins, 1973; Troiden, 1989) and that it is established early in life, often within the first 5 or so years, although it may be unrecognized until many years later or, perhaps, never (Bell, Weinberg, & Hammersmith, 1981; Jay & Young, 1979; Remafedi, 1987; Savin-Williams, 1990; Slater, 1988; Woodman & Lenna, 1980). In terms of the seduction myth, research has established that about 90% of all reported sexual abuse was perpetrated by heterosexuals (Herman, 1981; Nugent & Gramick, 1992) and that "gay men are no more likely than heterosexual men to molest children" (Herek, 1991, p. 156).

While these findings help many who are relatively low in homophobia to perceive lesbians and gay men in a more positive light, masses of adults and youths are so influenced by homophobia, either internalized or impacting on them environmentally, that they reject data in favor of the more negative views of homosexuality. Homophobia is particularly destructive when we are dealing with teachers at the high school or the college level, times when youths require healthful role models in order to proceed with personality development as they separate from their families of origin and individuate, partly through identification with significant adults in their lives. Research has indicated that many lesbian and gay high school teachers and college faculty/staff believe that if their identity were to be revealed, they would be in an endangered position vulnerable to verbal and/or physical attack, they could lose their employment, or their chance to advance academically would be jeopardized (President's Select Committee for Lesbian and Gay Concerns of Rutgers, 1989; Revelle, 1988; Savin-Williams, 1990; Task Force on Lesbian and Gay Concerns of the University of Oregon, 1990; Yeskel, 1985).

At the college level this fear of discrimination based on homophobia persists even in those schools which include sexual orientation as a protected category. Overall, only a handful of states and local jurisdictions have passed laws protecting persons from discrimination on the basis of sexual orientation (Herek, 1992; National Gay and Lesbian Task Force, 1991a), and some of those that do have such documentation specifically exclude teachers and other persons who work directly with children and adolescents. Elementary, middle, and high school teachers have reason to fear discrimination if they are identified as lesbians or gay men, or if they are even suspected of being other than heterosexual.

For example, an elementary principal who had received considerable praise for her effectiveness discovered in the spring of one year, much to her surprise, that there were rumors in her school that she was a lesbian although a lesbian sexual orientation was not something that she had ever acted upon or was aware of in her life. At the end of the school year, her contract was not renewed and she was told that she had not been effective as a principal. In another case, a gay male high school teacher was brought out or outed (orientation revealed) when he took part in a gay rights demonstration in another state and was seen by someone from his hometown who carried the information back and distributed it widely throughout the community. He was removed immediately from working on an after school activity with children although the activity had been highly successful under his tutelage and, the following fall, his long term assignment of working with gifted and talented students was changed and he found himself working exclusively with the lowest functioning youths in the school.

While over a hundred and fifty colleges and universities have included sexual orientation in their protected category in official documents, the majority of faculty and staff are left without specific protection set forth by the college/university, municipality, county, or state (Leonard, 1989; National Gay and Lesbian Task Force, 1991a; Political Committee of the Lesbian and Gay Student Alliance of Pennsylvania State University, 1991) in the face of numerous reported instances of loss of employment or loss of promotion. For example, a faculty member was notified that she had been promoted in rank only days before she presented a professional paper on lesbian issues in another state. A newspaper in the conference state identified her as a lesbian although she had never stated or even implied such. When she returned to her college, she was told that, if this presentation and "revelation" had happened before the promotion decision had been finalized, she might not have been promoted.

Fearing revelation of lesbian or gay status, as is common among many faculty members and staff, faculty tend to employ a variety of defensive strategies to conceal their identities (Task Force on Lesbian and Gay Concerns of the University of Oregon, 1990). They must separate their professional and personal lives completely. They cannot be part of university committees or other groups related to sexual orientation. They cannot recognize, support, or assist troubled students who are struggling with identity issues. They cannot include lesbian and gay issues in their courses and so they present a totally heterosexist (assumption that everyone is heterosexual and/or that non-heterosexual issues are irrelevant) view of the world. They cannot serve as role models or support persons for lesbian and gay students. They may even have to lie about their orientation if asked directly or if they believe that they are under suspicion. Even more destructively, many faculty members in this position actually handle homosexuality in a negative manner to provide additional camouflage, thus further damaging those students in their courses who are lesbian/gay or who are exploring their orientation. In the first instances we are dealing with damage by omission and in the last instance, damage by commission. College staff are faced with the same issues and may also resort to camouflage, resulting in decreased or non-existent services. For example, a residence supervisor may fail to discipline students engaging in homophobic harassment or a counseling center may fail to provide visible, or even available, lesbian and gay information.

Obviously the influences just described impact negatively on the well-being of all students exposed to them during their college careers, whether they are homosexual, heterosexual, bisexual, or in exploration. The destruction caused by such behaviors also impacts powerfully on the self-concept and dignity of those who feel forced to engage in them. Ultimately, it is hoped that discrimination against and homophobia among teachers and faculty/staff can be sufficiently reduced so as to provide youths who are exploring their orientation, are in the coming-out stage, or are self-identified as lesbian or gay with the necessary information and support systems so that they can go about their lives with a positive view of themselves. In order to accomplish this, curricula must present accurate information and information which treats lesbians and gay men equitably and these materials need to be integrated into the overall college program rather than being compartmentalized (Murphy, 1991). Direct contact with lesbian and gay faculty/staff role models and with faculty who present an equitable picture of the diversity of life can do much to mitigate the unfortunate effects of internalized homophobia and of external violence. Accordingly, heterosexual students and adults would also benefit: they would become less homophobic and more accepting of the diversity of life through contact with others who are low in homophobia and with lesbians and gay men.

KINDS OF VIOLENCE: EXTERNAL

Let us look first at some of the evidence of external violence against gay and lesbian youths. Pharr (1988) discussed the widely accepted perception that it is acceptable to express homophobia overtly in society, so that there is no ready mechanism for safety from verbal or physical attack. Whitlock (1989) concurred: "Homophobia is so pervasive that many people do not perceive mistreatment of gay and lesbian youth as wrong" (p. 4). The literature documents many incidents of victims reporting harassment or attacks who have faced skepticism or a lack of enthusiastic support on the part of officials contacted once homosexuality became a factor in the complaint. Studies of colleges have articulated the presence of this unacceptable behavior even on some campuses which include sexual orientation statements (D'Augelli, 1989; President's Select Committee for Lesbian and Gay Concerns of Rutgers, 1989; Revelle, 1988; Task Force on Lesbian and Gay Concerns of the University of Oregon, 1990; Yeskel, 1985). A current emphasis on the Constitutional right to express oneself, even in the face of emotional damage to the target of the verbal attacks, has increased the probability and the fact of verbal harassment. Lack of appropriate control mechanisms has also resulted in direct physical attacks.

The lack of clear procedural processes for recourse or protection has led to many victims not reporting experienced verbal or physical violence because they believe that they will face disbelief or further difficulties, that nothing will be done, or that the reporting itself will make it known that they are lesbian or gay (D'Augelli, 1989; Wall & Evans, 1991). Because of such failure to report, the full extent of external violence is unknown. However, from the verified accounts, it is clear that college students suffer from homophobic violence, whether they are the perpetrators of such violence or the victims.

By the time youths reach college, most of them already have been exposed to the concept or the reality of violence directed against lesbians and gay men or those suspected of being gay or lesbian. Newspapers and magazines, television programs, movies, and social organizations are rife with information either reporting violence or indicating that such violence is "normal." In addition, at the college level the environmental/academic stress is on heterosexuality or, as described by Mohr (1988), "compulsory heterosexuality" (p. 300). Until recently, even fiction depicting gay or lesbian lives portrayed them as evil, sick, hopeless, or in other negative ways (Zimmerman, 1990).

If we look at pre-college youths, the professional literature sufficiently documents the extent and results of violence against lesbian and gay adolescents as perpetrated by peers, the media, the government, families, social organizations, religious representatives, health/mental health professionals, and the schools (Anderson, 1985; Boxer & Cohler, 1989; Coleman, 1982; Comstock, 1991; D'Augelli, 1988; Gibson, 1982; Hammersmith, 1987; Herdt, 1989; Hetrick & Martin, 1987; Hunter, 1992; Malyon, 1981; Savin-Williams, 1990; Slater, 1988; Vergara, 1984; Weiss & Schiller, 1988; Whitlock, 1988). Remafedi (1987) reported that 30% of the gay male youths in his sample had experienced physical assaults, 55% had experienced verbal abuse from peers, and 37% had experienced some form of discrimination. The schools are widely known to be bastions of homophobia (Kaplan & Saperstein, 1985; Slater, 1988; Uribe & Harbeck, 1992) which, under the socio-political regime from 1980 through 1992, seems to be increasing.

Only a handful of schools have broken through the barrier so as to offer programs for gay and lesbian youths (the Harvey Milk School in New York), programs for youths within the school or system or training programs for faculty (for example: Project 10 in the Los Angeles Unified School District; Project 10 East, Boston School System; Support Services for Gay and Lesbian Youth of the San Francisco Unified School District; Fairfax County Public Schools, Fairfax, Virginia; Madison Public Schools, Wisconsin; Minneapolis, Minnesota; The School District of Philadelphia), or programs administered outside of the schools and brought into them at the request of the schools themselves (for example: The Human Rights Foundation, 1984; The National Education Association, 1991; The Sexual Minority Youth Assistance League, Washington, DC). Without accurate information and/or assistance, youths may reach college with the burden of feeling different, believing that their "condition" is unacceptable, and experiencing guilt and alienation, or a multitude of other negative feelings/beliefs/fears.

Berrill (1992) poignantly summarized conditions at the college/ university level by stating: "Although diversity and pluralism ideally should be cherished values in the academic environment, anti-gay prejudice and violence are serious problems at many colleges and universities. In 1989 alone, a total of 1,329 anti-gay episodes were reported to the NGLTF by lesbian and gay student groups on just 40 college campuses" (pp. 32-33). Negative attitudes and hate crimes against lesbians and gay men have been documented in all of the several campus studies cited by Herek (1989). Herek (1989) summarized three of these studies as follows:

In a study conducted by Herek (1986a) at Yale, 65% of the subjects reported verbal abuse, 25% verbal threats, 19% objects thrown, 25% chased or followed, 3% spat upon, 5% hit, kicked, or beaten, 1% assault with a weapon, 10% vandalism or arson, 12% sexual assault/harassment, and 90% incidents not reported.

In a study by D'Augelli (1989) at Pennsylvania State University, percentages in each of the above categories respectively were: 72%, 25%, 13%, 22%, 6%, 4%, 1%, 16%, 15%, 93%.

In a study by Cavin (1987) at Rutgers, percentages in each of the above categories respectively were: 57%, 16%, 11%, 16%, 1%, 4%, 1%, 6%, 8%, 88% (p. 950).

Yeskel (1985) reported on a study of gay/lesbian/bisexual student issues at the University of Massachusetts at Amherst as follows: 45% of the students reported having been victims of verbal threats or harassment, 21% reported that they had been the victims of physical assault or confrontation, 29% reported that they had been threatened with exposure of their orientation, and between 62 and 69% reported that they would not report the incident to school authorities if they were victimized again.

Duncan (1990) reported that, in a sample of 412 university students, "sexual victimization was significantly more common among . . . gay and lesbian than heterosexual students" (p. 65). Kurdek (1988), in a study looking at negative attitudes of heterosexual toward homosexual students, found that about 17% of his sample agreed with each one of 40 negative statements about homosexuals. He concluded that "negative attitudes toward homosexuals are part of a larger belief system regarding conventional social order" (p. 727). Similarly, Norris (1992), in a study of homophobia at Oberlin College, noted the paradox between the overall liberal attitude of Oberlin and the presence of considerable homophobic activity. He concluded that there was a conflict between two competing values, "a liberal ethos focused on equal rights, and a heterosexual orthodoxy" (p. 81). On a final note, Berrill (1989) reported that over 90% of the youths surveyed who had already experienced some form of violence anticipated that they would experience further homophobic harassment while they were in college.

The literature is filled with specific instances of violence such as the following (please note that the colleges/universities involved in these incidents are not named so as to protect students and faculty/staff).

Verbal/social/emotional violence: homophobic jokes made by a psychology faculty person in class; a literature professor making fun of the poetry of a gay poet on the basis of his lack of masculinity; an athletic coach stating that only heterosexual team members were acceptable; a student sending a BITNET message providing a rationale for killing homosexuals; demeaning notes related to homosexuality left under the doors and in the mailboxes of suspected gay and lesbian students; jeers yelled at students leaving gay/lesbian campus meetings; a banner proclaiming "help stop AIDS, kill a fag" hung from a dorm window; threatening telephone calls to a lesbian and gay campus organization.

Physical violence: Woman student struck in the face by an unknown male assailant because she supported the right of a gay faculty member to teach at the university (both she and the faculty member were later threatened in writing in a most violent fashion); female student suspected of being a lesbian badly roughed up by her teammates in field hockey practice, with accompanying homophobic comments; vandalizing of the home of a professor who had identified himself as gay in a student paper; paint splashed on the door of a gay student after his picture was published in a local gay newspaper; rocks thrown at the car of a gay student; suspected gay student attacked in his dorm hall and struck several times by his assailant while other students watched; items in a lesbian student's room destroyed by persons admitted to the room by a roommate after the student had revealed her orientation upon direct questioning; damage done to a car in the student parking lot with a homophobic message scratched in the finish next to a lesbian/gay bumper sticker.

Sexual violence: Lesbian student woke in her darkened room to find a male leaning over her–he stated that all she needed was a good "fuck" to cure her and then ran from the room; female student, suspected of being a lesbian, raped by several males with accompanying homophobic statements.

College students who are under legal age can be subjected to rejection, derision, parentally enforced psychotherapy or behavior modification (including sexual orientation conversion therapy), deprogramming, or hospitalization, all of which are considered as violence in that they are applied against the will of the youth by or at the direction of adults legally empowered to control these minority aged youths (Coleman, 1978; Pharr, 1988; Weiss & Schiller, 1988; Whitlock, 1988).

KINDS OF VIOLENCE: INTERNAL

Internalized homophobia may be even more destructive than external homophobia since it is often invisible, eroding the victim's self-concept, dignity, and ability to function, without any signs which can be seen by even those close to the target youth. According to Gonsiorek (1988), "One of the greatest impediments to the mental health of gay and lesbian individuals is 'internalized homophobia'" (p. 117). Obviously, internalized homophobia is a result of external or societal homophobia, whether it is aimed specifically at the youth or only present in the youth's environment. Focus is typically on the impact of violence experienced directly by the individual; however, we must not ignore the effects of modeling, as Gonsiorek (1988) noted: "Rejection by peers need not be experienced directly in order to be felt keenly. Many gay and lesbian youth observe the treatment of peers and clearly understand what could happen to them if they appear to be, or are known to be, different" (p. 117).

In a world essentially negatively inclined toward homosexuality, it requires a great deal of support from important others and, what might best be called, personality toughness to avoid internalizing enough homophobia to damage youths during the coming-out process. As discussed in the theoretical section, adolescent and young adult personality development is particularly vulnerable to distortion or interruption. Early adolescents struggle with their developing sexuality and lesbian and gay male adolescents must deal with both overall sexuality and the sense that their sexuality is different. This occurs whether they are aware of their orientation or only aware of a differentness within themselves. Because this sense of differentness can make itself known to the individual quite early in life, as young as age five, the emerging gay man or lesbian has the potential of many years of hearing, seeing, or experiencing homophobia before assumption of a lesbian/gay identity.

Dual minority youths, those experiencing ethnic minority status and sexual orientation minority status, face particular issues. Because they must struggle to find their places in three social/cultural communities (ethnic, gay/lesbian, and predominantly white heterosexual) (Morales, 1990), the expectations and conflicts they face are myriad and complex. Research on identity development of dual minority persons has found that they feel a need to "find validation in each community (ethnic and gay/lesbian) and a need to integrate both cultural identities. When presented with an 'either-or' choice of preference and/or dominance of one culture over another, many gay and lesbian people of color reported feeling stressed and pressured to make such a choice" (Rodriguez, 1991, p. 2). Rodriguez (1991) noted that some Chicano gay men must develop a split in their social lives to accommodate the "unacceptance, denial, and rejection by each community" (p. 120).

Chan (1989), studying identity development among Asian-American lesbians and gay men, also noted the complexities of dual status and the tendency of many of her subjects to identify more strongly with either ethnicity or orientation. Similarly, Loiacano (1989) discussed the challenges Black Americans who are lesbian or gay face and how some may fear that their gay identity could "compromise their acceptance in the Black community because of the homophobia there" (p. 24). One must keep in mind the additional issues, and perhaps burdens, faced by many dual minority youths who are struggling against internalized homophobia in their developmental processes. They require additional assistance and support in order to avoid internalization of sufficient negativity to block healthful personality growth.

All of the instances of external violence described in the previous section are examples of the negative influences which go into the hopper of self-esteem for our target population. As these bits of information are processed they interact with information related to other aspects of the self. If the adolescent years have been marked by overall acceptance and support, then the college years are approached with more ego or internal strength. This can act as a buffer against homophobia to at least some degree. If the adolescent years were marked by ostracization, discrimination, and rejection, then college is entered in a weakened, disadvantaged position.

Because our major concern is with the effects of violence, those college students who move into or continue a gay/lesbian identification without undue stress or problems will not be discussed. Under the most extreme situations, those in which the youth has received little or no support during adolescence and then is subjected to direct violence in college, serious deficits in functioning can be anticipated. Referring to the figures noted earlier, between 22% and 35% of lesbian and gay college students surveyed have been the victims of such severe violence as having objects thrown at them, having been hit, kicked or beaten, having been assaulted with a weapon, or having had arson or vandalism inflicted on them. We are not talking about a small number of persons but rather at least a quarter of the approximately 10% of all college students who are lesbian and gay, in addition to those students who are exploring their orientation and who will come out as lesbian or gay later in their lives.

Rabin and Slater (1991), in an unpublished paper presented at the 99th Annual Convention of the American Psychological Association, discussed preliminary results of a long range study of the effects of early support systems on adult lesbian characteristics. They found that those lesbians who had negative early experiences in terms of rejection or lack of acceptance from important others, when compared to lesbians who had considerable early support, had significantly less "affirmative lifestyles as signaled by community and cultural involvement and in terms of perception of lesbian lifestyles as positive in nature" (p. 7). There is no doubt that early experiences have a strong influence on later adjustment. Although the effects we see may be misinterpreted as internal and psychological in nature, they are actually reactions to an essentially negative society.

What kinds of effects can we anticipate from internalized homophobia? The effects range from mild self-doubt to extreme self-hatred and intra-punitive actions.

Students with internalized homophobia but with fairly good ego strength may defensively conceal their orientation to avoid direct discrimination or may come out only to a few trusted peers so as to ensure support. Such concealment is related to a sense that their orientation is unacceptable and that they will face rejection if it is revealed. In fact, there is a great deal of reality in this fear. This group of students is likely to move through their academic careers without major upset related to orientation although they may suffer considerable internal stress directly related to issues of concealment and fear of disclosure.

Moving up in severity of effects we find students who experience strong self-doubt, who dislike themselves, and who isolate themselves from peers and others or who attempt to enter a heterosexual world to prove that they are "normal." Such students may continue to succeed academically and in college-related spheres because these are relatively safe areas in which they can avoid the essential conflict by focusing attention on structured materials. However, in social contexts they cannot avoid the conflicts. A small sub-section of these students attempt to cover their identities by acting up sexually with members of the other sex.

At the next level are students who have such self-loathing that they are essentially unable to function socially or academically. They often withdraw into a depressed, isolated position and may fail to attend classes, may leave college, or may flunk out. If they are able to remain in school, they may do very poorly and they may not be able to retain sufficient information to benefit them. These students typically do not engage in non-academic activities.

At the most damaged level are those students who are so filled with self-loathing or hatred that they believe they do not deserve to lead a happy life or even, perhaps, to live. As a part of this perception, they may identify with the perpetrators, thus allowing themselves to be further abused because they "deserve" it. These youths are vulnerable to high risk-taking and to life-threatening actions and may abuse substances, engage in dangerous activities to the extreme, inflict wounds on their own bodies, and/or attempt or complete suicide.

Please keep in mind that those students who are not the victims of internalized homophobia are not represented here. Such healthy, well adjusted youths proceed through college with only minimal conflicts associated with their orientation although they may face innumerable other conflicts common to the college aged young person.

In looking at this menu of possible effects, one needs to keep in mind that being lesbian or gay can be overt or not known to others. In effect, those students experiencing difficulty related to the discrimination they face because of their orientation typically are assumed to be heterosexual unless they have overtly and clearly self-identified as lesbian or gay (Herdt, 1989; Ponse, 1978). This prevents support even if such support might be available to them. In order to offer quality education to college students and to provide a safe and supportive environment for them, colleges and universities must not foster or allow the kinds of external/institutional homophobia and heterosexist thinking, as described in this paper, which lead to internalized homophobia and the resultant self-doubt and/or self-hatred.

THEORETICAL ASPECTS

From an object relations perspective, early adolescence is a time of resurgence of separation-individuation issues during which youths tend to turn to peers in an attempt to resolve various aspects of individuation from the family of origin. For some youths, key teachers have an important role in this process. A second resurgence of these issues often occurs when the young person separates from home, family, and established peers to enter college. In the case of those opting not to attend college or a training program, the next separation-individuation struggle typically takes place at the point of entering the world of work or of parenting, often with accompanying loosening ties with the family of origin. At this stage of life both new peers and important adults serve as models for further individuation. Clearly individuation, a critical factor in healthful personality growth, cannot occur in the face of harassment, violence, and denigration from those very persons turned to for support and assistance.

Individuals in conflict may polarize negative and positive aspects of the conflict and then allow the polarization to become so extreme that they fix themselves at one of the poles, losing access to the opposite pole. Typically, under homophobic attack with accompanying diminution of self-concept, a young person would attach to the negative pole and see it as the total picture (part whole relationship). As Gonsiorek (1988) put it, "Negative feelings about a part of one's self (i.e., sexual orientation) may be overgeneralized to encompass the entire self" (p. 117). When this occurs, the affected youth may take on many or all of the negative aspects attached to being lesbian or gay in her or his mind, including identification with the aggressor (the homophobic world or individual homophobic persons). While this is occurring, the youth may be able to move ahead in a gay or lesbian identity, but it ensures increased assumption of negative characteristics as integral parts of the personality. Concomitant rejection from important others leaves the polarized youth objectless as his/her struggles to interact with others meet with consistent rebuffs. If this overall situation is not remedied, the youth becomes vulnerable to destructive defenses, as described earlier, to avoid experiencing the polarized sense of worthlessness and/or the trauma of becoming objectless.

From a slightly different perspective, as noted by Coleman and Remafedi (1989), "The central tasks of adolescence and young adulthood are, according to Erikson (1963), to find identity and to develop intimacy with another individual" (p. 37). For young persons to establish intimacy or even to reach out in that direction under conditions of self-doubt or self-hatred is generally impossible. Coleman and Remafedi (1989) also noted that many of the adolescents they have studied "expressed ambivalence toward their sexual identities" (p. 37); this ambivalence would further inhibit the accomplishment of developmental tasks requiring intimate contact with another. A further complication would be the belief that one is alone in the world, with no like person to reach out to, a particular problem for youths from rural areas or from restrictive families. When a youth is trapped in a situation in which there seems to be no means of finding others with whom to relate or with whom to enter into a relationship, a sense of hopelessness may inhibit functioning in a variety of other arenas, often including school performance. For those who have been able previously to use academic success as a positive measure of their self-worth, this social hopelessness also adds to the burden of negativity. As previously described from the object relations perspective, such youths are vulnerable to self destructive defenses unless offered massive support and assistance.

Notably, some lesbian and gay youths are strong enough to overcome adversities which would block the average person. They find the means to set aside an essentially negative societal impact and move ahead through the necessary phases of personality development. Research currently in process by Rabin and Slater (1991, 1992) has found that, while the positive or negative aspects of the coming-out process have profound impact on later lesbian adaptation, some lesbians have had almost completely negative coming out experiences and yet have highly adaptive later life styles as lesbians. We must take into consideration individual differences in adaptation in such cases. Furthermore, some youths do not encounter the negativity discussed in this paper. They are the fortunate individuals who receive the support of their families, friends, teachers, and important others in their identification process.

SUGGESTED SOLUTIONS

For colleges and universities to alter the homophobic environment presently existing on most campuses, major efforts must be made at the administrative, faculty/staff, and student levels. Only a genuine, campus-wide commitment will be able to effect significant change, and it must be anticipated that this will take sustained effort and that backsliding will occur if vigilance is not maintained. The following recommendations are made to schools wishing to alter their climate for lesbians and gay men, and for all students in general.

To reduce homophobia and heterosexism, colleges and universities must provide clear-cut, non-ambivalent administrative leadership, which requires inclusion of sexual orientation in the official affirmative action statement and inclusion of that statement in all published documents. A growing list of colleges and universities have already succeeded in taking this step. While some colleges and universities have used the issue of official military discrimination against homosexuals, as it is related to their ROTC programs, as a rationale for not including a sexual orientation statement, some have found ways to deal with this legally. The college or university president must issue a statement to all members of the academic community spelling out the unacceptability on the campus of any discrimination against lesbians and gay men and of heterosexism on the campus, and set in place means to ensure adherence to this policy.

Some preliminary work most likely will be required. The administration, preferably the president, likely will need to establish a working group or committee empowered to explore the overall situation on campus and to make specific recommendations. The working group must have a budget to accomplish its aim and its membership should include students, faculty/staff, and administration and both heterosexual and lesbian/gay persons. Specifically I suggest that the following representatives be included: undergraduate and graduate students, if relevant; members of the student government organization and the student newspaper; faculty from a variety of academic areas (preferably including psychology and education); staff from the counseling center, the health center, the police/security, and student housing; and administration. The group will need to set forth its aims and how best to accomplish them. Extensive collection of existing data from sources outside of the college/university will be needed and, most likely, some form of campus survey to build upon the data already available will be valuable. The group should produce a formal document articulating background information, the major campus issues, what is needed to remedy problems, and recommended solutions.

Once the working group has accomplished its objectives and an official statement is in place, the working group needs to become a permanent committee empowered to carry forth its major goals. At all levels of the campus, direct assistance must be given to ensure that homophobia is halted, heterosexism is avoided, and heterosexuality is never assumed. It must be clearly established that, regardless of one's personal beliefs, discrimination is not acceptable and that the campus will be a safe, supportive environment for all students, including those who are lesbian and gay.

Specific methods of implementation include workshops and meetings for students, staff, and faculty (particularly staff from the counseling and health centers and residence halls); distribution of material providing accurate, factual information about alternative lifestyles, for use in classes and in student services areas; articles and papers which provide accurate, factual information about alternative lifestyles published in student, faculty, and staff newsletters and presented on radio and television stations; media presentations which are non-homophobic and non-heterosexist, for example student dramas; and distribution of gay/lesbian related material across campus in such places as the counseling center, health center, student union, dorms, cafeterias, class buildings, and other places where students, staff and faculty are apt to gather.

A student organization, clearly recognized by the university and sponsored by a lesbian and/or gay faculty/staff person(s) or if such a person is not available, a gay/lesbian affirmative individual, needs to be formed. As part of the student support network, lesbian and gay cultural events such as speakers, discussion and support groups, movies, drama, dances, social events, and sports events should be sponsored by the university and supported by the student government organization.

Often a frightened student has no one to go to for assistance in sorting out feelings and fears associated with homophobia and heterosexism or to report such behaviors and the same may hold true for staff and faculty members. Thus a mechanism for handling stress/fears, complaints, and problems should be set in place, including publicizing the names of contact persons who are gay/lesbian supportive and knowledgeable about lesbian/gay lifestyles and who have agreed to serve as contact persons for anyone in the campus community who needs support in dealing with any form of sexual orientation related discrimination. Such persons serve as sounding boards and resources, although not empowered to act upon problem situations. It is essential that confidentiality be strictly adhered to if this process is to be successful.

A clear and publicized official mechanism for dealing with homophobic violence is also needed. Campus security persons/ police need to be provided with training to handle issues related to gay/lesbian orientation in a confidential, sensitive, and respectful manner. Often lesbians and gay men have faced additional stress and discrimination at the hands of homophobic or unsophisticated officials or have had their orientation revealed, resulting in further pain and rejection from important others, including their families. Assistance in this training is available from the American Psychological Association, the National Lesbian and Gay Task Force, and lesbian and gay community centers located in most urban areas. Procedures for investigating incidents need to be carefully spelled out, including protection of the victim's identity unless she or he chooses to "go public." Although prosecution cannot occur if the victim needs to remain unidentified, it is still possible to deal with homophobia on a local or campus level. In cases where the victim is willing to come forth, legal action or college action against the perpetrator is necessary.

The overall process of effectively dealing with homophobia and heterosexism on a campus is involved and difficult. However colleges and universities should engage in the efforts which will make it possible for gay and lesbian students to pursue their academic careers free from orientation based destructive influences.

CONCLUSIONS

As the result of an increasing body of literature, it has become clear that most of our colleges and universities are strongholds of homophobic discrimination and heterosexism which impact directly on lesbian and gay students, staff, and faculty, upon those exploring their orientation, and upon the entire campus community. The scope and seriousness of violence perpetrated against gay men and lesbians, or those thought to be other than heterosexual, have been sufficiently documented for us that we can no longer ignore its extent and impact. The negative effects of internalized homophobia have been clearly established and include self-doubt, isolation, engaging in attempts at heterosexuality in order to survive, identifying with the aggressors and allowing further abuse, inability to function socially or academically, self-hatred or self-loathing, and engaging in serious self-destructive behaviors including substance abuse, eating disorders, serious risk taking, self-mutilation, and suicide attempts.

Colleges and universities can establish policies and procedures to combat homophobia and heterosexism across the entire campus community provided that institutional administrative support is available for strenuous and long-term efforts. Resources and assistance are available to those schools wishing to make their campus a safe environment for all students, staff, and faculty including those members of the academic community who are not heterosexual.

While this paper merely touches the surface of the immensity of the issue, it does provide some information for those wishing to embark upon homophobia/heterosexism proofing their campus. It is hoped that it will provoke thought and stir readers to action, including examination of their own campus communities to determine what problems and solutions exist and what needs to be done to ensure the emotional and physical safety of campus members who have alternative lifestyles.

REFERENCES

Anderson, C. (1985). Males as sexual assault victims: Multiple levels of trauma. In J. C. Gonsiorek (Ed.), *A guide to psychotherapy with gay and lesbian clients* (pp. 145-162). Binghamton, NY: Harrington Park Press.

Bell, A. P., Weinberg, M. S., & Hammersmith, S. K. (1981). *Sexual preference: Its development in men and women.* Bloomington, IN: Indiana University Press.

Berrill, K. T. (1985). *Anti-gay violence and victimization.* New York, NY: National Gay and Lesbian Task Force.

Berrill, K. T. (1992). Anti-gay violence and victimization in the United States: An overview. In G. M. Herek & K. T. Berrill (Eds.), *Hate crimes: Confronting violence against lesbians and gay men* (pp. 19-45). Newberry Park, CA: Sage Publications Inc.

Berrill, K. T. (1989, March). *Combating homophobia.* Presentation at the annual meeting of the American College Personnel Association, Washington, DC.

Berzon, B. (1979a). Achieving success as a gay couple. In B. Berzon (Ed.), *Positively gay* (pp. 30-40). Los Angeles, CA: Mediamix Associates.

Berzon, B. (1979b). Developing a positive gay identity. In B. Berzon (Ed.), *Positively gay* (pp. 1-14). Los Angeles, CA: Mediamix Associates.

Boxer, A. M., & Cohler, B. J. (1989). The life course of gay and lesbian youth: An immodest proposal for the study of lives. *Journal of Homosexuality, 17,* 315-355.

Cass, V. C. (1985). Homosexual identity: A concept in need of definition. In J. P. De Cecco & M. G. Shively (Eds.), *Origins of sexuality and homosexuality* (pp. 105-126). New York, NY: Harrington Park Press.

Cavin, S. (1987). Rutgers sexual orientation survey: A report on the experiences of the lesbian, gay and bisexual members of the Rutgers community. Unpublished manuscript. New Brunswick, NJ: Author.

Chan, C. S. (1989) Issues of identity development among Asian-American lesbians and gay men. *Journal of Counseling and Development, 68,* 16-20.

Coleman, E. (1982). Developmental states of the coming out process. *Journal of Homosexuality, 7,* 31-43.

Coleman, E. (1978). Toward a new model of treatment of homosexuality: A review. *Journal of Homosexuality, 3,* 345-359.

Coleman, E., & Remafedi, G. (1989). Gay, lesbian, and bisexual adolescents: A critical challenge to counselors. *Journal of Counseling & Development, 68,* 36-40.

Comstock, G. D. (1991). *Violence against lesbians and gay men.* New York: Columbia University Press.

D'Augelli, A. R. (1988). The adolescent closet: Promoting the development of the lesbian or gay male teenager. *The School Psychologist, 32,* 2 & 9.

D'Augelli, A. R. (1989). Lesbians' and gay men's experiences of discrimination and harassment in a university community. *American Journal of Community Psychology, 17,* 317-321.

D'Augelli, A. R. (1991). Teaching lesbian/gay development: From oppression to exceptionality. *Journal of Homosexuality, 22,* 213-227.

De Cecco, J. P. (1981). Definition and meaning of sexual orientation. *Journal of Homosexuality, 6,* 51-67.

Duncan, D. F. (1990). Prevalence of sexual assault victimization among heterosexual and gay/lesbian university students. *Psychological Reports, 66,* 65-66.

Evans, N. J., & Wall, V. A. (1991). *Beyond tolerance: Gays, lesbians, and bisexuals on campus.* Alexandria, VA: American College Personnel Association.

Erikson, E. (1963). *Childhood and society* (2nd ed.). New York: Norton.

Freiberg, P. (1987, September 1). Sex education and the gay issue: What are they teaching about us in the schools? *The Advocate,* 42-48.

Gibson, P. (1982). Developing services to gay and lesbian youth in a runaway shelter. In National Network of Runaway and Youth Services (Ed.). *Gay youth counseling manual.* San Francisco: Author (Unpublished manual).

Gonsiorek, J. C. (1988). Mental health issues of gay and lesbian adolescents. *Journal of Adolescent Care, 9,* 114-122.

Gross, L., Aurand, S. K., & Addessa, R. (1988). *Violence and discrimination against lesbian and gay people in Philadelphia and the Commonwealth of Pennsylvania.* Philadelphia, PA: Philadelphia Lesbian and Gay Task Force.

Hammersmith, S. K. (1988). A sociological approach to counseling homosexual clients and their families. In E. Coleman (Ed.). *Integrated identity for gay men and lesbians: Psychotherapeutic approaches for emotional well-being* (pp. 173-190). Harrington Park Press, New York.

Herdt, G. (Ed.). (1989). Introduction: Gay and lesbian youth, emergent identities, and cultural scenes at home and abroad. In G. Herdt (Ed.), *Gay and lesbian youth* (pp 1-42). Binghamton, NY: Harrington Park Press.

Herek, G. M. (1986a). Sexual orientation and prejudice at Yale: A report on the experiences of lesbian, gay and bisexual members of the Yale community. Unpublished manuscript.

Herek, G. M. (1986b). *Violence against lesbians and gay men.* Statement presented on behalf of the American Psychological Association before the United House of Representatives Committee on the Judiciary Subcommittee on Criminal Justice. Washington, DC: American Psychological Association.

Herek, F. M. (1989), Hate Crimes Against Lesbians and Gay Men: Issues for Research and Policy. *American Psychologist, 44*(6), 948-955.

Herek, G. M. (1991). Myths about sexual orientation: A lawyer's guide to social science research. *Law and Sexuality: A Review of Lesbian and Gay Legal Issues, 1* (Summer), 133-172.

Herek, G. M. (1992). The social context of hate crimes: Notes on cultural heterosexism. In G. M. Herek & K. T. Berrill (Eds.), *Hate crimes: Confronting violence against lesbians and gay men* (pp. 89-104). Newberry Park, CA: Sage Publications Inc.

Herek, G. M., & Glunt, E. K. (1988). An epidemic of stigma: Public reaction to AIDS. *American Psychologist, 43,* 46-53.

Herman, J. (1981) *Father-daughter incest.* Cambridge, MA: Harvard University Press.

Hetrick, E. S., & Martin, A. D. (1987). Developmental issues and their resolution for gay and lesbian adolescents. In E. Coleman (Ed.), *Integrated identity for gay men and lesbians: Psychotherapeutic approaches for emotional well-being* (pp. 25-43). Binghamton, NY: Harrington Park Press.

Hoult, T. F. (1985). Human sexuality in biological perspective: Theoretical and methodological considerations. In J. P. DeCecco & M. G. Shively (Eds.), *Origins of sexuality and homosexuality* (pp. 137-153). New York: Harrington Park Press.

Human Rights Foundation, Inc. (1984). *Demystifying homosexuality: A teaching guide about lesbians and gay men.* New York: Irvington Publishers.

Hunter, J. (1992). Violence against lesbian and gay male youths. In G. M. Herek & K. T. Berrill (Eds.), *Hate crimes: Confronting violence against lesbians and gay men* (pp. 76-82). Newberry Park: CA: Sage Publications Inc.

Jay, K., & Young, A. (1979). *The gay report.* New York: Summit Books.

Kaplan, S., & Saperstein, S. (1985). Lesbian and gay adolescents. In H. Hidalgo, T. L. Peterson, & N. J. Woodman (Eds.), *Lesbian and gay issues: A resource manual for social workers* (pp. 17-20). Silver Spring, MD: American Association of Social Workers.

Kurdek, L. A. (1988). Correlates of negative attitudes toward homosexuals in heterosexual college students. *Sex Roles, 18,* 727-738.

Leonard, A. S. (1989). *Gay & lesbian rights protections in the U.S.: An introduction to gay and lesbian civil rights.* Washington, DC: National Gay and Lesbian Task Force.

Loiacano, D. K. (1989). Gay identity issues among Black Americans: Racism, homophobia, and the need for validation. *Journal of Counseling and Development, 68,* 21-25.

Malyon, A. K. (1981). The homosexual adolescent: Developmental issues and social bias. *Child Welfare, 60,* 321-330.

Mohr, R. D. (1988). *Gays/justice: A study of ethics, society, and law.* New York, NY: Columbia University Press.

Money, J. (1988). *Gay, straight, and in between.* New York: Oxford Univ. Press.

Morales, E. S. (1990). Ethnic minority families and minority gays and lesbians. In F. W. Bozett & M. B. Sussman (Eds.). *Homosexuality and family relations* (pp. 217-239). Binghamton, NY: Harrington Park Press.

Murphy, B. C. (1991). Educating mental health professionals about gay and lesbian issues. *Journal of Homosexuality, 22,* 229-246.

National Education Association. (1991). *Affording equal opportunity to gay and lesbian students through teaching and counseling: A training handbook for educators.* Washington, DC: Author.

National Gay and Lesbian Task Force (1988). *Anti-gay violence and victimization in 1988.* Washington, DC: Author.

National Gay & Lesbian Task Force. (1990). *Anti-gay violence, victimization & defamation in 1989.* Washington, DC: Author.

National Gay and Lesbian Task Force Policy Institute. (1991a). *Anti-gay/lesbian violence, victimization & defamation in 1990.* Washington, DC: Author.

National Gay and Lesbian Task Force Policy Institute (1991b). *Count and counter hate crimes: A fact sheet on violence against lesbians and gay men.* Washington, DC: Author.

Norris, W. P. (1992). Liberal attitudes and homophobic acts: The paradoxes of homosexual experience in a liberal institution. In K. Harbeck (Ed.) *Coming out of the classroom closet: Gay and lesbian students, teachers and curriculum* (pp. 81-120). Binghamton, NY: Harrington Park Press.

Nugent, R., & Gramick J. (1992). *Building bridges: Gay and lesbian reality and the Catholic church.* Mystic, CT: Twenty Third Publications.

Political Committee of the Lesbian and Gay Student Alliance of Pennsylvania State University. (1991). Unpublished document prepared at Pennsylvania State University in support of the inclusion of sexual orientation in the university policy. *Chapter II. Schools with sexual orientation clauses: Summary.* State College, PA: Author.

Pharr, S. (1988). *Homophobia: A weapon of sexism.* Inverness, CA: Chardon Press.

Ponse, B. (1978). *Identities in the lesbian world: The social construction of the self.* Westport, CT: Greenwood.

President's Select Committee for Lesbian and Gay Concerns of Rutgers. (1989). *In every classroom: The report of the president's select committee for lesbian and gay concerns.* New Brunswick, N. J.: The State University of New Jersey at Rutgers.

Rabin, J. S., & Slater, B. R. (August, 1991). *Impact of early developmental experiences on adult lesbians.* Unpublished paper presented at the 99th Annual Convention of the American Psychological Association. San Francisco, CA.

Rabin, J. S., & Slater, B. R. (August, 1992). *Consequences of early and later coming-out patterns in lesbian development.* Unpublished paper presented at the 100th Annual Convention of the American Psychological Association. Washington, DC.

Remafedi, G. (1987). Adolescent homosexuality: Psychosocial and medical implications. *Pediatrics, 79,* 331-337.

Revelle, R. (1988). *Report on gay and lesbian youth in Seattle.* Seattle, WA: Department of Human Resources.

Rodriguez, R. A. (1991). *A qualitative study of identity development in gay Chicano males.* A dissertation completed at the University of Utah. Salt Lake City, UT: Author.

Rofes, E. E. (1983). *"I thought people like that killed themselves": Lesbians, gay men and suicide.* San Francisco, CA: Gray Fox Press.

Ruse, M. (1981). Are there gay genes? Sociobiology and homosexuality. *Journal of Homosexuality, 6,* 5-34.

Saghir, M. T., & Robins, E. (1973). *Male and female homosexuality: A comprehensive investigation.* Baltimore, MD: Williams & Watkins.

Savin-Williams, R. C. (1990). *Gay and lesbian youth: Expressions of identity.* New York, NY: Hemisphere Publishing Corp.

Schaecher, R. (1989, Winter). Stresses on lesbian and gay adolescents. *Independent School,* 29-35.

Slater, B. R. (1988). Essential issues in working with lesbian and gay male youths. *Professional Psychology: Research and Practice, 19*, 226-235.

Slater, B. R. (1989). Special needs of today's adolescents. In C. D. Kain (Ed.), *No longer immune: A counselor's guide to AIDS* (pp. 93-113). Washington, DC: American Association of Counseling and Development.

Task Force on Lesbian and Gay Concerns of the University of Oregon. (1990). *Creating safety, valuing diversity: A report to the University of Oregon.* Eugene, OR: Author.

Troiden, R. (1989). The formation of homosexual identities. *Journal of Homosexuality, 17*, 43-73.

United States Department of Health and Human Services. (1989). *Report of the secretary's task force on youth suicide.* Rockville, MD: Author.

Uribe, V., & Harbeck, K. M. (1992). Addressing the needs of lesbian, gay, and bisexual youth: The origins of PROJECT 10 and school-based intervention. In K. Harbeck (Ed.). *Coming out of the classroom closet: Gay and lesbian students, teachers and curriculum* (pp. 9-28). Binghamton, NY: Harrington Park Press.

Vergara, R. L. (1984). Meeting the needs of the sexual minority: One program's response. *Journal Social Work and Human Sexuality, 2*, 19-38.

Wall, V. A., & Evans, N. J. (1991). Using psychosocial developmental theories to understand and work with gay and lesbian persons. In N. J. Evans & V. A. Wall (Eds.), *Beyond Tolerance: Gays, lesbians and bisexuals on campus* (pp. 25-38). Alexandria, VA: American College Personnel Association.

Weiss, A., & Schiller, G. (1988). *Before Stonewall: The making of a gay and lesbian community.* Tallahassee, FL: Naiad Press.

Whitlock, K. (1988). *Bridges of respect: Creating support for lesbian and gay youth.* Philadelphia, PA: American Friends Service Committee.

Woodman, N. J., & Lenna, H. R. (1980). *Counseling with gay men and women: A guide for facilitating positive life-styles.* San Francisco: Jossey-Bass Inc., Publishers.

Yeskel, F. (1985). *The consequences of being gay: A report on the quality of life for lesbian, gay and bisexual students at the University of Massachusetts at Amherst.* Amherst: University of Massachusetts.

Zimmerman, B. (1990). *The safe sea of women.* Boston, MA: Beacon Press.

Chapter 9

Violence and the Male Gender Role

Donald L. Marshall

SUMMARY. The nature of the culturally defined male gender role is reviewed, followed by an examination of ways gender role and gender role conflict and strain contribute to violent behaviors. Environmental supports for adoption and adherence to the problematic aspects of the male gender role are reviewed. Implications for intervention at individual, group and institutional levels are explored.

This chapter addresses how the male gender role, as understood in late twentieth century North American culture, contributes to violent behaviors on and off college campuses, beginning with a review of recent work on understanding the structure of the male gender role. Next is a review of research and theorizing about how the assigned roles encourage violent behaviors in men, and ways in which gender roles are perpetuated. This chapter concludes with observations about prevention and suggested treatment strategies designed to interrupt gender-based violent tendencies.

Donald L. Marshall, PhD, is a psychologist in the Counseling Center at the University of Puget Sound, 1500 North Warner St., Tacoma, WA 98416. Donn helped develop a community-based treatment program for batterers and studied a batterer population as a part of his doctoral research. On college campuses Donn has developed sexual assault education and prevention programs for men and women, designed programs to encourage men to take responsibility for ending sexual violence, and helped organize a regional conference on sexual assault prevention and treatment.

[Haworth co-indexing entry note]: "Violence and the Male Gender Role." Marshall, Donald L. Co-published simultaneously in *Journal of College Student Psychotherapy* (The Haworth Press, Inc.) Vol. 8, No. 3, 1993, pp. 203-218: and: *Campus Violence: Kinds, Causes, and Cures* (ed: Leighton C. Whitaker and Jeffrey W. Pollard) The Haworth Press, Inc., 1993, pp. 203-218. Multiple copies of this article/chapter may be purchased from The Haworth Document Delivery Center [1-800-3-HAWORTH; 9:00 a.m. - 5:00 p.m. (EST)].

203

THE MALE GENDER ROLE

What does it mean to be a man? How do males learn to be *men*? How are those lessons passed on from generation to generation, and how are the minimal acceptable standards of masculinity assessed and maintained? What counts as masculine? What are the rewards for displaying masculinity and what are the penalties for failing to live up to this elusive measure of maleness?

Following the lead of others (cf. O'Neil, 1990) I refer to the male gender role as the set prescribed and proscribed "behaviors, expectations and values" (p. 24) deemed appropriate for men in our culture, as distinct from sex roles, which refer to a much narrower range of sexual behaviors. Masculinity is considered the embodiment and enactment of the male gender role.

Meth (1990) notes the culture's "script" prescribing acceptable masculine thought, feeling and behavior. The messages contained in this script are thought to provide guidance in the transitions from childhood to adulthood. Because the scripts are provided and followed in many varied, subtle and non-conscious ways from very early in a boy's life, the scripts become deeply ingrained and transformed into prescriptive notions about what a boy must be in order to be accepted as a man. Unfortunately for both the individual boy and for society at large, many of these prescriptions are unhealthy, conflictual, or impossible to achieve. I now turn to the content of the culture's script(s) for masculinity.

In the late 1960s and early 1970s much work was done on the development of masculinity/femininity scales (e.g., Bem, 1974; Broverman, 1972). Cicone and Ruble (1978) summarized and synthesized these studies as they address the normative description of the male gender role; they group the qualities describing masculinity as (a) active and achievement-oriented; (b) dominant; and (c) level-headed, and they further note the importance of avoiding the feminine.

In an early work specifically examining the make-up of the male role Sawyer (cited in Pleck, 1976) posited that the two primary themes of masculinity are an emphasis on achievement and the suppression of affect. Pleck (1976) added to those themes by suggesting a distinction between traditional and modern notions of masculinity. Modern expectations are often more complex, and may contradict the traditional norms. For example, Pleck suggested that within the traditional male norms interpersonal skills were rejected in favor of anger and impulsiveness. However, within modern expectations interpersonal skills which promote achievement are highly valued and "losing one's cool" is prohibited. The increasingly complex and internally contradictory messages about manhood add to gender role strain which is discussed further below.

Brannon (1976) provided an often-cited formulation of the components of the male gender role. Brannon colorfully labels the four identified primary attributes of masculinity as (a) "No Sissy Stuff: The Stigma of Anything Vaguely Feminine" (which includes prohibitions against male intimacy, and especially excludes homosexuality); (b) "The Big Wheel: Success, Status, and the Need to Be Looked Up To"; (c) "The Sturdy Oak: A Manly Air of Toughness, Confidence, and Self-Reliance"; (d) "Give 'em Hell: The Aura of Aggression, Violence, and Daring." These intuitively-formulated dimensions were expanded and operationally defined in the Brannon Masculinity Scale (BMS; Brannon & Juni, 1984).

In a subsequent study examining the factorial structure of the BMS, Thompson and Pleck (1987) reported three factors which were described as "Status" (consisting of items from the "Big Wheel" and "Sturdy Oak" dimensions), "Toughness" (derived from items in the "No Sissy Stuff," "Sturdy Oak" and "Give 'em Hell" dimensions) and "Antifemininity" (with other items from "No Sissy Stuff"). Interestingly, the subjects in the Thompson and Pleck study (undergraduates attending two liberal arts colleges, almost all Caucasian (96%), and socioeconomically "middle to upper class" (p. 26) identified these attributes as constituting the normative male role, but fell short of affirming them; they found the factors loaded together without the respondents necessarily owning the attributes as descriptive of their own beliefs. Responses to these items about the male role were complexly related to questions about attitudes toward women's roles, suggesting that attitudes toward changing roles for men and women may vary independently of each other. However, the results do support the earlier theorizing that the male gender role has identifiable components.

O'Neil (1982) wrote about *gender-role conflict* defined as "a psychological state in which gender roles have negative consequences or impact" (p. 203) and *gender role strain* which he defined as "excessive mental or physical tension caused by gender role conflict" (p. 203). He suggested that gender role strain and conflict in men evidence as six patterns of functioning: (a) restrictive emotionality; (b) homophobia; (c) socialized control, power and competitiveness; (d) restricted sexual and affectionate behaviors; (e) obsession with achievement and success; and (f) health problems. Although seemingly a mixture of gender-role driven attitudes and behaviors and negative consequences of adhering to those prescriptions and proscriptions, the overlap of O'Neil's patterns with the other formulations is obvious. O'Neil, Helms, Gable, David and Wrightsman (1986) asserted that the fear of femininity could be considered a unifying theme in the study of men's gender role conflict.

Although no definitive list of male gender role characteristics has been formulated, there is considerable overlap in the intuitive and empirical efforts to do so, as described above. Of course these characteristics may vary in importance to individual men (and women), and may vary in salience to men at different times of their lives, and in different situations (Pleck, 1976). However, there is an identifiable, if shifting, cultural press for men to embody characteristics deemed appropriate for the male gender role.

THE MALE GENDER ROLE AND VIOLENCE

It is important to distinguish between the emotional response of anger and the violent behaviors that sometimes accompany those feelings. Whereas violent behaviors may be deemed inappropriate and unacceptable in most contexts (college campuses being a prime example), the feeling of anger is in itself posited to be a value neutral response to internal and external stimuli. Violent behaviors may well demand legal, administrative and/or therapeutic attention. For the purposes of this article *violence* or *violent behavior* will be defined as "behavior that is intended to hurt another person" (Roark, 1987). Violence, and threats of violence, can be manifested in many forms including physical assault, sexual assault, harassment, and hazing.

The connection between violent behavior and the qualities linked to masculinity will be considered in two ways: (a) the direct contribution of masculine attributes to violent behavior; and (b) gender role conflict and strain as a contributor to male violence in the modern world.

Several male gender role characteristics described earlier, particularly those Pleck (1976) described as the more traditional role expectations, require that men be action-oriented, aggressive and restrict emotional expression other than to act out anger. A readiness to actively aggress while experiencing anger seems a prescription for violent behavior. Similarly, behaving in a physically threatening or aggressive manner puts to rest, at least temporarily, any doubts about appearing feminine.

Feminist researchers (Herman, 1981; Martin, 1976; Walker, 1979) in the 1970s and early 1980s questioned the then-prevailing notions about men who were sexually assaultive, physically abusive with women partners, or child molesters. Until that time these violent men were generally considered rare and sociopathic. In short, they were thought to be very different from the "normal" man. However, these writers began making explicit connections between the male role and the abuses men inflicted. Thus men's needs for control and dominance, and propensity for acting aggressively led Russell to write, "Rape is not so much a deviant act as an over-conforming act" (quoted in Pleck, 1981; p. 146). Similarly, Herman (1981) wrote an incisive analysis indicting male gender roles in incestuous abuse. She concluded that sexual aggressiveness was inevitable as long as traditional gender roles and gender inequality within families remained.

Acceptance of a rigidly defined male role has been described as one of the "most salient characteristics" (Hofeller, 1982) of men who batter women partners. Because of the role-generated demands that a man be in control or "wear the pants" in a relationship, any perceived loss of power may be seen as a threat. The resulting need to re-establish control may require using whatever means available, including violent, abusive behaviors. The more often violence is used, the more likely it will be used in the future with increasing ferocity (Walker, 1979). Several studies have shown that holding to more traditional attitudes about male and female gender roles distinguishes between abusive and non-abusive men (Marshall, 1988; Telch & Lindquist, 1984; Thompson, 1990). Similarly, Yllo (1984) found that respondents who reported relative equality in decision-making power within a relationship also reported lower rates of physical violence. A loosening of rigid attitudes about appropriate roles for men and women is an important criterion for long-term change in many treatment programs (Feazell, Mayers & Deschner, 1984). In a study of men who completed a batterers' treatment program, a change to more egalitarian attitudes about men and women has been identified as an important component of successful "recovery" (Gondolf & Hanneke, 1987). Finally, in their review, Hotaling and Sugarman (1986) suggest that the reason rigid, traditional gender role attitudes do not evidence as a more consistent correlate of partner abuse may be that expectations for male dominance are so pervasive that measurements are not sufficiently sensitive to distinguish between abusive and nonabusive men.

One area of consensus among scholars of the male gender role is the belief that men (and boys) experience a gap between that which they believe to be expected of them and their experience of self in the world (O'Neil, 1981). Young boys evidently experience greater pressure to conform to gender-specified role demands earlier and more rigidly than girls, and boys more often evidence anxiety about their failures to adhere to those expectations (Hartley, 1959). It is also argued that the experience of gender role strain is inevitable in men's lives since it is impossible to live up to poorly defined requirements (e.g., do not be feminine) and because some requirements conflict with others (e.g., be aggressive vs. be "cool"). As a result of experienced inadequacy in meeting role demands, some men may experience gender role conflict and strain as a loss of control which they feel compelled to correct. These men may display dysfunctional masculinity in exaggerated and over-compensated forms, taking clearer behavioral prescriptions such as control and aggressiveness to stereotyped extremes. These "hypermasculine" displays of violence may target perceived threats to men's masculine identity. Thus, strong or liberated women, or gay or effeminate men, may become victims.

ORIGIN AND MAINTENANCE
OF THE MALE GENDER ROLE

How one acquires the behavioral and attitudinal attributes considered appropriate for one's sex continues to be a matter of debate, without sign of resolution. In her renowned cross-cultural study, Margaret Mead (1935/1963) believed she had uncovered solid evidence of the pliability of gender-linked behaviors, and thus she held that masculinity and femininity are entirely constructed and taught by cultures. However, doubts about the validity of Mead's observations have emerged. More recent studies on the impact of heredity on behavior suggest genetic propensities for a wide variety of behaviors.

Developmental psychologists have known for over twenty years that from the moment of their births children are treated and described differently based on their sex. In experimental conditions in which subjects are presented infants randomly assigned as male or female, subjects describe perceptions and treat infants consistent with assigned sex (reviewed in Maccoby & Jacklin, 1974). Predictably, these differential perceptions and treatments are in the direction of culturally prescribed norms for the sexes. Boys are more likely to be described as more robust and active, and treated more roughly than girls.

In their fascinating and painstaking review of the relevant research available at that time, Maccoby and Jacklin (1974) concluded that although genetic predispositions could not be ruled out as influential in the development of observed gender differences, learning and socializing were clearly operating from the first moments following birth. In short, both nature and nurture are at work, the former influencing the latter as a prepared readiness to learn certain responses (Seligman & Hager, 1972). The strength of those biological predispositions versus the influence of the cultural insistence that the predispositions be realized in each male child has not been definitively measured. However, it is clear that culture acts to differentially encourage and discourage sex-linked behaviors, and defines those behaviors as appropriate and inappropriate (acceptable and unacceptable) dependant on one's biological make-up. Because the selectively perceived attributes are reinforced from the moment of birth (perhaps even prenatally) in so many varied ways, both subtle and obvious, the nature-nurture question has remained elusive. It is sufficient for the current discussion to acknowledge the pervasiveness of the cultural press for boys to be perceived and act in ways defined as appropriate for their gender. I now turn to ongoing cultural influences.

Following an infancy and an early childhood replete with direct ("big boys don't cry") and indirect (gender-specific toys) messages about how a boy is to be behaviorally distinguished from girls, a wide variety of institutions (e.g., schools, religious groups, extended families) continue to reinforce boys for conformance to male norms, and punish those who do not measure up. If this assertion is true, then the socializing forces should be particularly apparent in groups which are traditionally predominated by males. Such groups as the Boy Scouts (Hantover, 1978) and sports teams such as Little League baseball and Pop Warner football abound from boyhood (Sabo & Runfola, 1980). Through adolescence and young adulthood, sports teams, fraternities and the military (Arkin & Dobrofsky, 1978) remain bastions of male dominance. To illustrate the ongoing socialization process in environments most relevant for this readership, I next examine how sports teams and fraternities serve to promote gender role conformance expectations which lend themselves to violent behaviors.

Sports provide an arena in which boys can be taught and can display what is expected of them. They are called on to compete, often ruthlessly, and to win at all costs, thus learning lessons about achieving. Successful competitors learn to exploit weaknesses while exhibiting none, and often hurt others while remaining impervious to pain themselves ("walk it off"), thus they learn about displaying a cool toughness without regard for the feelings of self or others. In part because of the differences in physical strength, and largely because of strong social prohibitions, girls rarely compete alongside boys in sports and the sex segregation can lend itself to feelings of superiority. This is further reinforced in the way girls are often included as cheerleaders, clearly a secondary, supportive role designed to make the winning boys feel adulation for their "manly" displays. The cheers themselves often refer to fighting, hitting ("Hit 'em a lick. Hit 'em a lick. Harder. Harder."), and being strong.

In a fascinating compendium, Sabo and Runfola (1980) explore the relationship between masculinity and sports. They recount a story about Knute Rockne, a legendary Notre Dame football coach, disgustedly appearing before his poorly-performing team at half time. Instead of a roaring, challenging speech the team had expected, Rockne reportedly only said, "Oh, excuse me, ladies. I was looking for the Notre Dame football team" (p. 1). The direct challenge to the players' manhood purportedly worked, and the team went on to win the game. Clearly, the coach found an effective way to enliven his team by suggesting that they needed to prove they were not of the "fair sex."

Brannon (1974) and O'Neil (1981) suggested that the avoidance of femininity ("No Sissy Stuff") was the most salient of the male gender role characteristics. Relatedly, Morin and Garfinkle (1978) explored how homophobia powerfully serves to force men into behavior which complies with traditional roles. Thus, Rockne used one of the strongest motivators possible. Insisting that men live up to the antifemininity requirement is in part so motivating because it is not clearly defined. It was not enough that Rockne's team was playing a sport which epitomizes competitive toughness and near complete disregard for their physical bodies; their masculinity was still challengeable. They still had to do more, play harder, more aggressively, to prove they were not like girls. Any behaviors short of total annihilation of the other in competition can leave men vulnerable to accusations of weakness with the implications of femininity and thinly disguised implications of homosexuality.

College fraternities serve as another example of environments developed and maintained by and for men. At their best, fraternities offer structure for public service, provide fertile ground for valued, life-long friendships, offer support and guidance to younger members, and encourage study and self improvement. However, Ehrhart and Sandler (1985) point out that "nearly all of the recent reported gang rape incidents have involved fraternities" (p. 6). That finding does not indict all fraternities and fraternity members as gang rapists, but it does clearly suggest that some acculturating forces which do not live up to explicitly stated fraternal ideals are operating in many of these settings.

Stimulated by one reported gang rape and the subsequent cover-up by members of a fraternity, Martin and Hummer (1989) conducted a study of the socialization process within fraternity organizations. They found that fraternities were "vitally concerned–more than with anything else–with masculinity . . . Valued members display, or are willing to go along with, a narrow conception of masculinity that stresses competition, athleticism, dominance, winning, conflict, wealth, material possessions, willingness to drink alcohol, and sexual prowess vis-a-vis women" (p. 460). They concluded that "fraternities are a physical and sociocultural context that encourages the sexual coercion of women" (p. 458). Similarly, Merton (1985) cautions that "gang rapes should not be viewed as a separate phenomenon; they are simply the most spectacular manifestation of a pervasive and virulent hostility toward women" (p. 62). Ehrhart and Sandler (1985) add that "Gang rape is the 'ultimate proof' of men's power–they are dominant over women. Sex is not seen as an expression of love and friendship but as a way of expressing dominance" (p. 6). Thus, male sexual violence against women is revealed as an expression of men's needs to demonstrate their masculine ability and willingness to dominate and control others.

It is well known, if not always acknowledged, that a primary function of fraternities is meeting members' social goals, with much of the socializing centered around alcohol consumption. Consuming quantities of alcohol is itself often a way of establishing a reputation for masculinity, in and out of fraternities. Substance abuse is also strongly associated with battering (Marshall, 1988) and sexual assault (Harney & Muehlenhard, 1991). Although the causal nature of the relationship between alcohol and violence continues to be debated (Richardson & Hammock, 1991) it is generally accepted that much violence occurs under the influence. In an environment in which rigid gender role stereotypes (including expectations of male control and dominance) are enforced, where women are seen as sexual prey or even bait to help recruit potential pledges (Martin & Hummer, 1989), and in which alcohol flows freely, sexual violence is inevitably fostered.

It is important to point out that although fraternities may embody and, because of their membership may well intensify troublesome characteristics of the male gender role, they are examined here and elsewhere because they make for identifiable examples, not because they are the sole, or even primary, perpetrators of campus assaults. Other, less formally recognized groups of men engage in similar socialization and violence-perpetuating activities.

PREVENTION AND TREATMENT OF MALE VIOLENCE

The preceding discussion suggests methods for preventive programming and interventions to reduce male violence. The specific suggestions which follow come from the perspective that efforts to live up to some vaguely formed notions about what it means to be a man underlie and motivate, directly or indirectly, a significant amount of male-perpetrated violence. Strategies to reduce violence must take into account what is known about the male gender role.

Because existing male standards have been the established and accepted norms, an unquestioning acceptance of male gender roles will serve to perpetuate existing violence-inducing gender role expectations (Good & May, 1987). Change for individuals, groups, institutions and the culture at large requires active affirmation and modeling of acceptable alternatives to overcome the historical and ongoing cultural press. Thus, a hands-off policy allowing men to develop their own sense of masculine identities without an active effort to present alternatives, capitulates, and via silence endorses, the powerful status quo. Effective change strategies must engage a target audience in exploring the limitations and problematic elements of extant gender role norms. Models of alternative norms should be sought out, acknowledged, and supported.

Roark (1987) wrote that "Violence occurs in a cultural and social context and is both a community and individual phenomenon" (p. 370). Therefore, intervention efforts must address both. The campus community should present highly visible programmatic efforts focused on relevant topics such as rape prevention, sexual decision-making, communication in relationships and substance abuse. The role of gender role socialization should be explored in all related programming. Trained peer leaders can model and be supportive of men stretching beyond rigidly defined male gender roles while presenting relevant material, and may thereby increase audience identification and the potential for change (Walter-Brooks,

Jaynes, & Marshall, 1990). Male-dominant groups such as fraternities and male sports teams are powerful socializing influences on many campuses. Too often they are seen as beyond the reach of traditional programming efforts and so they represent real challenge as well as potential.

Institutions should confront the restrictive power of homophobia via public support for sexual minorities. This support should include recognition and financial support for gay, lesbian and bisexual student organizations and explicit anti-discrimination policy statements.

Codes of student conduct should include clear statements about the unacceptability of violent behaviors or threats of any kind. In some forms of gender-based violence, such as sexual harassment and assault, legal definitions often lag behind developing social norms, or behind standards of conduct expected of students on a college campus. Perpetrators sometimes attempt to rely on the more restrictive legal definitions of criminalized violence in order to rationalize and justify their behaviors. Explicit policy and codes of conduct establish the norms of the campus community and are important preventively and remedially. To have preventive power these codes must be publicized to the campus community several times each year. Campus administrations and student courts must be educated about the dynamics of violence and the impact of assaults on victims. Administrators and campus hearing boards must be prepared to support codes of conduct with expulsion if necessary.

Good, Gilbert and Scher (1990) have written about psychotherapy in which awareness of gender informs case conceptualization and the treatment process. When men present for psychotherapy, or in less formal counseling contacts in residence halls or course conferences, it is important to listen closely for themes related to gender role strain and conflict. It is important to move beyond a simple willingness to accept any feelings male clients may express since male socialization strongly limits that expression. Armed with awareness of the press of the male gender role, counselors should actively encourage men to become more emotionally attuned and expressive in order to help clients move beyond those gender role limitations. Robertson and Fitzgerald (1992) suggest that we go even further: Since we are aware that holding traditional masculine attitudes is negatively related to a lack of willingness to seek traditional counseling services (cf. Good, Dell & Mintz, 1989), we should market counseling services in ways more acceptable to male constituents. Their suggestions include developing outreach programs marketed as "classes, workshops and seminars" (p. 245) instead of relying on men to present for personal counseling. It is imperative that therapists develop awareness of their own blind spots which may result in overlooking or discounting issues not typically associated with men (e.g., surviving sexual abuse).

Treatment for men who abuse partners may be undertaken selectively in college and university counseling centers where staff have the necessary expertise. Clear treatment agreements and behavioral contracts which guarantee safety of past and potential victims, and specify consequences for failure to comply with the agreements, are critical components for this work. Treatment for men who are sexually assaultive is an increasingly specialized area of psychotherapy and generally should not be undertaken without training and supervision. This treatment often includes contact with the legal system, some forms of evaluation and supervision (e.g., plethysmograph) and long-term follow up for which most colleges and universities are ill prepared. It should be noted that many men who present for treatment for other reasons (e.g., depression, motivational problems, etc.) also may be violent. Remaining alert for cues to those behaviors, and the underlying dynamics, is important to ongoing assessment as men are not likely to present that information from the outset (Scher & Stevens, 1987).

From the perspective of a victim being assaulted, whether the assailant is acting out an exaggerated display of angry, dominating, and controlling hypermasculinity as compensation for underlying doubt about his manhood (i.e., homosexual panic), or he is a sadistic sociopath, is not particularly meaningful. Survival is. Later, during a recovery process in which developing an understanding of the possible motivations of an attacker as a way to diminish self-blame and reassert a sense of predictability and control in one's life, these distinctions may be profitably explored with a survivor. However, to prevent male-perpetrated violence, or to help violent men understand and change their behaviors, one must address these issues as important components of a program of recovery from a malignant masculinity.

REFERENCES

Arkin, W., & Dobrofsky, L. R. (1978). Military socialization and masculinity. *Journal of Social Issues, 34*, 151-168.

Bem, S. The measurement of psychological androgyny. *Journal of Consulting and Clinical Psychology, 42*, 155-162.

Brannon, R. (1976). The male sex role: Our culture's blueprint of manhood, and what it's done for us lately. In D. S. David & R. Brannon (Eds.), *The forty-nine percent majority: The male sex role* (pp. 1-45). New York: Random House.

Brannon, R., & Juni, S. (1984). A scale for measuring attitudes about masculinity. *Psychological Documents, 14*, 6-7.

Broverman, I. K., Vogel, S. R., Broverman, D. M., Clarkson, F. E., & Rosenkrantz, P. S. (1972). Sex-role stereotypes: A current appraisal. *Journal of Social Issues, 28*, 59-78.

Cicone, M. V., & Ruble, D. N. (1978). Beliefs about males. *Journal of Social Issues, 34*, 5-16.

Ehrhart, J. K., & Sandler, B. R. (1985). *Campus gang rape: Party games?* Washington, D.C.: Association of American Colleges.

Feazell, C. S., Mayers, R. S., & Deschner, J. (1984). Services for men who batter: Implications for programs and policies. *Family Relations, 33*, 217-223.

Gondolf, E. W., & Hanneke, J. (1987). The gender warrior: Reformed batterers on abuse, treatment, and change. *Journal of Family Violence, 2*, 177-191.

Good, G. E., Gilbert, L. A., & Scher, M. (1990). Gender aware therapy: A synthesis of feminist therapy and knowledge about gender. *Journal of Counseling and Development, 68*, 376-380.

Good, G. E., Dell, D. M., & Mintz, L. B. (1989). Male role and gender role conflict: Relations to help seeking in men. *Journal of Counseling Psychology, 36*, 295-300.

Good, G. E., & May, R. (1987). Developmental issues, environmental influences, and the nature of therapy with college men. In M. Scher, M. Stevens, G. Good, & G. A. Eichenfield (Eds.), *Handbook of counseling and psychotherapy with men* (pp. 150-164). Newbury Park, CA: Sage Publications Inc.

Hantover, J. P. (1978). The Boy Scouts and the validation of masculinity. *Journal of Social Issues, 34*, 184-195.

Harney, P. A., & Muehlenhard, C. L. (1991). Factors that increase the likelihood of victimization. In A. Parrot & L. Bechhofer (Eds.), *Acquaintance rape: The hidden crime* (pp. 159-175). New York: Wiley.

Hartley, R. E. (1959). Sex-role pressures and the socialization of the male child. *Psychological Reports, 5*, 457-468.

Herman, J. L. (1981). *Father-daughter incest.* Cambridge, MA: Harvard University Press.

Hofeller, K. H. (1982). *Social, psychological and situational factors in wife abuse.* Palo Alto, CA: R & E Research Associates.

Hotaling, G. T., & Sugarman, D. B. (1986). An analysis of risk markers in husband to wife violence: The current state of knowledge. *Violence and Victims, 1*, 101-124.

Maccoby, E. E., & Jacklin, C. N. (1974). *The psychology of sex differences.* Stanford, CA: Stanford University Press.

Marshall, D. L. (1988). *Characteristics of men who abuse their partners: A comparative study.* Unpublished doctoral dissertation, The Ohio State University, Columbus.

Martin, D. (1976). *Battered wives.* New York: Pocket Books.

Martin, P. Y., & Hummer, R. A. (1989). Fraternities and rape on campus. *Gender and Society, 3,* 457-473.

Mead, M. (1935/1963). *Sex and temperament in three primitive societies.* New York: Dell.

Merton, A. (1985, September). Return to brotherhood. *Ms.,* pp. 60-65, 121-122.

Meth, R. L. (1990). The road to masculinity. In R. L. Meth & R. S. Pasick (Eds.), *Men in therapy: The challenge of change* (pp. 3-34). New York: The Guilford Press.

Morin, S. F., & Garfinkle, E. M. (1978). Male homophobia. *Journal of Social Issues, 34,* 29-47.

O'Neil, J. M. (1981). Patterns of role conflict and strain: Sexism and fear of femininity in men's lives. *Personnel and Guidance Journal, 60,* 203-210.

O'Neil, J. M. (1990). Assessing men's gender role conflict. In D. Moore & F. Leafgreen (Eds.), *Men in conflict.* Alexandria, VA: AACD.

O'Neil, J. M., Helms, B. J., Gable, R. K., Laurence, D., & Wrightsman, L. S. (1986). Gender-Role Conflict Scale: College men's fear of femininity. *Sex Roles, 5/6,* 335-350.

Pleck, J. H. (1976) The male sex role: Definitions, problems, and sources of change. *Journal of Social Issues, 32,* 155-164.

Pleck, J. H. (1981). *The myth of masculinity.* Cambridge, MA: MIT.

Richardson, D. R., & Hammock, G. S. (1991). Alcohol and acquaintance rape. In A. Parrot & L. Bechhofer (Eds.), *Acquaintance rape: The hidden crime* (pp. 83-95). New York: Wiley.

Robertson, J. M. & Fitzgerald, L. F. (1992). Overcoming the masculine mystique: Preferences for alternative forms of assistance among men who avoid counseling. *Journal of Counseling Psychology, 39,* 240-246.

Roark, M. L. (1987). Preventing violence on college campuses. *Journal of Counseling and Development, 65,* 367-371.

Sabo D. F., & Runfola, R. (1980). *Jock: Sports & male identity.* Englewood Cliffs, NJ: Prentice Hall.

Scher, M., & Stevens, M. (1987). Men and violence. *Journal of Counseling and Development, 65,* 351-355.

Seligman, M. E. P., & Hager, J. (1972). The biological boundaries of learning: The Sauce-Bearnaise syndrome. *Psychology Today,* pp. 59-61, 84-87.

Telch, C. F., & Lindquist, C. U. (1984). Violent versus nonviolent couples: A comparison of patterns. *Psychotherapy, 21,* 242-248.

Thompson, E. H. (1990). Courtship violence and the male role. *Men's Studies Review, 7,* 4-13.

Thompson, E. H., Jr., & Pleck, J. H. (1987). Reformulating the male role. In M. S.

Kimmel (Ed.), *Changing men: New directions in research on men and masculinity.* Newbury Park, CA: Sage Publications Inc.

Walker, L. E. (1979). *The battered woman.* New York: Harper & Row, Pub., Inc.

Walter-Brooks, T. J., Jaynes, J. H., & Marshall, D. L. (1990, April). *Acquaintance rape education and prevention: A peer programming model.* Paper presented at the meeting of the American College Personnel Association, St. Louis, MO.

Yllo, K. (1984). The status of women, marital equality, and violence against wives. *Journal of Family Issues, 5,* 307-320.

Chapter 10

The Topography of Violence in College Men: Frequency and Comorbidity of Sexual and Physical Aggression

Kerry Erway Hannan
Barry Burkhart

SUMMARY. This chapter (a) summarizes previous studies on the epidemiology of sexually aggressive and physically aggressive behavior directed against women by college men; (b) provides additional data regarding the topography of violent behavior, e.g., what is its form and quality; and (c) estimates the degree of comorbidity between these two forms of violence. Specifically, are men who physically

Kerry Erway Hannan, PhD, is a psychologist working at Johns Hopkins Hospital in the Community Psychiatry Program. She is also a consultant for the Baltimore Child Abuse Center. Her current interests include the areas of sexual abuse and bereavement. Barry Burkhart, PhD, is Professor of Psychology at Auburn University. His research interests span several areas of violence and victimization including child sexual abuse, sexual violence, and treatment of victims of trauma.

This article is based on a doctoral dissertation by the first author under the direction of the second author in partial fulfillment of the requirements for the doctoral degree in psychology at Auburn University.

Correspondence may be addressed to: Barry Burkhart, Department of Psychology, 4082 Haley Center, Auburn University, AL 36849.

[Haworth co-indexing entry note]: "The Topography of Violence in College Men: Frequency and Comorbidity of Sexual and Physical Aggression." Hannan, Kerry Erway, and Barry Burkhart. Co-published simultaneously in *Journal of College Student Psychotherapy* (The Haworth Press, Inc.) Vol. 8, No. 3, 1993, pp. 219-237; and: *Campus Violence: Kinds, Causes, and Cures* (ed: Leighton C. Whitaker and Jeffrey W. Pollard) The Haworth Press, Inc., 1993, pp. 219-237. Multiple copies of this article/chapter may be purchased from The Haworth Document Delivery Center [1-800-3-HAWORTH; 9:00 a.m. - 5:00 p.m. (EST)].

219

aggress against women more or less likely to aggress sexually against women and is there a distinct group who are both physically and sexually aggressive toward women? Subjects were 261 male college students who completed a comprehensive questionnaire assessing their involvement in sexually and physically aggressive conduct. Forty-seven percent (n = 124) of the sample did not meet the criteria for assignment to either the sexually or physically aggressive group. Twenty-five percent (n = 65) and eleven percent (n = 28) of the sample met the criteria for assignment to the sexually or physically aggressive group, respectively. Seventeen percent (n = 44) of the sample exceeded criterion levels for both sexual and physical aggression. Designated the combined aggression group, these men formed a very distinct, clinically and socially, critical subgroup.

A rose is a rose is a rose, but is violence, by any other name, still violence. This question is less rhetorical when the question becomes one of defining violence in terms of motivational foundations. For example, is sexual violence defined by sexual motives or by aggressive motives (Brownmiller, 1975; Groth, 1979)? As scholars and researchers have begun to examine critically forms of violence, particularly violence perpetrated against women by men, simple, obvious answers to such questions have become hard to find. Instead, conceptual and empirical accounts of violence are characterized by their complexity and the use of multidimensional, multivariate models (Burkhart & Fromuth, 1991; Hall, 1990; Malamuth, 1988).

Curiously, however, an obvious interconnection between physically aggressive behaviors and sexually aggressive behaviors has received very little attention in the empirical literature. Though some conceptual accounts have defined sexual aggression as a form of aggression, per se (Brownmiller, 1975; Russell, 1984; Groth, 1979), there has been little empirical examination of the strict empirical link between forms of physical aggression and forms of sexual aggression. The primary purpose of the present paper is to redress this basic deficit in the literature; to examine, empirically, the frequency of and the comorbidity between physical and sexual aggression perpetrated by college aged men against women.

In a recent review, Burkhart and Fromuth (1991) identified three curious common denominators among the various events defined as sexually aggressive. Despite the apparent diversity of such behaviors, these three basic facts were clear: "(a) sexual aggression is extraordinarily common, (b) it appears to adhere to the central but ordinary social roles of women and children, and (c) the perpetration of it is primarily a male phenomenon" (Burkhart & Fromuth, 1991, p. 76).

The "commonness" of sexual aggression derives from two basic observations: (a) that sexual aggression is not limited to the stereotyped notions of sexual violence, e.g., the deranged perpetrator who lurks in dark alleys, rather, by count, the majority of sexually aggressive events occur between people who are known to each other (Koss, Gidycz, & Wisniewski, 1987) and, (b) that these events typically occur is the context of an ordinary social situation, for example, a date (Burkhart & Stanton, 1988; Craig, 1990; Koss & Burkhart, 1989). Additionally, another critical feature of such events is that they are hidden in that they are rarely reported to conventional social authorities. Consequently, only recently have the characteristics of these sexual aggressive events and of their perpetrators been examined (Koss, Leonard, Beezley, Dana, & Oros, 1985).

Most of this research has been conducted with college men and has revealed several basic findings. First, a relatively high percentage of college men engage in some form of sexually coercive behavior (Rapaport & Burkhart, 1984). A relatively lower but still substantial percentage of men are involved in sexually aggressive behavior meeting the legal definition of rape. Less is known about the topography of these sexually aggressive events, particularly the nature of force used in the pursuit of different sexual goals.

Physical violence, also, has been recognized as a significant problem in marital relationships. Recent work, moreover, has identified dating violence to be widespread in courtship contexts among college students (Lane & Gwartney-Gibbs, 1985; Roscoe & Callahan, 1985; Sigelman, Berry, & Wiles, 1984). Though dating violence has been reported as mutual or reciprocal (Sigelman et al., 1984) males have been found to use more extreme forms of aggression and to have engaged in aggressive conduct with multiple partners (Lane & Gwartney-Gibbs, 1985).

In comparing the high school and college student, Roscoe and Callahan (1985) found that though some similarities were evident, the rate and severity of violence for high school students was lower. Assuming college students tend to have more intimate relationships than high school students, these data are consistent with the finding that violence is more likely to occur in more intimate relationships (Arias, Samios, & O'Leary, 1987). For example, Cate, Henton, Koval, Christopher, and Lloyd (1982) found that, in over 70 percent of the cases, violence was initially experienced only after the relationship had progressed beyond casual dating. Interestingly, of those subjects still dating the person with whom they reported experiencing violence, over 80 percent reported the violence first occurred after the relationship became sexual.

Only a few studies have examined specifically, however, the direct relationship between physically and sexually aggressive behavior. In part, this neglect is a side-effect of the narrow observational focus of different researchers. Researchers in violence tend to be separated not only by their different disciplinary contexts (e.g., sociologists study social norms, psychologists examine individual differences) but, also, by the behavioral category in which they are interested. Thus, research tends to be event focused, that is organized by referent to a particular class of aggressive behaviors and tends not to examine aggressive behavior across categories.

The few exceptions to an exclusive focus on one specific behavioral class typically include only modest measures of one class in the context of the research focus. Representative of this work is a study by Sigelman et al. (1984), who included two questions related to sexual aggression in their study of dating violence. Respondents were asked whether they had ever "used strong physical force to try to engage in a sex act against another's will" or "used violence to try to engage in a sex act against another's will" (p. 535). These measures were intended to measure moderate and severe sexual aggression, respectively. The results showed that among men, there was a small but significant association between having been sexually aggressive toward a female partner and having been physically aggressive.

In another study focused on dating violence, Lane and Gwartney-Gibbs (1985) utilized a modified version of Koss's Sexual Experiences Survey (Koss & Oros, 1982), in attempting to identify participants of courtship violence. Their hypothesis was that disputes over sexual activity was an important and extensive source of conflict and aggression. They found that males were more likely than females to inflict a variety of forms of sexual aggression. They did not, however, specifically examine whether males who coerce sex are, also, physically assaultive.

Given these sparse empirical data, it is difficult to come to any firm conclusions. Tentatively, there appears to be some empirical association between physical and sexual assaultiveness. Conceptually, however, there is good reason (Brownmiller, 1975; Burkhart & Stanton, 1988) to expect linkage between physically and sexually aggressive behavior. Thus, we expected to find considerable comorbidity of physical and sexual aggression as well as distinct subgroups of men who were either sexually aggressive or physically aggressive only.

METHOD

Subjects. Participants in this study were male college students recruited from undergraduate psychology and business classes at Auburn University. Subjects were asked to participate in an investigation of past and present dating relationships, in which they would be questioned about how conflict is resolved in their relationships and about their sexual attitudes and behaviors. Subjects were told that because of the sensitive nature of this study and the desire for honest reporting, all responses would be anonymous. In addition, subjects were asked to sign consent forms before participating. All subjects received extra credit for their participation according to respective departmental procedures.

Of the 266 subjects who participated in the study, 261 were retained for the analyses. Five were excluded due to incomplete data. The ages ranged from 18 to 30 years; the average age was approximately 21, and 86% of the men were 22 or younger. Approximately 97% of the men were unmarried. Ninety-six percent of the men were White, 3% were Black, and approximately 1% fell into the "Other" category.

Materials. Data collection was conducted anonymously through the use of questionnaire booklets and debriefing sheets. The questionnaire booklets contained the following materials:

Demographic Information. The demographic questionnaire consisted of items of age, marital status, race, and year of college.

Sexual Conflicts Measure (SCM). The Sexual Conflicts Measure used in this study was based on several previously developed sexual experience surveys (Koss & Oros, 1982; Rapaport & Burkhart, 1984). The measure was modified in order to parallel behaviors used to resolve nonsexual conflicts and had behavioral anchors for aggressive conduct ranging from ignoring a partner's protest to a high degree of physical violence, i.e., choking or hitting. Subjects were asked to report the frequency with which they had engaged in specific aggressive behaviors on a five-point scale ranging from (0) *never* to (5) *more than 10 times.* The SCM was divided into three parallel forms. The three forms requested type and frequency of aggressive behavior used in three domains of sexually aggressive behavior: (a) sexually coercive conduct; (b) attempted sexual intercourse; and (c) completed sexual intercourse. Both unweighted and weighted scores were calculated, with the weighted scores accounting for the severity of coercion used and the degree of sexual contact made (i.e., fondling, attempted intercourse, and intercourse), in addition to frequency of the acts. Despite the additional loading given to the weighted scoring procedure, the unweighted scores were highly correlated with the weighted scores (r = .96, p < .0001).

Self-report measures of sexual experiences which delineate specific behavioral acts have been found to have a high correlation with information obtained in individual interviews (Koss et al., 1987). When discrepancies were found, they tended to show denial of behaviors in face to face interviews which were reported on self-report measures, particularly for sexually aggressive and coercive methods.

Conflict Tactics Scales (CTS). The Conflict Tactics Scales, (CTS; Straus, 1979) were designed to assess strategies or actions that a family member might use during a conflict with another member. The behaviors range from those low in coerciveness (e.g., discussed the issue calmly) to those high in aggressiveness and violence (e.g., used a knife or gun). A modified version of the CTS (Form N) was used in the present study because it has been used extensively in previous courtship violence studies. Subjects were asked to report the number of times each action had occurred, ranging from (0) *never* to (6) *more than 20 times.*

Interpersonal Conflicts Measure (ICM). The Interpersonal Conflicts Measure was a modification of the CTS. The measure was condensed from eighteen strategies to six, in order to parallel the behaviors used in Sexual Conflicts Measure to define aggressive conduct. Subjects were asked, as with the SCM, to report the frequency with which they had engaged in specific behaviors. To determine the validity of the ICM, the correlation between the ICM and the Straus CTS was calculated. The obtained correlation (r = .78, p < .01) suggested that the ICM was a reasonable parallel form for the CTS.

PROCEDURE

Subjects completed the materials in groups of approximately 15 to 20 people. All subjects were given a consent form that indicated they were willing to answer questions about their sexual and dating experiences. The form guaranteed that subjects' responses would be anonymous and that they might leave the experiment at any time without penalty. No subjects left early. After completion of the materials, debriefing sheets were distributed. Subjects were encouraged to contact the principal investigator if they had questions or concerns about the experiment.

RESULTS

Prevalence of Coercive and Aggressive Sexual Behavior. Of the 261 men in the sample, 224 (86%) reported engaging in at least one consensual experience of sexual intercourse. Involvement in some form of nonconsensual sexual activity, ranging from touching and fondling to rape, was admitted by 144 men (55%). The nonconsensual sexual behaviors reported most frequently were those having to do with sexual fondling, such as touching of the breast, thigh or genital area, and removal of clothing or underclothing. The frequency and degree of coerciveness or forcefulness used to engage in sexual fondling are shown in Table 1. The most frequently

TABLE 1. Nonconsensual Sexual Fondling: Number of Subjects by Level of Coercive Method Utilized*

Tactics	Never	Once	Twice	More than 3 times**
Ignored her wishes to stop	148 (57%)	42 (16%)	26 (10%)	45 (18%)
Verbal coercion	185 (71%)	32 (12%)	14 (5%)	30 (11%)
Threats of physical force	257 (98%)	2 (.8%)	1 (.4%)	1 (.4%)
Low to moderate degree of physical aggression	247 (95%)	10 (4%)	1 (.4%)	3 (1.2%)
High degree of physical aggression	255 (98%)	6 (2%)	0	0

*From Sexual Conflicts Measure
**Because of the low frequencies the categories of 6-10 and > 10 times were included in this category.

endorsed tactic was to ignore her wishes. Examples provided for this category included: "I went ahead and just did it even though I knew she didn't want to; I ignored her protests and statements that she wanted me to stop." One hundred thirteen men (44%) reported having used this method at least once. The second most frequently endorsed tactic was to use verbal coercion. Examples given for this category included: "I said something to spite/hurt her; I persuaded her through continued verbal arguments or by telling her things I did not really mean; I used verbal threats such as 'You'll have to walk home.'" Seventy-six men (28%) reported using this method on at least one occasion. The method of threatening to use physical aggression was endorsed by only four men (1.5%). The method of using physical aggression and force was divided into low to moderate and high degrees. Low to moderate physical aggression was defined by the following examples: "I twisted her arm; I held her down; I slapped her." A high degree of physical aggression was defined as: "I kicked, bit, or hit her with my fist; I hit or tried to hit her with something; I beat her up; I choked her; I threatened to use or I used a weapon." A total of 14 men (5%) engaged in a low to moderate degree of force while six men (2%) used a high degree of physical aggression.

Nearly one-third of the sample (85 men) reported at least one uncompleted attempt to have sexual intercourse against a woman's consent. Approximately the same number of men (n = 84) also reported engaging in at least one nonconsensual act of completed intercourse. The methods and number of times the methods were used are presented in Table 2 for nonconsensual acts of attempted intercourse and in Table 3 for nonconsensual acts of completed intercourse. The methods of ignoring her wishes and using verbal coercion were the most commonly endorsed by the men reporting involvement in nonconsensual sexual intercourse. Only approximately 2% of the total sample of men admitted using any degree of physical aggression in an effort to obtain sexual intercourse against a woman's consent.

Prevalence of Conflictual Courtship Behavior. The majority of the sample men (n = 196) reported that they date at least two to three times per month or more. Slightly more than half of the men (n = 145) reported they had a current, steady dating partner. Of those men with steady partners, almost half (n = 76) have been with their partners for more than one year.

The men were asked to report the behaviors they had engaged in when attempting to settle disputes with their partners. Coercive methods of conflict resolution are delineated in Table 4. Behaviors ranged from passive aggressive tactics (e.g., ignoring her) to physically violent acts (e.g., hitting). A total of thirty-five men (13%) reported that they had threatened to physically harm their partners at least once. Approximately half of those men reported threatening their partners on more than one occasion. Physically aggressive tactics were divided into low to moderate and high categories.

TABLE 2. Attempted Non-Consensual Intercourse: Number of Subjects by Level of Coercive Method Utilized*

Tactics	Never	Once	Twice	More than 3 times**
Ignored her wishes to stop	186 (71%)	31 (12%)	22 (8%)	22 (9%)
Verbal coercion	217 (83%)	19 (7%)	7 (3%)	18 (7%)
Threats of physical force	259 (99%)	1 (.4%)	1 (.4%)	0
Low to moderate degree of physical aggression	257 (98%)	2 (.8%)	1 (.4%)	1 (.4%)
High degree of physical aggression	260 (99%)	1 (.4%)	0	0

*From Sexual Conflicts Measure
**Because of the low frequencies the categories of 6-10 and > 10 times were included in this category.

Approximately one-quarter of the total sample (64 men) reported using a low to moderate degree of aggressiveness toward their partners at least one time. Thirty-four men (13%) reported doing so only once, while thirty men (11%) admitted to engaging in these behaviors two times or more. A total of eight men (3%) admitted to having used a high degree of physical aggression against their partners on at least one occasion.

Group Membership. The criteria for group memberships were based on the endorsement of nonconsensual sexual behaviors on the Sexual Conflicts Measure, and the endorsement of physically aggressive tactics in dealing with relationship conflicts on the Interpersonal Conflicts Measure. Four groups were formed: men who

TABLE 3. Non-Consensual Intercourse: Number of Subjects by Level of Coercive Method Utilized*

Tactics	Never	Once	Twice	More than 3 times**
Ignored her wishes to stop	185 (71%)	33 (13%)	15 (6%)	28 (10%)
Verbal coercion	224 (86%)	11 (4%)	7 (3%)	19 (7%)
Threats of physical force	256 (98%)	4 (1%)	1 (.4%)	0
Low to moderate degree of physical aggression	256 (98%)	3 (1%)	1 (.4%)	1 (.4%)
High degree of physical aggression	260 (99%)	1 (.4%)	0	0

*From Sexual Conflicts Measure
**Because of the low frequencies the categories of 6-10 and > 10 times were included in this category.

reported no or "low" levels of involvement in either sexual aggression or courtship aggression (Non-aggressive Control Group), men who reported engaging in nonconsensual sexual activity but no or limited involvement in courtship aggression (Sexual Aggression Group), men who reported engaging in courtship aggression but no or limited involvement in sexual aggression (Courtship Aggression Group), and men who reported involvement in courtship violence and sexual aggression (Combined Aggression Group).

Men assigned to the Sexual Aggression Group reported involvement in at least one of the following nonconsensual sexual behaviors: (a) obtaining nonconsensual sexual touching through the use

TABLE 4. Number of Men Endorsing Conflict Resolution Tactics*

Tactics	Never	Once	Twice	More than 3 times**
Ignored her side of things	66 (25%)	36 (14%)	43 (16%)	116 (45%)
Verbal arguments	75 (29%)	47 (18%)	41 (16%)	98 (37%)
Threatened to physically harm her	226 (87%)	16 (6%)	10 (4%)	9 (3%)
Low to moderate degree of physical aggression	197 (75%)	39 (13%)	11 (4%)	19 (8%)
High degree of physical aggression	253 (97%)	5 (2%)	1 (.4%)	2 (.8%)

*From Sexual Conflicts Measure
**Because of the low frequencies the categories of 6-10 and > 10 times were included in this category.

of physical force or threats of physical force (e.g., hitting, holding her down), and (b) obtaining nonconsensual sexual intercourse, or attempting to, through the use of any means, including ignoring her protests, verbal arguments, and threats or actual use of physical force. These acts were considered high sexual aggression behaviors. Men assigned to this group had to report no significant courtship aggression behaviors.

Men assigned to the Courtship Aggression Group reported engaging in at least one of the following behavioral clusters: (a) use of threats of physical harm, and (b) actual use of physical aggression (e.g., shoving, beating her up). These acts were considered high courtship aggression behaviors. Men assigned to the Courtship Aggression Group had to report no significant sexually aggressive behaviors.

Men assigned to the Combined Aggression Group reported engaging in high courtship aggression behaviors and high sexual aggression behaviors. Assignments to all groups were dependent on the most aggressive behavior endorsed. All males not meeting the criteria for assignment to one of the three research groups were assigned to the non-aggressive control group.

The frequencies and percentages of men for each of the four groups are presented in Table 5. Just under one-half of the sample (124 subjects) were in the Control Group. Approximately one-quarter of the sample (65 subjects) met the criteria for the Sexual Aggression Group, twenty-eight men (10.7%) for the Courtship Aggression Group, and forty-four men (16.9%) for the Combined Aggression Group.

Frequency of Aggressive Acts. In order to test group differences on reported frequency of aggressive acts, a univariate analysis of variance (ANOVA) was computed. The total number of aggressive behaviors was obtained for each of the men by summing their

TABLE 5. Group Frequencies and Percentages

Sexual Aggression

	Low	High
Low Courtship Aggression	Non-aggressive Control Group 124 (47%)	Sexual Aggression Group 65 (25%)
High Courtship Aggression	Courtship Aggression Group 28 (11%)	Combined Aggression Group 44 (17%)

reported frequencies of acts across both the sexual aggression and conflictual aggression measures. A significant group effect was found for the overall aggression index (F = 104.46, p < .0001). Table 6 presents the means, standard deviations, F value and significance level of the three aggression groups and non-aggressive control group. The ANOVA was followed by Tukey's HSD post hoc comparisons, using an alpha level of .05. All pairwise differences between the aggression groups and non-aggressive control group were found to be significant, with the exception of the difference between the Sexual Aggression Group and the Courtship Aggression Group, which was not statistically significant. The Combined Aggression Group reported significantly more acts of aggression than either of the single aggression groups or the non-aggressive control group. Men in both Courtship Aggression and Sexual Aggression groups reported significantly more violent behaviors than the men who reported no aggressive involvement.

DISCUSSION

Consistent with previous findings, college males engage in a wide variety of sexually (Koss et al., 1985; Muehlenhand & Linton, 1987; Rapaport & Burkhart, 1984) and physically (Lane & Gwartney-Gibbs, 1985; Makepeace, 1981, 1983; Roscoe & Callahan, 1985) aggressive behaviors. In fact, by frequency count, mild forms of sexually aggressive and physically aggressive behavior can be best described as normative (Burkhart & Fromuth, 1991). It is well known that males are "supposed" to be persistent, controlling, and active in pursuit of sexual interactions; that is, such conduct is normative (Weis & Borger, 1973). It appears, based on these data, wherein one-quarter of this sample of men had slapped, pushed, or restrained their partner at least once, that physical aggressiveness, also, may be characterized as having a normative quality. Though normative in the sense that such behavior is common and normative in the sense that college males and females expect such behavior, it is clear that the behavior has harmful impact.

A substantial proportion, 17 percent, of the present sample of men reported having committed both sexually and physically aggressive acts against their partners. Comparable findings for other studies are

TABLE 6. Group Means and Standard Deviations for Frequency of Aggressive Acts

Measure	Non-aggressive Control (n = 124)		Courtship Aggression (n = 28)		Sexual Aggression (n = 65)		Combined Aggression (n = 44)		F Value
	M	SD	M	SD	M	SD	M	SD	
Frequency of Aggressive Acts	3.39	3.01	9.12	4.90	10.40	5.69	20.32	9.72	104.46*

*p < .0001

surprisingly limited; few researchers have tried to examine the co-morbidity of these two forms of sexual aggression. Such neglect is likely to be a function of two primary reasons. Conceptually, researchers in the general area of violence tend to be event focused and thus, define their research domain by the particularly behavioral event, be it rape or physical violence, in which they are interested. Additionally, research tends to become methodologically driven. For example, the most widely used instrument used in studies of courtship and family violence is the Conflict Tactics Scale (Straus, 1979) which does not include items measuring sexual aggression. Similarly, the measure which has become the prototype for most research in sexual aggression, The Sexual Experiences Survey (Koss & Gidycz, 1985), has no items specific to physical aggression.

One of the purposes of the present study is to encourage the integration of studies in physically and sexually aggressive behavior. Accordingly, we tried to develop parallel instruments which would allow for more direct comparisons across these behavior domains. This turned out to be a difficult task. Though the development of the measure of physical aggression was relatively straightforward, the development of a measure of sexual aggression was more complicated. Sexual aggression, by definition, is composed of both an aggressive component (type and method of force or coercion used) and a sexual component (extent of sexual contact obtained). Thus, unlike the physical aggression measure, simply listing degrees of physical force in order of severity is insufficient. To account for the sexual component, the degree of force applied in three types of sexual contact, sexual touching, attempted sexual intercourse, and completed sexual intercourse, were obtained. For the purposes of this study, high vs. low degree of sexual aggression was defined by reference to both the degree of coercion or force and the sexual act accomplished. This procedure is not without its problems. Is a man who obtains sexual intercourse by ignoring a woman's protest psychologically similar to a man who slaps a woman in order to remove her clothes? At least, however, this procedure may allow such questions to begin to be examined.

The degree of comorbidity of physical and sexual aggression found in this study was relatively high. The only precursor to the present study (Sigelman et al., 1984) found a comorbidity rate of about 10%.

However, we attribute this discrepancy to the insensitive measure of sexual aggression used in their study. This discrepancy does illustrate how significant methodological and definitional criteria are to obtaining reliable data in this area of research (Fromuth & Burkhart, 1987; Koss & Harvey, 1991). We recommend that researchers continue to develop and utilize measures with explicit operational definitions and, in so far as possible, directly assess the comparability of measures across studies.

The comorbid group was significantly more aggressive than either of the other clinical groups. In part, this is an expected consequence of how the groups were defined, but the degree of difference was striking. The rate of violent behavior was twice as high for the comorbid group as either the physically or sexually aggressive groups and six times greater than the non-aggressive group. Additionally, we have found that the distinctiveness of this group by count is corroborated by the construct distinctiveness of this group (Hannon & Burkhart, in preparation). Across a number of conceptually relevant measures, the comorbid group consistently was significantly differentiated from not only the control group but both the physically and sexually aggressive groups.

Based on these findings, we encourage researchers to look beyond their specific event behavior of aggression and consider the proposition that there may be a commonality in aggressive behavior. This commonality may be particularly evident between physically and sexually aggressive behaviors. Furthermore, this commonality would suggest that we might be well served to examine violent men as well as violent behaviors.

REFERENCES

Arias, I., Samios, M., & O'Leary, K.D. (1987). Prevalence and correlates of physical aggression during courtship. *Journal of Interpersonal Violence*, 2(1), 82-90.

Brownmiller, S. (1975). *Against our will: Men, women, and rape.* New York: Simon & Schuster Inc..

Burkhart, B.R. & Fromuth, M.E. (1991). Individual psychological and social psychological understandings of sexual coercion. In E. Grauerholz & M.A. Koralewski (Eds), *Sexual coercion: A sourcebook on its nature, causes, and prevention* (pp. 75-89). Lexington: D.C. Heath & Company.

Burkhart, B.R. & Stanton, A.L. (1988). Sexual aggression in acquaintance relationships. In G.W. Russell (Ed.), *Violence in intimate relationships* (pp. 43-65). New York, PMA Press.

Cate, M., Henton, J.M., Koval, J., Christopher, F.S., & Lloyd, S. (1982). Premarital abuse: A social psychological perspective. *Journal of Family Issues, 3,* 79-90.

Craig, M.E. (1990). Coercive sexuality in dating relationships: A situational mode. *Clinical Psychology Review, 54*(4), 454-460.

Fromuth, M.E. & Burkhart, B.R. (1987). Childhood sexual victimization among college men: Definitional and methodological issues. *Violence and Victims,* 2(4), 241-253.

Groth, A.N. (1979). *Men who rape: The psychology of the offender.* New York: Plenum.

Hall, G.C.N. (1990). Prediction of sexual aggression. *Clinical Psychology Review, 10,* 229-246.

Hannon, K.E. & Burkhart, B.R. (in preparation). Psychological characteristics of aggressive college men.

Koss, M.P. & Burkhart, B.R. (1989). A conceptual analysis of rape victimization: Long-term effects and implications for treatment. *Psychology of Women's Quarterly, 13,* 27-40.

Koss, M.P. & Gidycz, C.A. (1985). Sexual Experience Survey: Reliability and validity. *Journal of Consulting and Clinical Psychology, 53,* 422-423.

Koss, M.P., Gidycz, C.A., & Wisniewski, N. (1987). The scope of rape: Incidence and prevalence of sexual aggression and victimization in a national sample of higher education students. *Journal of Consulting and Clinical Psychology, 55,* 162-170.

Koss, M.P. & Harvey, M.R. (1991). *The rape victim: Clinical and community interventions* (2nd ed.). Newbury Park: Sage Publiccations Inc.

Koss, M.P., Leonard, K.E., Beezley, D.A., Dana, A., and Oros, C.J. (1985). Nonstranger sexual aggression: A discriminant analysis of the psychological characteristics of undetected offenders. *Sex Roles, 12,* 981-992.

Koss, M.P. & Oros, C. (1982). The sexual experiences survey: A research instrument investigating sexual aggression and victimization. *Journal of Consulting and Clinical Psychology, 50,* 455-457.

Lane, K.E. & Gwartney-Gibbs, P.A. (1985). Violence in the context of dating and sex. *Journal of Family Issues, 6,* 45-59.

Makepeace, J.M. (1981). Courtship violence among college students. *Family Relations, 32,* 97-102.

Makepeace, J.M. (1983). Life events stress and courtship violence. *Family Relations, 32,* 101-109.

Malamuth, N.M. (1988). A multidimensional approach to sexual aggression: Combining measures of past behavior and present likelihood. In R.A. Prentsky and V.L. Quinsey (Eds.), *Human sexual aggression: Current perspectives,* (pp. 123-132). New York: New York Academy of Science.

Muehlenhand, C.L. & Linton, M.A. (1987). Date rape and sexual aggression in dating situations: Incidence and risk factors. *Journal of Counseling Psychology*, *34*, 186-196.

Rapaport, K. & Burkhart, B.R. (1984). Personality and attitudinal characteristics of sexually coercive college males. *Journal of Abnormal Psychology*, *93*, 216-221.

Roscoe, B. & Callahan, J.E. (1985). Adolescents' self-reports of violence in families and dating relationships. *Adolescence*, *20*, 545-553.

Russell, D.E.H. (1984). *Sexual exploitation*. Beverly Hills, CA: Sage Publications.

Sigelman, C.K., Berry, C.J., and Wiles, K.A. (1984). Violence in college students' dating relationships. *Journal of Applied Social Psychology*, *5-6*, 530-548.

Straus, M.A. (1979). Measuring intrafamilial conflict and violence: The Conflict Tactics (CT) Scale. *Journal of Marriage and the Family*, *41*, 75-88.

Weis, K. & Borges, S. (1973). Victimology and rape: The case of the legitimate victim. *Issues in Criminology*, *8*, 71-115.

Chapter 11

College Men and Sexual Violation: Counseling Process and Programming Considerations

Mark A. Stevens

SUMMARY. A variety of methods are used to reduce sexual violence on our college campuses. This article discusses remedial and prevention programs designed to educate and change men's sexual violating attitudes and behaviors. A conceptual and practical guideline followed by case examples of counseling college men accused or convicted of sexual violence is discussed. Ideas and resources for sexual violence prevention programming are also provided.

INTRODUCTION

Sexual violence continues to be an important issue on college campuses (Koss et al., 1987). As the campus culture becomes more educated and sensitive to the issues of sexual violence, the number of reported rapes and rape-like behaviors has increased. According to directors of Student Conduct offices, the number of reported

Mark A. Stevens, PhD, is Assistant Director and Coordinator of Training at the University of Southern California Student Counseling Center, YWCA Building, 857 West 36th Place, Los Angeles, CA 90089-0051.

[Haworth co-indexing entry note]: "College Men and Sexual Violation: Counseling Process and Programming Considerations." Stevens, Mark A. Co-published simultaneously in *Journal of College Student Psychotherapy* (The Haworth Press, Inc.) Vol. 8, No. 3, 1993, pp. 239-258: and: *Campus Violence: Kinds, Causes, and Cures* (ed: Leighton C. Whitaker and Jeffrey W. Pollard) The Haworth Press, Inc., 1993, pp. 239-258. Multiple copies of this article/chapter may be purchased from The Haworth Document Delivery Center [1-800-3-HAWORTH; 9:00 a.m. - 5:00 p.m. (EST)].

239

rapes and other sexual violating behavior complaints against college men has increased approximately 50% during the last 5 years (S. Rhoten, personal communication, October, 1992). Subsequently, university conduct offices are faced with a number of new issues and dilemmas, including, the practice of the university (specifically the counseling center) of providing educational/prevention services to men accused/convicted of sexual violence.

I will first present an overview of therapeutic issues and considerations related to counseling college men who are accused or convicted of sexual violence and subsequently self-referred or mandated to go to the university counseling center. Then I will provide an overview of sexual violence (rape) prevention programs for college men.

COUNSELING PROCESS

Context. It is important to address several contextual issues in order to better understand the counseling process with college men accused/convicted of sexual violence.

The first contextual issue is that of terminology. Rape is a legal term, denoting a crime. Often the word rape is interchanged with such terms as sexual assault and sexual imposition by colleges and universities, and when developing their student conduct codes, their terminology may not coincide with the legal definition of rape in their city or state codes. Consequently, the (alleged) perpetrator, no matter what he is being charged with, believes he is being viewed as a "rapist" by the community. He rejects this label because he has a stereotypic view of a rapist as being a "sleazy, deranged" male who sneaks through women's bedroom windows at night (Burt, 1991).

While the term rape may be helpful in a court of law or in university conduct hearings, a more elaborate definition is needed to understand the goals and process of counseling. Legal definitions must be expanded to include moral, psychological and socio-political perspectives on sexual violence. These definitions would include, but not be limited to, the following concepts:

1. Sexual violence stems from the individual's confusion of sexuality and violence and has nothing to do with mutual intimacy or pleasure.

2. Sexual violence is an act of power and control.
3. Sexual violence is degrading and humiliating to the victim.
4. Sexual violence has negative consequences for men and women.

This definition would be inclusive of behaviors/attitudes such as physically forced intercourse, sexual harassment and unwanted sexual attention (e.g., staring, frottage). While it may not be specific enough for a court of law, the definition does help the counselor and client better understand the nature of sexual violation (Scher & Stevens, 1987). In this article the term sexual violence is used as an inclusive working definition.

The second contextual issue is that of understanding statistics about reported acts of sexual violence. Since the number of complaints by college women against college men has increased over the past five years (Berkowitz, 1992), have college men become more sexually violent? The most likely explanation for the increase in reporting is public attention, expanded definitions of sexual violence and friendlier, more accessible judiciary reporting and review procedures on college campuses (Koss & Dinero, 1989).

Third, we need to understand the background reasons for referral to counseling. College men, who are convicted of sexual violence, come into counseling primarily because they are referred by a university conduct panel. Students may be required to see a therapist at the university counseling center, in order to remain or reenter the university. Sometimes a specific number of sessions is mandated, although typically it is left open to the counselor's discretion. A significant number of college men, who are self referred, seek counseling after a sexual violation charge has been or is threatened to be filed against them. The college male who self-refers, without external pressure, because he is concerned about his sexual violating behavior (past or present), is rare.

Mandatory counseling for college students convicted of violating student conduct codes is an important and controversial issue, which university administrators and counseling centers have struggled with over the years (see chapter 5 by Gerald Amada). While I am not a strong advocate for mandatory counseling, I have found that many students who come for a required one-time only counseling interview will continue treatment. This may be a result of being educated about confidentiality and assured that the university will only know they came in for the one required session. A variety of sexual violating behaviors may prompt a university conduct panel to refer a student for counseling, presuming they have that power. Typically students are referred because they (allegedly) engaged in behaviors/attitudes such as: inappropriate touching; taking "advantage" of an intoxicated person; "silently" participating in gang sexual violence, and other behaviors that are degrading to women and reinforce the males confusion of sexuality and violence (O'Sullivan, 1991 & Koss & Dinero, 1989, Martin & Hummer, 1989, Malamuth, 1986). Violations that involve weapons, excessive physical force and sexual intercourse call for expulsion, and therefore the student is usually not referred to counseling.

Fourth, an alarming percentage of the sexual violating behaviors in which college men engage occur while under the influence of alcohol (Richardson & Hammock, 1991). While alcohol intoxication by no means excuses their behavior, it does expand treatment considerations to include assessment and lessening of alcohol abuse and/or dependency (See chapter 4 by Timothy Rivinus and Mary Larimer).

The final contextual issue involves an understanding of the relationship between traditional male sexuality socialization and sexual violence (Rapaport & Burkhart, 1984). Generally speaking, the male socialization process emphasizes sexual relations as a conquest and a way to build self esteem and gain peer acceptance (O'Neil, 1981), rather than the process of developing intimacy and emotional connection (Fracher & Kimmel, 1987). This type of self-expression is reinforced and taught by the media, pornography and "locker room lies," so male sexuality becomes objectified and performance and conquest-driven. Potential sex partners become objectified, e.g., as numbers, body parts and notches on the belt. As potential sexual partners become objectified, men are less empathetic and as empathy goes down and self-centeredness goes up, men are more likely to commit acts of sexual violence. Initially men are often confused about why their behavior is considered offensive. Because myths of male sexuality are so ingrained in their way of thinking, men believe they are "doing what guys are supposed to do" (Muehlenhard & Linton, 1987).

Counselors need to understand their personal beliefs as well as have a professional understanding of the influence of male sex-role socialization, male sexuality training and consequent propensity towards sexual violence. Such understanding does not excuse violent behavior; it increases empathy for perpetrators and provides guidelines for treatment interventions.

Treatment guidelines and considerations. I will now provide a developmental perspective as an overview of the counseling process with college males accused/convicted of sexual violence, and then briefly present two case examples with discussion of relevant clinical issues and outcomes.

I. First Treatment Phase
    A. Relationship Building.
    B. Clarification of confidentiality.
    C. Clarification of student's expectations.
    D. Clarification of counselor's role.
    E. Clarification of university conduct panel demands.

These steps in the first phase of treatment are essential for helping establish the boundaries of the therapeutic relationship, which involve these questions: (1) Is the student mandated to come into counseling and, if so, for how many sessions; and (2) What type of documentation does the university conduct panel need and/or want? For example, the student may be under the assumption that the counselor will report back to conduct panel his/her opinions whether the sexual violence occurred. With students mandated to counseling it is important to clarify with the student what the counselor is willing to submit in writing or verbally to the conduct panel. This is also the phase of treatment in which the counselor can communicate his/her role to the student. For example, it is important for the counselor to let the student know that he/she is there to support him through the judiciary process while also hoping to serve as a catalyst for his personal growth during the crisis.

II. Second Treatment Phase
     A. Relationship Building.
     B. Hearing his story.
     C. Not taking sides.

    D. Acknowledging and encouraging feelings, whatever
        they may be associated with.
    E. Assessment of relevant history.

This phase sets the tone which will influence the degree of personal sharing and risk taking by the student. Most students feel a deep sense of embarrassment, shame and confusion, anticipating that they will not be understood and will have a "critical finger" pointed at them. The student may feel victimized and unjustly treated by the system. He may feel impending doom, such as the loss of respect from others and punishment from school official (e.g., expulsion, suspension or eviction from housing). Although he may show some remorse, the client is typically self-absorbed in shame, confusion and fear. By carefully listening to his story and acknowledging his feeling, without taking sides, the counselor earns "credibility and trust tokens" which will come in handy during the next phase of treatment.

III. Third Treatment Phase
    A. Continue relationship building and support.
    B. Challenge student to take more responsibility in
        relation to his sexual violating behaviors and
        attitudes.
    C. Look more closely at the impact of alcohol on his life.
    D. Introduce student to men's issues, in particular,
        male sex role socialization and male sexuality.

This phase is intended to help the student move out of the victim/victimizer role, as accomplished through increasing the student's willingness and ability to empathize with the feelings/thoughts of the individual who was the target of his behaviors/attitudes.

Through learning about male socialization issues, a student can better understand the roots of their sexual violating behaviors/attitudes which may lower his internal voice that says he is a "bad boy." In other words, the student increases his own capacity for "self empathy." His fear of the critical finger may indicate a projection of his internal voice. Assignments to read men's issues articles or books may help facilitate this process.

A thorough assessment of the client's alcohol and other drug use and attitudes is crucial. Students should be educated about the myths and facts of alcohol use and sexual violence (Richardson & Hammock, 1991). Many students want to excuse their behaviors if they are intoxicated, while at the same time place blame on the woman if she has been drinking. This double standard also contributes to the perception that women who get drunk are "easy."

Most clients are unaware of the laws related to consent and intoxication. In many states if a person is alcohol impaired they cannot give consent for sex and thus the partner can be convicted of sexual violation (rape) if they have sex in these circumstances. The assessment of alcohol dependence and abuse is critical to the treatment process and interventions to reduce drinking may take precedence over other concerns.

IV. Closing Phase of Treatment
  A. Continue relationship building and support.
  B. Refer to rape education and prevention program.
     Discuss assigned readings.
  C. Discuss how the crisis has been integrated
     into a learning opportunity.
  D. Discuss where to go from here?

During this phase of treatment the student attempts to "make peace." The edge of criticalness toward the system, victim and self is reduced. He is ready to move on and does so by finding some answers about himself and understands larger psycho-social issues.

Referral to rape prevention programs helps reinforce some of the concepts discussed in counseling. More importantly, it gives the student an opportunity to make public his struggles and learning, which often is relieving and shame reducing. He is no longer a man in hiding and knows that he can talk about the event as a learner rather than victim. As with most therapy termination, it is important to review the process of treatment including, left over feelings and identified new learning.

Case example #1: Rick is a 21 year old junior, from a large mid-western university and a member of a fraternity who does not live in the house. He was referred to counseling by a university conduct panel for sexual misconduct and alcohol abuse. No charges were filed against him through the district attorney's office. Rick indicated that while at a fraternity party he met a young woman who was "partially" drunk. They both continued to drink and went upstairs and had sexual intercourse. According to Rick the young woman gave full consent and there was no indication that she did not want to have intercourse with him. A short time later a friend of his came into the room and Rick left and went down to the party. Later that evening the young woman came down the stairs and said with considerable emotion that she had been raped by Rick's friend.

Counseling process and outcome. Rick was obviously anxious about coming into counseling. The first phase of treatment revealed that he assumed the counselor had control of his future: the counselor would decide whether he could stay in school. Clarification of the counselor's role was needed. The counselor explained to Rick about confidentiality and agreed that the university conduct panel would only be sent a note that Rick came into counseling; Rick double checked with the conduct panel to see if that was enough for them. But Rick was confused and angry about the university conduct hearing decision which suspended him for one semester. He did not understand why he was punished. He disclosed that he was sexually active and had similar experiences without any complaints. He was not sure what happened between his friend and the woman; yet he was positive that he did not rape the woman.

After the initial tension subsided, Rick became quite enthusiastic about counseling. He felt relieved that he could openly talk about his feelings and confusion. He had been "hiding" from others out of shame, and the hiding was very uncomfortable.

Rick contracted to meet for five sessions, read *Men on Rape* (Beneke, 1982) and attend a rape prevention workshop. He appeared to find relief in discussing personal issues that he had not paid much conscious attention: alcohol use, sexuality and intimacy, and definitions of legal and moral consent.

Rick saw himself as an above average "party person." He was accepted and felt proud of his reputation of being a guy who could easily "get" women. He had not given much conscious thought or feeling to what it meant to have so many casual sexual experiences, without real intimacy. He revealed that being sexually active helped him with the illusion that he was a likable guy, while underneath he felt unsure of his ability to be liked in a long-term relationship. He was envious of his fraternity brothers who were in long-term relationships.

Rick was unaware of the laws regarding consent while intoxicated. When asked if he thought the woman would have had intercourse with him if she had not been drinking, Rick seemed quite affected. He had never asked himself that question before. The question produced a moral dilemma, which was important for Rick, as was another moral issue: whether Rick had encouraged his friend to have intercourse with the woman. If so, could he be held morally accountable for the sexual violation? Rick's actions showed little empathy for the woman. She was somebody that was "easy" and a stimulus for "male bonding." Although Rick never admitted saying directly to his friend that he should try to have intercourse with the woman, he did reveal that he was not concerned about her well being and thought she would have intercourse with his friend under his (Rick's) definition of consent. Clearly part of Rick's lack of empathy was connected to his self centeredness; it was also compounded by his alcohol abuse.

His alcohol use was not a major issue in our counseling process, but he was required to attend AA meetings. It appeared that Rick saw alcohol as a problem only because "it" reduced his judgment abilities. Though his day to day life was not impacted by alcohol use, he clearly has the potential for developing severe alcohol problems, but was not motivated to explore that potential.

Rick appeared to benefit from the counseling contract. He shared openly with others in the workshop what he had been through. By that time, he had four sessions and was clear about his role in the sexual violation. He appeared to have increased his empathy toward women in terms of viewing them as important in their own right, not just sexual objects for his self esteem. He realized that it is important to gain sexual consent and be sexual with somebody who is not drinking. Others in the group responded to him quite positively and he was reinforced for his self-disclosure by others sharing their personal stories.

The termination phase was short. Rick was appreciative of having a place to share his story and not feel negatively judged. He recounted what he had learned and was thankful that his bitterness toward the system had significantly reduced.

Case example #2: Kent is a 20 year old junior who was on the sailing team. He came into counseling on his own after being accused of sexual assault by a female team member. Kent does not remember the event because he was intoxicated, yet he strongly denies that he would ever try to hurt another person. Kent was a good friend of the women and volunteered to walk her home after a party. Both individuals had been drinking. According to the female student, Kent tried to kiss her and touch her breasts without her consent. She tried to run away, but he wrestled her to the ground. When she did get away, she ran into her on-campus residence and Kent broke a window trying to get to her. Security was called and a report was taken. A few days later Kent called and made an appointment to see a counselor.

Counseling process and outcome. Kent was quite distraught when he came into counseling. He was fearful of losing his academic scholarship and his friends. Kent worried that his parents would find out and disown him. He had never been in "trouble" before and characterized himself as a "goody two shoes." His immediate concern was whether or not to hire a lawyer.

The first phase of treatment was to clarify confidentiality and his expectation of the terms of counseling and of the counselor. Kent clarified that he wanted someone to talk who was "anonymous." He was having difficulty concentrating on school and was experiencing loss of appetite and sleep. He was not suicidal, but did show clinical signs of acute depression. He was crying throughout most of the initial sessions and was focused on how the charges against him were going to ruin his life.

Kent was seen for fifteen sessions. Early phases of treatment concentrated on crisis intervention and stabilization. A clinical history revealed the student grew up in a strict, close-knit, second generation Slavic family. He feared his father's temper and became the "obedient" child. He was afraid of being sexual and described himself as shy and awkward with women, never having been in a long-term relationship, and he was a virgin. Kent said he drank on social occasions, but never before college. He said that recently he began drinking larger amounts of alcohol at social gatherings.

Our sessions weaved together several foci: (1) coping with and understanding the alleged sexual violation; (2) the father-son relationship; (3) and social discomfort with females. Because Kent had been intoxicated, his memory for the event was limited. He said he would have no trouble feeling remorse for what he allegedly did, but he thought he was not capable of such actions. He believed that, because the woman was drunk, she had distorted the events. Around the fourth session, Kent realized that the counselor had some doubts about the certainty of his account. This was an important transition in the counseling process. Kent was fearful of not being trusted (akin to his fear of his father) by the counselor. But he became willing to confront his counselor and that appeared to help lift the acute depression and empower him out of the victim role, which perpetrators often experience.

Kent appeared to benefit from counseling. By the time the university conduct hearing took place, he was able to articulate his confusion and remorse even though he did not remember what occurred. He made a commitment to work further on himself, specifically in the area of relationships with women and his father. He accepted and followed through on a referral for outside counseling. He decided to stop his drinking, motivated by his fear of losing control and having to go through another ordeal.

SEXUAL VIOLENCE PREVENTION PROGRAMS

Historically, sexual violence (rape) prevention programming on college campuses (and in the community) were done by women and for women, including self-defense, safety and awareness workshops, with the primary goals being protection and education (Cummings, 1992). Not until the early 1980s was programming on college campuses directed towards the perpetrators of sexual violence, those being college men (Koss et al., 1987). In 1983, the Ohio State University Rape Education Prevention Project (R.E.P.P.) created a men's curriculum task group that developed prevention workshops for college men (Stevens & Gebhart, 1984). Currently, many colleges have sexual violence prevention programming for men–including mixed gender and male only workshops. I will next highlight the goals, strategies and facilitation issues associated with sexual violence prevention workshops for college men.

Why do men attend sexual violence prevention programs? Some come to the programs because they have been *mandated* to attend. For example, a fraternity has violated a conduct code associated with sexual violence, and part of the reprimand is to provide education programming for its' members. Mandatory prevention programs have also included campus groups such as athletic teams, band and other male groups who have been known to have had its members perpetuate sexual violence.

Another group of men attending prevention programs are the *curious men* who attend a campus wide or residential life sponsored program and come on a volunteer basis with a sense of suspiciousness and curiosity. Finally, there are the *leadership men*, R.A.'s, student senators or presidents of campus organizations. Part of their leadership development includes education in the area of sexual violence prevention. They typically have participated in other social issue training such as racism, sexism, and homophobia which often allows them to bring a deeper understanding of sexual violence issues.

How can men benefit from participating in programs designed to prevent sexual violation? Three conceptual premises are needed to help understand the potential benefits for male workshop participants. First, we live in what Susan Bownmiller (1977) calls a "Rape Culture." This culture is perpetuated and endorsed by sexist attitudes, the media's stereotypic depiction and sexual objectification of women and the male socialization process that confuses sexuality and violence (Beneke, 1982). The second premise is that, to a certain extent, all men contribute to the perpetuation of the rape culture, often without willful intent to harm. Third, all men have something to gain if the rape culture is reduced.

Most men have never consciously thought how sexual violation (rape) affects their lives. When it is suggested in an experiential exercise (Stevens, 1987) that one imagines living the next 24 hours in a rape-free environment, almost all male (and female) participants respond with a sense of relief. Men typically report a sense of relief over not having to worry as much about a girlfriend, sister, friend or mother being raped. Their sense of needing to be the "protector" is reduced. Men are also relieved not to be perceived as a potential rapist. In a rape-free environment men think they can be friendlier to women without being afraid she may be "taking it" the wrong way. Men describe feeling uncomfortable about seeing a woman walk across campus at night, with a look of fear on her face. The men describe wanting to put up a sign stating "I am not a rapist, please don't judge me that way just because I am male."

On another level some male workshop participants identified that living in a rape-free environment would take away some of the pressures around initiating romantic physical involvement. For example, the men would not have the same internal demands to go out on a date and "score." Women in a rape-free environment would more likely initiate sexual involvement without the fear of being perceived as "easy." Still, on another level, some male participants discussed how their friendships with men would improve in a rape-free environment. They thought that conversations between men would be on a more intimate level since the men would not feel a need to bond through objectifying women and engaging in other types of "locker room talk."

Male participants may also learn different ways to build self-esteem. Traditional masculine socialization has taught men that being sexually active–the earlier and more the better–defines a "real man" (Pleck, 1981). Unfortunately, this type of behavior creates a false illusion of self-esteem. "Scoring" creates a temporary high without the conscious recognition of pain inflicted on self and others. Anecdotal information and research (Muehlenhard & Cook, 1988) suggest that a high percentage of males lose their virginity under non-intimate circumstances such as: being intoxicated; going to a prostitute; or being with someone with whom they have no emotional intimacy. Having something to gain from living in a rape-free environment probably provides men the greatest incentive to change their behaviors and attitudes. Whereas pointing a critical finger and coercing them and making them feel guilty may only provide temporary change.

Though perhaps motivated to change, men often are not aware of their behaviors and attitudes that perpetuate sexual violation. Furthermore, the men are not aware of alternative behaviors and attitudes that would promote a rape-free environment. Exercises that incorporate the Rape Domains (See Diagram 1) and Sexual Justice Domains (See Diagram 2) provide participants with specific ideas about what they can do to reduce the "rape culture." In other

Diagram 1

Rape Domain

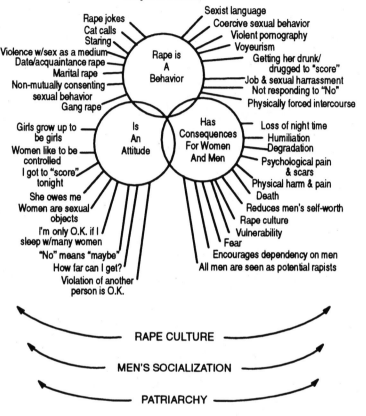

Rape jokes
Cat calls
Staring
Violence w/sex as a medium
Date/acquaintance rape
Marital rape
Non-mutually consenting
sexual behavior
Gang rape

Sexist language
Coercive sexual behavior
Violent pornography
Voyeurism
Getting her drunk/
drugged to "score"
Job & sexual harrassment
Not responding to "No"
Physically forced intercourse

Rape is
A
Behavior

Girls grow up to
be girls
Women like to be
controlled
I got to "score"
tonight
She owes me
Women are sexual
objects
I'm only O.K. if I
sleep w/many women
"No" means "maybe"
How far can I get?
Violation of another
person is O.K.

Is
An
Attitude

Has
Consequences
For Women
And Men

Loss of night time
Humiliation
Degradation
Psychological pain
& scars
Physical harm & pain
Death
Reduces men's self-worth
Rape culture
Vulnerability
Fear
Encourages dependency on men
All men are seen as potential rapists

RAPE CULTURE

MEN'S SOCIALIZATION

PATRIARCHY

Stevens, 1984

words, it is not enough to tell men how they contribute to the "rape culture," without giving them specific and doable options.

Male-female audiences. The major goal of this type of workshop is to clarify the faulty communication patterns that may lead to sexual violation. In a workshop titled "I Know You Said No But I Thought You Meant Maybe" (Stevens, 1987), the audience is asked to discuss how they attempt (or others have attempted with them) to initiate romantic physical involvement. It becomes clear that the communication patterns are often non-verbal and confusing to both

Diagram 2

Sexual Justice Domain

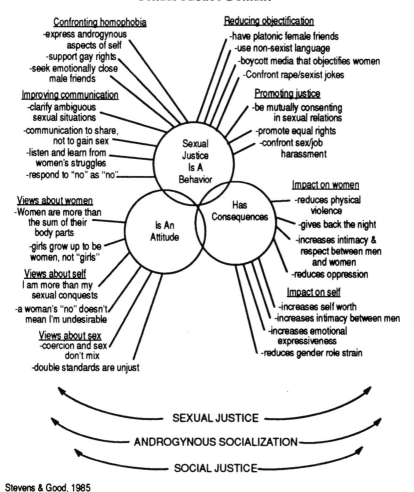

Confronting homophobia
-express androgynous
aspects of self
-support gay rights
-seek emotionally close
male friends

Improving communication
-clarify ambiguous
sexual situations
-communication to share,
not to gain sex
-listen and learn from
women's struggles
-respond to "no" as "no"

Views about women
-Women are more than
the sum of their
body parts
-girls grow up to be
women, not "girls"

Views about self
I am more than my
sexual conquests
-a woman's "no" doesn't
mean I'm undesirable

Views about sex
-coercion and sex
don't mix
-double standards are unjust

Reducing objectification
-have platonic female friends
-use non-sexist language
-boycott media that objectifies women
-Confront rape/sexist jokes

Promoting justice
-be mutually consenting
in sexual relations
-promote equal rights
-confront sex/job
harassment

Impact on women
-reduces physical
violence
-gives back the night
-increases intimacy &
respect between men
and women
-reduces oppression

Impact on self
-increases self worth
-increases intimacy between men
-increases emotional
expressiveness
-reduces gender role strain

Sexual
Justice
Is A
Behavior

Is An
Attitude

Has
Consequences

SEXUAL JUSTICE

ANDROGYNOUS SOCIALIZATION

SOCIAL JUSTICE

Stevens & Good, 1985

parties. Discussion can lead to breaking some pre-conceived myths. For example, men think that if they are verbally direct about wanting to become romantically involved, women will view them as "uncool." Questioned about how they would feel about a man asking if it would be O.K. to kiss or touch them, etc., women overwhelmingly approved of that form of communication.

Mixed gender workshops facilitate dialogue that normally does not occur (Abbey & Melby, 1986). Men can hear, directly, women's feeling about being sexually objectified. Women tell men that it is not a compliment or "turn on" to be whistled at or be the target of cat calls. Men discuss the pressure of having to be "in charge" and they want women to be more assertive in terms of initiating and paying for dates. Women share how they are concerned that, if they are too "forward" it will be taken as if they are "easy." Ultimately, this type of workshop clarifies and engenders understanding of what is mutual consent. While attending to needs for spontaneity and romance, participants are asked to create definitions and scenarios of mutual consent. The topic of alcohol use is brought into the discussion in terms of how it hinders the ability to differentiate consent from coerciveness (Richardson & Hammock, 1991). A further goal of the workshop is to encourage a continuing dialogue with other peers and in other settings.

Male only workshop. Sexual violation (or rape) prevention workshops, for men only, offer a unique environment to discuss issues of male sexuality, friendships and homophobia. Many men are afraid of and have not risked having an intimate conversation with another male (Pleck, 1981). Men find it safe to discuss sports, objectification of women and other non-intimate topics. Their homophobia prevents men from getting "too close" to one another and perpetuates some myths of male sexuality that encourage sexual violation (Lehne, 1976). The all male workshop is designed to give men a different kind of experience. The content of the workshops include: defining consent; defining sexual violation; and the interaction of male socialization and sexual violence. While the content component of the workshops is important, it may be the process experiences of the participants that better enable desired behavioral and attitudinal changes. For example, participants frequently comment that they expect to be laughed at by other male participants when they disclose something personal. Men share that in most all male groups it is difficult to be taken seriously when discussing personal issues like fears and confusion. Similarly, most of the participants express a fear of confronting other males who engage in sexist or homophobic behaviors. The combination of unwillingness to confront others and a fear of being humiliated for sharing personal issues, creates a type of emotional distance. Encouraging men to break this pattern of silence is a major goal of all male groups. As this silence is broken, men can become more intimate with one another and not rely so much on women's providing emotional support. Furthermore, it is the breaking of silence that will allow and encourage men to confront the sexist attitudes and behaviors that perpetuate the "rape culture."

Facilitation issues. Optimally a male and female facilitation team should be provided for mixed audiences. All male facilitators are essential for all male programs.

Because men come to all male workshops with a certain defensiveness and concern, facilitators are often confronted initially with a variety of obstacles, such as side talk and group joking interchanged with long periods of silence. When the tension rises and men start to feel guilty or picked on, it is common for someone to ask, out of nowhere, if a man can be raped.

When the men know one another it may be more difficult for them to self-disclose. Participants fear of being humiliated and desire to appear "cool" are obstacles that facilitators will need to gently maneuver with or around. Facilitators should respect the defensiveness of male participants. Getting into early power and control battles creates a tense tone that is difficult to overcome. It is helpful for male facilitators to do a fair amount of self-disclosure and let the male participants know how difficult it may be to personally respond to the questions and comments made during the workshop. While there are no set criteria for being a facilitator of sexual violence prevention workshops for men, here are some guidelines that may be useful to consider. Facilitators should be:

1. Well read in the area of men's issues, feminism and sexual violence with a "big picture" understanding of the psycho-social issues of male socialization and the construction of masculine identity.
2. Have empathy with and sensitivity to the male experience be willing to view men, in general, as constricted by the myths of masculinity.

3. Like men and have a positive sense of male pride. Homophobia must be low.
4. Knowledgeable about the variety of resources available to enhance personal growth in the area of men's issues.
5. Have insight and willingness to share their own growth edges, struggles and stories about being a man.
6. Have a high tolerance for typical "male group bonding" behaviors, while also be able to clearly share their boundaries of acceptable workshop behaviors.

CONCLUSIONS AND FUTURE DIRECTIONS

Sexual violence has become a larger public issue in recent years. The attention and subsequent dialogues created in reaction to the Tyson, Kennedy and Thomas-Hill trials has been significant, if not profound. Men, now more than ever, are thinking they will be held more accountable for their sexual violating behaviors, and this is a gigantic step forward. The grass root efforts of feminist communities in the 60s and 70s, along with the college campus date/acquaintance rape research and the media splash of the 80s is paying off.

Finding ways to help educate and empower men to change their attitudes and behaviors that promote/perpetuate our "rape culture" is the call of the 90s. We must hold men accountable for their behaviors by being both firm and affirming. Promoting change must incorporate compassion and understanding of male socialization along with sensitivity to the destructiveness and power differential of male sexism.

Campus communities must find creative ways to reach college men and provide all-male forums of "alternative locker rooms" that promote dialogue. These "alternative locker rooms" can help break down the isolation created by homophobia, competition and hypermasculinity training (Harris & Gertner, 1992, Stevens, 1992). Continuing programs are needed to encourage dialogue between women and men, whereby directness and honesty is valued more than political correctness. Berkowitz (1992) has proposed a model that helps clarify the complex inter and interpersonal interactions of men and women that promote sexual violence.

This article has provided ideas and guidelines for helping college men better understand and to be able to change their sexual violating attitudes and behaviors. Research is needed to better understand the effectiveness of interventions directed to promote such changes. In other words, how can it be determined that sexual violence prevention programs are working. Attitudinal changes that are theoretically linked to sexual violating behaviors can be measured over time, yet how do we know such attitudinal changes translate into behavioral changes. Measuring such changes is a difficult endeavor and should include not only self reports but also observations from others.

REFERENCES

Abbey, A. & Melby, C. (1986). The effects of nonverbal cues on gender differences in perceptions of sexual intent. *Sex Roles*, (5)15, 283-298.

Beneke, T. (1982). *Men on rape*. New York: St. Martins Press.

Berkowitz, A. (1992). College men as perpetrators of acquaintance rape and sexual assault: A review of recent research. *Journal of American College Health*, (4)40, 175-181.

Brownmiller, S. (1977). *Against our will*. New York: Simon & Schuster Inc.

Burt, M. (1991). Rape myths and acquaintance rape. In A. Parrot & L. Bechofer (Eds.), *Acquaintance rape: The hidden crime*. New York: Wiley.

Cummings, N. (1992). Self-defense training for college women. *Journal of American College Health*, (4)40, 183-188.

Fracher, J. & Kimmel, M. (1987). Hard issues and soft spots: Counseling men about sexuality. In M. Scher, M. Stevens, G. Good & G. Eichenfield (Eds.) *Handbook of Counseling and Psychotherapy With Men*. Newbury Park: Sage Publications Inc.

Harris, J. & Gertner, D. (1992). *Exploring masculinity: Experiential exercises to help students explore men's issues*. Fort Collins: Colorado State University Residential Life.

Koss, M. & Dinero, T. (1989). Predictors of sexual aggression among a national sample of male college students. In R. Prentky & V. Quinsley (Eds.), *Human sexual aggression: Current perspectives*. Annals of the New York Academy of Science, 528-133-146.

Koss, M., Gidycz, C. & Wisniewski, N. (1987). The scope of rape: Incidence and prevalence of sexual aggression and victimization in a national sample of higher education students. *Journal of Counseling and Clinical Psychology*, (2)55, 162-170.

Lehne, G. (1976). Homophobia among men. In D. David & R. Brannon (Eds.). *The forty-nine percent majority: The male sex role*. Reading, MA: Addison-Wesley Pub. Co., Inc.

Malamuth, N. (1986). Predictors of naturalistic sexual aggression. *Journal of Personality and Social Psychology*, (6)50, 953-962.

Martin, P. & Hummer, R. (1989). Fraternities and rape on campus. *Gender and Society*, 3, 457-473.

Muehlenhard, C. & Linton, C. (1987). Date rape a sexual aggression in dating situations: Incidence and risk factors. *Journal of Counseling Psychology*, (2)34, 186-196.

Muehlenhard, C. & Cook, S. (1988). Men's reports of unwanted sexual activity. *Journal of Sex Research*, 24, 58-72.

O'Neil, J. (1981). Male sex role conflicts, sexism and masculinity: Psychological implications for men, women and the counseling psychologist. *The Counseling Psychologist*, (2)9, 61-80.

O'Sullivan, C. (1991). Acquaintance gang rape on campus. In A. Parrot & L. Bechhofer (Eds.). *Acquaintance rape: The hidden crime*. New York: Wiley.

Pleck, J. (1981). *The myth of masculinity*. Cambridge, MA: MIT press.

Rapaport, K. & Burkhart, B. (1984). Personality and attitudinal characteristics of sexually coercive college males. *Journal of Abnormal Psychology*, (2)93, 216-221.

Richardson, D. & Hammock, G. (1991). Alcohol and acquaintance rape. In A. Parrot & L. Bechhofer (Eds.). *Acquaintance rape: The hidden crime*. New York: Wiley.

Scher, M. & Stevens, M. (1987). Men and violence. *Journal of College Development*. (7)65, 351-356.

Stevens, M. & Gebhart, R. (1984). *Rave education for men curriculum guide*. Columbus: The Ohio State University Rape Education and Prevention Program.

Stevens, M. (1987). *24 hours without rape*. In C.A.R.E. manual. Los Angeles: University of Southern California Office of Women's Advocacy.

Stevens, M. (1992). *Introducing college men to men's issues*. Symposium presentation at the 100th annual convention of the American Psychological Association, Washington, D.C.

Chapter 12

Psychological Challenges and Responses to a Campus Tragedy: The Iowa Experience

Gerald L. Stone

SUMMARY. The multiple murder tragedy at The University of Iowa on November 1, 1991, caused a major crisis. This article describes the tragedy, the psychological response, and unplanned consequences from a public and a private perspective. As a result of this experience, the author offers practical suggestions for emergency preparedness and implementing a responsive campus culture.

Viewing the campus as a place where bad things happen is disturbing. Whether the campus was ever a sanctuary, safely cloistered away from the tensions of the world, is debatable. The current political correctness controversy and date rape concerns surely point to conflict. Yet murders on campus are something else! Although the recent tragic experiences within the communities of Ecole Polytechnique de Montreal, the University of California at Berkeley, and the University of Florida (Archer, 1992) underscore

Correspondence may be addressed to: Gerald L. Stone, PhD, Director, University Counseling Service, The University of Iowa, 330 Westlawn Bldg. S., Iowa City IA 52242.

[Haworth co-indexing entry note]: "Psychological Challenges and Responses to a Campus Tragedy: The Iowa Experience." Stone, Gerald L. Co-published simultaneously in *Journal of College Student Psychotherapy* (The Haworth Press, Inc.) Vol. 8, No. 3, 1993, pp. 259-271; and: *Campus Violence: Kinds, Causes, and Cures* (ed: Leighton C. Whitaker and Jeffrey W. Pollard) The Haworth Press, Inc., 1993, pp. 259-271. Multiple copies of this article/chapter may be purchased from The Haworth Document Delivery Center [1-800-3-HAWORTH; 9:00 a.m. - 5:00 p.m. (EST)].

the scope of violence on campus, the association of murder and campus life is still shocking and an unbelievable experience. As one colleague voiced in response to our multiple murder tragedy, "Hell, Iowa City, no way!"

This paper articulates an experience of such a tragedy (see Mann, 1992) in the hope of raising our collective consciousness about the importance of campus climate and emergency preparedness. To do this, the tragedy will be described, followed by a public and a private perspective of the emergency response. The final section covers the unplanned challenges that often accompany such crises, and the author makes recommendations for emergency preparedness.

SITUATION

On Friday, November 1, 1991, at 3:52 p.m., shootings were reported at two locations on campus: the physics and administration buildings. Within 30 minutes, all of the shooting victims and the suspect had been identified. Three persons, later identified as two physics professors and a recent Ph.D. graduate from the People's Republic of China, were found dead in a seminar room in the physics building. In an office one floor below, the Chairman of the Physics Department was found dead. In the Office of Academic Affairs in the administration building, about a block and a half west of the physics building, two persons were found shot; one, an Associate Vice President for Academic Affairs, was rushed to the hospital, but died the next day. The other victim, a temporary replacement employee and a former student, was also rushed to the hospital. She is permanently paralyzed from the neck down due to the gunshot wound she received. The suspect, a recent physics Ph.D. recipient from the People's Republic of China, was found one floor above the Office of Academic Affairs and died from a self-inflicted gunshot. Later, it was conjectured that the suspect was upset about the treatment he received concerning his dissertation and the awarding of a dissertation prize. He blamed his professors and the central administration for not responding to his work and grievances the way he wished. Thus he felt compelled to do some-thing, leading to his mission of destruction on November 1, 1991.

RESPONSE

Within minutes, police, fire and rescue units, coroner, and the media were on the scene. Also, within minutes, the administrative team of the University was activated and calls were made, buildings secured, and incoming calls from parents and the media were handled. After the confusion of the first wave of emergency response, a second wave occurred including the gathering and ongoing meeting of a crisis management team that planned the emergency response approach. During the early phases of responding and planning, the major issues were: (a) assisting the families of the victims and eye witnesses; (b) handling calls from students' parents and concerned others; (c) dealing with the media and the public; (d) helping with the ongoing criminal investigation; and (e) planning responsive services. This last issue will be the focus, but it needs to be noted how well the University and community, including law enforcement, responded. For instance, psychologists from the community and representatives from the victim assistance program in the county attorney's office did most of the work with the families of the victims. The Vice President for University Relations along with others held timely and informative news conferences to update the public. Campus and community efforts were made, through the campus Office of International Education and Services, to reach out to the Iowa City Chinese community, especially the students, to reassure them.

As the person responsible for coordinating the psychological services effort, I have a public and a private story to communicate. The public story consists of a log of psychological activities, while the more private story concerns my personal reactions and feelings.

Public log. There were a number of responsive services and interventions planned and implemented. These interventions are grouped under two categories: debriefing; and community interventions.

As a metaphor for the delivery of debriefing interventions, the "fan" consultation strategy is appropriate. That is, the families of the victims and the departments directly affected were debriefed, and then asked who they thought needed to be contacted. This fan or spread-like procedure was then implemented again and again with expanding groups over time. For example, in discussion with the Dean of Liberal Arts and with the advice of the Acting Chair of the Physics Department, a physics faculty meeting was held on Saturday, November 2, 1991 with campus and community psychological personnel. After some debriefing and information about resources, the faculty were asked about what our next steps in developing our intervention plan should be. These meetings led to additional debriefings with the eye-witnesses, teaching assistants, and support staff. Additionally, recommendations were made for the placement of psychologists in the physics building for consultations and services the following week, including attending the classes of the slain professors and making brief educational presentations on coping with stress and providing information about resources. This same fan-like consultation procedure was used in Academic Affairs and with the families of the victims, leading to ongoing individual and group counseling interventions.

The model for our debriefing interventions was similar to those described by Mitchell (1988a, 1988b) although we did not become familiar with Mitchell's work until later. Our time-limited approach combined elements of what Mitchell refers to as defusings and debriefings. The purpose of our interventions was prevention of serious problems (e.g., anxiety disorders such as Post-Traumatic Stress Disorder–PTSD) through exploration, education, screening, and referral to appropriate mental health resources. We focused on psychological education, *not* psychotherapy. Typically, the intervention process included several stages. During the introduction phase, personal introductions were made and the purpose, rules, and procedures of the intervention were outlined. For example, rules and procedures such as confidentiality and freedom (e.g., "you do not have to speak") and responsibility (e.g., "do not leave while intervention is ongoing") were outlined. The exploration section provided an opportunity for participants to hear the facts ("what happened") and share their thoughts ("My first thought . . ."), followed by personal reactions ("My worst feeling . . .") and symptoms ("I am having trouble sleeping . . ."). The last and very important task was education. Information about mental health resources and self-help material was provided. The information covered diet, exercise, social support, and sleep recommendations. Those needing more assistance were referred to appropriate sources such as the University Counseling Service (UCS).

In addition to these stages, the facilitators often had pre-debriefing meetings concerned with planning. All the facilitators had post-debriefing meetings that included cathartic and sharing discussions immediately after their interventions and, later, more formal debriefings by an outside facilitator.

A major provider of the debriefing interventions was the UCS which is staffed by psychologists, interns in professional psychology, and doctoral students in counseling psychology. The UCS is the primary mental health center (in collaboration with the Mental Health Unit in the Student Health Service) on campus. The usual hours are 8 a.m. to 5 p.m., Monday through Friday. In response to Friday's tragedy, the UCS was open on Saturday (1-5 p.m.) and remained open Sunday and most of the week from 8 a.m. to 8 p.m. Regular clinical work was put on hold while the staff's attention turned to crisis intervention work. One of the first accomplishments was the production and distribution of written self-help material (e.g., "Taking Care of Yourself After a Traumatic Event" and "Coping With Trauma–Skills for Facilitators") based on the stress and trauma literature (e.g., Figley, 1986). These materials, along with a Mental Health Resource List, a referral list based on community resources, and material for working with children, were ready for distribution within 36 hours. This material was available for all interventions including the community interventions on Monday. Some colleges and departments reprinted the material and sent it to all faculty members for their use. A total of 42 debriefings were conducted by the UCS staff, serving 1,162 participants. These debriefings ranged from the department chairs of the College of Liberal Arts to the Iowa City Fire Department. Some were serial, while others were one-time interventions. It must be also noted that the UCS was only one provider source of intervention; for example, the Faculty and Staff Services office on campus (similar to an employee assistance program) also held debriefings with faculty and staff.

Within the Iowa City community, an office of private practitioners established the Mental Health Resource Network through a meeting of area practitioners on Sunday following the tragedy. More than 40 professionals agreed to join the network and offered their services. In addition, they developed resource material for children, contacted area school counselors and informed them about coping with trauma, and published educational material in newspapers. Some of the practitioners joined the on-campus debriefings and one of the practitioners led a debriefing for UCS professionals. Through this experience, campus and community professionals came together, recognizing and valuing each other's contribution.

The next cluster of interventions could be labeled community interventions and addressed the following question: How do we regain a sense of community within a large university? In consultation with the President and Vice President for Academic Affairs, it was decided to create opportunities for community solidarity in the face of our common tragedy. The first planned community event was on Monday, November 4, following the tragedy of Friday, in which a morning open town meeting and afternoon opportunities for education and consultation were provided in lieu of classes. During the morning meeting, the President and Vice President for Academic Affairs defined the tragedy as a community experience (i.e., "We are all in this together."). The Vice President spoke about stress reactions. Finally, I spoke about a healing community and presented in person the numerous resource representatives from the campus and the community (e.g., psychological, spiritual, international, family and child resources) that were available to help and meet with individuals throughout the day. In the afternoon follow-up session, all the rooms in the student union were staffed with campus and community resource persons for education and counseling about stress reactions and provision of resource lists for assistance. Concurrently, the Office of International Education and Services provided sessions for international students, especially the Chinese community since there was growing concern about possible racial discrimination.

A televised service of remembrance and support for the families and survivor was held in the sports arena on Thursday, six days after the tragedy. At this occasion, attended by many of the families, colleagues, friends, and students of those killed and harmed, representatives spoke of the victims' professional and personal contributions. A student representative also provided a voice for the survivor and spoke of her contributions. Campus and community support through fund-raising activities continue to this day for the survivor's medical and rehabilitation costs.

Private log. To give the public record a more personal touch, let me share some of my experiences based on my written log of events.

On Friday, November 1, 1991, I was at home doing editorial work. A little after 4 p.m., I heard (at this time I am still not sure how I heard) about the shootings and experienced a numbness of disbelief, if not a minor dissociative reaction. After my initial shock and numbness, as I watched the television, I began to experience a number of feelings such as sadness ("I know these people"). But the overwhelming experience was a growing frustration, arousal, and sense of urgency to do something ("I need to be there." "Why are they not calling?").

I was called at 6:45 p.m. and arrived at 7 p.m. in the President's Conference Room. Energy was high. The buzz of activity was a bit overwhelming ("Who is in charge?" "What can I do?" "Where is the plan?"). My behavioral mode in the Conference Room, and one that continued for the next several days as my role was further defined, was the "take charge mode." In this role, my emotions were delayed, if not put on hold, as I focused externally on "things to do," "places to go," and "plans to be made."

As the take charge mode evolved, I began to notice some of my reactions. Cognitively, as I fielded a number of phone calls at home, I kept forgetting phone numbers and asked my spouse to take notes. I wore the wrong shoes for a formal meeting. As indicated earlier, I forgot how I heard about the shootings. Emotionally, as I was in the helping mode, I discovered during my debriefings that feelings of sadness started to well up as I mentioned the Associate Vice President for Academic Affairs to whom I often reported. I was also a little irritable in dealing with professionals and experts who expected me to find them a role (e.g., "let me have access to the families since I have done this kind of work before"). And behaviorally, I was easily distracted, hyperactive, and had difficulty sleeping. Despite these various reactions, I also felt highly charged and "good" about the involvement, the engagement, and the action.

Over time, slowly things returned to "normal," whatever that was or will be. I was finally able to focus on my own sense of loss, but time had passed and I detected a little resentment and feeling deprived of timely grieving. I also experienced another sense of loss, the loss of the action.

As I write this a few months after the fact, it is clear to me that many of my reactions fit the descriptions of a post-traumatic stress experience, including increased arousal and initial numbing of general responsiveness. A challenge for me (perhaps other crisis workers as well) is to be able to integrate the public and private experience of a tragedy.

CHALLENGES

There were other challenges. Many unplanned challenges emerged. I have selected a few to consider. These challenges include dealing with experts and the media, debriefing, and some consequences of a tragedy for the academy.

Experts and the media. As one colleague mentioned when I told him of my encounters with experts, "Sometimes we need to be saved from the helpers." I might add that "hell hath no fury like a spurned professional." What these comments underscore is that many well-intentioned, highly skilled, and experienced professionals are available and willing to come to your crisis and "be helpful." On the first night of our tragedy, I was inundated with calls from national organizations, state government, professional experts on crisis and murders, and so on. Each of these sources of goodwill was willing to fly in and take charge at a moment's notice. On the one hand, I felt a lot of support from these groups and individuals and used much of their material. On the other hand, I got the distinct impression that these organizations and experts were not very informed about the resources available in Iowa City and assumed that we were less than competent to carry this off without their assistance. Moreover, their agenda did not always ring true because they were most concerned about being included in public documentation and press briefings. In communicating our plan for careful, step-by-step needs assessment accompanied by a formulated plan based on such assessment and under local authorization, many professionals felt closed out and undervalued, if not a little irritated, with the politics.

The media was another mixed blessing. They were on the scene in minutes, providing news to a national audience almost instantaneously. The need for information was great and reporters were tying up phone lines and television cameras intruded into interventions. At the same time, reporters provided timely information to the public, often addressing fears of loved ones and concerned others.

Debriefing. In conducting debriefing sessions, the primary goals were concerned with assisting individuals in coping with their experience through "normalizing" and providing resources for assistance. Many times during the debriefing sessions, individuals would express strong emotions (e.g., "Why was our office not immediately identified?"). Little prior thought was given about the context of the group debriefing sessions in which such strong emotions were expressed. For instance, if administrators of the various groups were present, the aftereffects of the expression of strong feelings could create difficult issues in those offices (e.g., confidentiality, trust, and questions of loyalty).

Another observation from the debriefing sessions concerned the variability of coping with the tragedy: some persons were overcome with emotions including sadness and anger while others were quiet and passive. These variable reactions were also apparent in the University community including the student body, and among the professional helpers. People tended to wonder about, if not judge, people whose reactions were different from their own. For instance, if people are not visibly upset and tearful, does this automatically mean they are in denial? What happens when the pattern of reactions does not fit our theory of crisis and coping? Do we really value individual differences? How do we actually distinguish valid healthy individual differences from unhealthy coping strategies?

CONSEQUENCES

Several consequences of the tragedy were observed, including a temporary reduction in confidence in students, faculty, and administrators about their ability to manage their role-relevant tasks. Students were at a temporary loss as to how to respond to faculty who were obviously emotionally distraught. For instance, one student asked, "should I ask if everything is okay?" Another student voiced a common yet challenging concern for educators: "This is very troubling to me. I don't usually see my professor express such emotions. What am I to do?" Faculty expressed similar concerns. "How do I speak about the tragedy in class?" "Should I mention it or give my scheduled examination?" "How do I communicate my concern to my Chinese students?"

By far, the most time consuming activity involved the increased consultation to faculty and administrators about disturbed and disturbing students. After the tragedy, the University community, some more, some less, filtered events through the lens of tragedy. Thus students with a grievance and displaying an aggressive style including voicing a direct or indirect reference to the tragedy (e.g., "The November 1 incident could occur again if this doesn't get straightened out") got attention, usually unwanted attention. Before the tragedy, faculty and administrators usually dealt with these students in a confident and competent manner without much consultation.

This temporary loss of faith in a safe and predictable world voiced by students, faculty, and administrators is a normal response to trauma and victimization. For the University community, a basic trust had been violated and people we cared about died in "the line of duty." Line-of-duty deaths are reported to be the most stressful by police and fire and rescue personnel. For many of us in the academy, their deaths and injury may particularly affect us because these individuals were killed as they were fulfilling their roles as faculty, administrator, or student.

RECOMMENDATIONS

What did we learn? An important lesson is that preparation and planning are necessary, but one is never really fully prepared for tragedy and its aftermath. There are many types of preparations. One approach focuses on developing a specific plan of emergency preparedness and another on creating a "culture of responsiveness" on campus and within the community in which individuals are empowered to respond to unplanned circumstances.

Let me share a few thoughts about these preparations. Each campus should develop a written emergency preparedness manual, including the specific designation of a coordinating emergency response team. Additionally, the manual should describe a process by which individuals are designated responsible for media, psychological services, liaison to criminal investigations and community/government/governance relations, and relating these designated individuals to the coordinating response team. Of course, there are many more ingredients to a good plan including procedures germane to the local setting and a protocol for informing significant governance bodies. But clear designations of responsibility are key. It would also be helpful to have the development of the specific plan be a collaborative effort with broad campus, governing board, and community participation (e.g., a general town meeting). Wide circulation of the plan, once completed, would also be important. Timely updates and audits of the plan should be systematically incorporated. Wide circulation and timely updates become important since tragedies do not lend themselves to quiet reflection on the emergency intervention. While my recommendation about emergency response plans may not be new, I wonder if colleges and universities have actually developed such plans and if these plans are in working order.

My other suggestions concern developing a responsive culture by providing timely and ongoing continuing education, staff development, and student programming about trauma and coping with stress. Administrators, deans, faculty, and teaching assistants could benefit from a workshop on "Dealing With Difficult People." Professional service providers on campus and within the community need to be educated about crisis theory, post-traumatic stress disorders, responding to tragedies (e.g., multiple homicides), and dealing with one's own reactions. University and college personnel can be provided guidelines for service in public, media-intense, high energy, and politically charged environments. Such educational activities would set the groundwork for a culture of responsiveness.

The following lessons were learned in developing a culture of responsiveness. These lessons involve the preparation, intervention plan, and process. Although each tragedy or disaster is unique, I believe that these lessons are applicable to equally serious and less serious crisis situations.

Preparation

- Establish an ongoing administrative coordinating team for crisis management that meets regularly.
- Develop a written emergency plan based on collaborative efforts, broad representation, wide circulation, and timely updates.
- Designate capable and trained individuals to coordinate responsibilities for the media, psychological services, and other vital areas.
- Identify campus and community agencies and personnel to respond to crises.
- Provide training for crisis personnel (e.g., critical incident stress debriefing–CISD; Mitchell, 1988a, 1988b), campus faculty and staff (e.g., dealing with difficult people workshops), and students (e.g., coping with stress programs).

Intervention Plan

- Develop informational and educational material and lists of resources.
- Create opportunities for community interventions (e.g., town meetings, educational meetings, services of remembrance).
- Implement crisis intervention work that is immediate, provides control and safety in the situation, and leads to assessment, disposition, and referral (see Caplan, 1964; Greenstone, J. L., & Leviton, 1982; Klein & Lindeman, 1961; Slaikeu, 1984).
- Provide debriefing procedures including debriefing for emergency, mental health, and administrative personnel.
- Include systematic follow-up procedures to the crisis work in order to check on victims, improve response strategies, and deal with unexpected challenges (e.g., tragedy anniversaries).

Process. Up to this point, the lessons appear to be rational and · logically formulated. The process variables tap into components of tragedy work that are often difficult to anticipate. Several examples were discussed in the Private Log section including issues related to experts and debriefing. One variable worth elaboration is the personal factor. No matter how planful or trained in crisis work, people will not always respond the way you expect. Some people experience a profound emotional and cognitive disruption, while others experience a more transitory disruption. These differences could be associated with proximity to the precipitating event and/or are related to the dynamic meaning of the crisis situation in the person's history including line-of-duty deaths. Moreover, personal expressive style based on situational norms may lead some individuals and mental health professionals to experience certain emotions as inappropriate, leading to differential expressiveness of emotions in debriefing sessions. We need to pay attention to "feeling rules" at the personal and institutional level (Hochschild, 1979) when dealing with tragedy on campus so as to be more accepting of the range of emotional expressiveness.

In conclusion, bad things do happen and they do occur on our campuses. Such a view is not meant to create an alarmist situation, but it is a call for responsible action, to create a culture in which we are able to reasonably and humanely respond to the serious and often unpredictable crises on campus.

REFERENCES

Archer, J., Jr. (1992). Campus in crisis: Coping with fear and panic related to serial murders. *Journal of Counseling and Development 71*, 96-100.

Caplan, G. (1964). *Principles of preventive psychiatry.* New York: Basic Books.

Figley, C. R. (Ed.). (1986). *Trauma and its wake: Traumatic stress theory, research, and intervention.* New York: Brunner/Mazel Inc..

Greenstone, J. L., & Leviton, S. C. (1982). *Crisis intervention: A handbook for interveners.* Dubuque, IA: Kendall.

Hochschild, A. R. (1979). Emotion work, feeling rules, and social structure. *American Journal of Sociology, 85,* 552-575.

Klein, D., & Lindeman, E. (1961). Preventive intervention in individual and family crisis situations. In G. Caplan (Ed.), *Prevention of mental disorders in children: Initial exploration* (pp. 283-306). New York: Basic Books, Inc.

Mann, J. (1992, June 7). The physics of revenge. *Los Angeles Times Magazine,* pp. 26-48.

Mitchell, J. T. (1988a). Development and functions of a critical incident debriefing team. *Journal of Emergency Medical Services, 13,* 43-46.

Mitchell, J. T. (1988b). The history, status and future of critical incident stress debriefings. *Journal of Emergency Medical Services, 13,* 47-52.

Slaikeu, K. A. (1984). *Crisis intervention: A handbook for practice and research.* Boston: Allyn & Bacon.

Chapter 13

Homicide in the University Residence Halls: One Counseling Center's Response

Michael Waldo
Marsha J. Harman
Kathleen O'Malley

SUMMARY. On May 15, 1990, two students were murdered by a third student in the residence halls of a public university. The campus counseling center's attempt to assist the university community to adjust in the aftermath, including services to students, resident halls' staff and residents, university officials, and victims' families, is discussed. Responses to the anniversary of the homicides a year later, recommendations for counseling centers, and a stress management handout for students are provided.

Michael Waldo, PhD, is Associate Professor, Health & Human Development, Montana State University, Bozeman, MT 59717. Marsha J. Harman, PhD, is Assistant Director, Counseling Services, Box 2059, Sam Houston State University, Huntsville, TX 77341. Kathleen O'Malley, PhD, is Training Director, Counseling & Psychological Services, Montana State University, Bozeman, MT 59717.

The authors wish to acknowledge the contributions of Patrick Donahoe, Priscilla Roberts, James Murphey, Jim Collins, and Casey McVay in preparation of this manuscript.

[Haworth co-indexing entry note]: "Homicide in the University Residence Halls: One Counseling Center's Response." Waldo, Michael, Marsha J. Harman, and Kathleen O'Malley. Co-published simultaneously in *Journal of College Student Psychotherapy* (The Haworth Press, Inc.) Vol. 8, No. 3, 1993, pp. 273-284: and: *Campus Violence: Kinds, Causes, and Cures* (ed: Leighton C. Whitaker and Jeffrey W. Pollard) The Haworth Press, Inc., 1993, pp. 273-284. Multiple copies of this article/chapter may be purchased from The Haworth Document Delivery Center [1-800-3-HAWORTH; 9:00 a.m. - 5:00 p.m. (EST)].

273

And now
    that Death has left this black, poisonous imprint
        upon my life
            and on the lives of so many others
                I realize that we
                    will forever toss
                        in its wake
    For this breed of Death
        not only sucks the life from its victims
            but also
                targets the hearts of those
                    close by[1]

Traumatic violence on university campuses is a devastatingly and increasingly high profile phenomenon facing university counseling centers (Roark, 1987). In 1990, alone, a shooting occurred at a dance at Alabama A&M University, five female students were murdered in off-campus housing at the University of Florida (Kalette, 1990), and a group of students were held hostage at gun point at the University of California at Berkeley, resulting in one death, eight injuries, and several incidents of sexual molestation (Feinberg, 1991). In each of these situations, the university counseling center struggled to provide assistance to the survivors.

Many authors have described survivors' (including victims, their friends and families, and people who help them) responses to trauma (Davis & Friedman, 1985; Figley, 1983, 1988; Lipp, 1980; Rose & Rosow, 1978; van der Kolk, 1987; White & Hatcher, 1988) and goals for assisting them (Downing, 1988; Gilliland & James, 1988; Scurfield, 1985). Survivors are seen as progressing through stages in response to trauma such as impact, recoil, and reorganization (White & Hatcher, 1988) and being at risk of developing maladaptive patterns for dealing with the fear, anger and helplessness the trauma generates (Anderson & Bauer, 1987; Gilliland & James, 1988). Maladaptive patterns include sensation seeking, guilt, desensitization to violence, enjoying violence, estrangement and inability to find significance in life. Survivors may be reluctant to seek help (Roark, 1987). Goals for assisting survivors include remediation, prevention, and development (Downing, 1988). Both direct service and consultant roles are suggested for counselors (Nuttall & Kalesnik, 1987). Group interventions with survivors are thought to be particularly helpful because of their ability to reduce isolation and stigma and provide opportunities to express emotions, process unfinished business and exchange reality based confrontations (Scurfield, 1985).

Although traumatic events are dramatically documented in public media, and theories for understanding and assisting victims are offered in the professional literature, little has been written regarding counseling centers' responses when violence occurs on campus (Collins, Bowden, Patterson, Snyder, Sandall, & Wellman, 1987). This paper will describe shotgun murders of two students by a third student in the residence halls of a public university and the counseling center's attempt to assist the university community's adjustment in the aftermath. Initially, a description of the tragedy and the counseling center's response will be provided, followed by recommendations for university counseling centers' preparation and procedures for responding to traumatic violence.

DESCRIPTION OF THE HOMICIDES

At 2:15 a.m., May 15, 1990, one male freshman took a sawed-off shotgun from his truck. He proceeded to the dorm room of another freshman whose room, this particular night, was shared by a friend. The gunman knocked on the door and when it was opened, shot the answering student, the visitor, in the stomach. The gunman then proceeded to the other student, the resident of this room, who lay on the bed in a defensive position, and shot that student in the arm and leg. The gunman left the room, headed down the hallway, and suggested to the resident assistant and another student responding to the gunshots that they call the police because there had been a murder. The gunman left the building and drove away in his truck. One victim staggered from the room. The other was unable to rise. One asked a first responder why anyone would want to do this to him. He then collapsed on the hallway floor. The campus police were called; and they, in turn, called an ambulance and then called the counseling center director and assistant director. First responders to the scene, a neighbor student and a Resident Assistant, attempted to comfort the victims until the ambulance arrived. One victim, the guest in the room, died at 3:15 a.m., shortly after arriving at the hospital. The other victim died two hours after the shooting at 4:15 a.m.

COUNSELING CENTER RESPONSE

Residence Hall. The male director and female assistant director of the university counseling center arrived at the residence hall shortly after 3 a.m. The two victims had been taken by ambulance to the hospital just prior to their arrival. Initially, the counselors interviewed the first responders to the scene, both of whom were in a state of shock and denial. The counselors attempted to assess the first responders' psychological states and to offer them an opportunity to express emotions and normalize responses. The interviews also enhanced the counselors' understanding of the traumatic events and initiated relationships between the first responders and the counselors.

The counselors next organized a meeting of the building's resident advisors (RAs) to discuss the shootings, allow them to emote, delineate likely psychological responses to a traumatic event, and discuss how the counselors and RAs might respond to the residents. As the meeting was being organized, news of one victim's death was received. As the RAs processed this news, word came that the second victim had died. News of the second death was emotionally devastating to the RAs and counselors. Belief that one victim might survive had served as a reservoir of hope for everyone involved. Loss of the second victim punctured that hope, unleashing despair and anger.

Throughout the morning, the counselors worked to achieve a balance between being available to RAs and residents and avoiding intrusiveness. The counselors offered the RAs time alone as a group to react, analogous to giving a family time alone to register a loss, and to allow uninhibited expression of feelings and bonding among the RAs. The RAs talked among themselves for 30 minutes and then asked the counselors to rejoin them. The counselors then led a meeting with the RAs to help them process their own reactions and to prepare them to assist residents. Much time was spent expressing and processing feelings to assist RAs in avoiding denial which could negatively affect both their own adjustment and their ability to assist the residents. The counselors then educated the RAs about possible responses residents might have, including denial, fear, anger, and acting out. Suggestions to RAs included providing residents opportunities to talk about feelings, encouraging residents to support one another, directing them to additional assistance from counselors, and encouraging the RAs themselves to talk about their own feelings and to support one another.

The two counselors remained a presence in the residence hall where the shootings occurred, from 8 a.m.-10 p.m., which allowed one to have a private individual meeting while the other counselor was available for more casual contacts. Their presence also allowed having a male and female counselor available to meet with students and for the counselors to offer each other consultation and support. They made a point of being in the walkway to the building and the lobby as much as possible, and found that many contacts which started out as casual conversation turned into requests for help, referral of an affected student to counseling and/or an opportunity to inform students about potential psychological responses to trauma.

That evening the counselors held a meeting for interested students and RAs. The meeting began with a review of the event, and participants were encouraged to share details of the chronological events to the time of the meeting. Mutual sharing served to assist participants to overcome gaps in knowledge of the homicides and the ensuing events. Once information was shared, the staff encouraged expression and exploration of emotions. It was stressed that nothing more could be done for the victims but that the survivors had some control over how they reacted and would be responsible for their reactions. Modeling of openness and emotional expression by the counseling center staff and senior residence hall staff stimulated student examination of personal experiences. The staff also distributed a handout regarding reactions the students might have to the trauma and coping strategies they might employ (see Table 1).

Stages of response to violence and loss including denial, anger, sadness, and resolution were discussed. It was also explained to students that others (family, friends, instructors, etc.) who were not close to the tragedy might not understand their experience. Students

TABLE 1. Coping Guidelines Sheet

Below are listed some of the typical psychological reactions to trauma such as you have experienced, followed by various coping strategies that might help you get through this experience.

Reactions to Trauma

1. *Heightened fear:* This might include reduced feelings of personal safety, fears of being alone, apprehensions around strangers, and feeling uneasy with people you do not know well.
2. *Sleep problems:* These might include problems with falling asleep, waking up early in the morning, fitful sleep, bad dreams, and sometimes excessive sleep.
3. *Irritability:* Feeling on edge, snapping at others, and being annoyed by little things that previously were not as troublesome.
4. *Concentration problems:* Experiencing difficulty remembering, forgetting assignments, forgetting deadlines, or being in the middle of a task and not being able to focus.
5. *Guilt:* Feeling that you could have done something differently before the crisis or feeling that you should have responded differently as the crisis emerged.
6. *Increased vulnerability:* Feeling more open to a sense of pain and hurt.
7. *Startle reactions:* Jumpy reactions to noises, voices, and sudden movements.
8. *Preoccupation with the incident:* Constantly replaying the incident, subsequent scenes, and memories in your head.
9. *Intrusive memories:* Uncontrollable thoughts and flashbacks related to either the incident or the victims.

Coping Strategies

The following are some recommended ways to cope with this trauma.

1. *Talk:* It is important to talk about the incident and your feelings as much as necessary with supportive family members and friends.
2. *Pacing:* It is important to pace oneself in resuming regular routines and not assume that you should be able to immediately return to life as normal.
3. *Stress reduction for physical side effects:* It is important to deal with physical side effects by using positive stress management techniques, such as exercise, relaxation training, and appropriate dietary measures vs. negative ones such as increased alcohol and other drug use.

were warned that these people might try to cheer them up or distract them and, although these efforts might be well intended, they might result in people who were close to the tragedy feeling misunderstood and alienated. Additionally, it was stated that, while there would be some general reactions to trauma, each person's experience would be unique. The meeting ended with encouragement for the students to be permissive and supportive for themselves and one another, to continue to talk about their reactions, and to make use of the counseling center staff. The counseling center extended its hours and opened times for persons reacting to the trauma to drop in without an appointment. Two counselors stayed on site in the residence hall for three days.

Victims' Families. Later on the morning of the murders, two counselors were requested to come to the hospital to talk with students who had accompanied the victims to the emergency room, but the students had left by the time the counselors arrived. However, the emergency room physician requested that the counselors remain for the arrival of one victim's family, that was not yet aware of their son's death. Meanwhile, the medical staff discussed their reactions with the counselors. Although the counselors were having strong reactions to the tragedy themselves, they attempted to lay aside their reactions and respond empathically to the hospital staff.

When the family arrived and asked to see their son, they were informed that their son had died. The counselors took the roles of supportive advocates, assistants, information providers and compassionate companions to the family, but tried not to intrude or control. The counselors' rationale for these procedures was that one impact of their son's murder was a terrible loss of control, and it was the counselors' goal to empower the family as much as possible to deal with their loss. The counselors helped locate the son's body at the county morgue, arranged transportation for the family, and assisted the family in deciding how, when and who would view the body. The counselors discussed with the coroner preparation of the victim for presentation to the family and accompanied the family during the viewing. The family and the counselors all stayed by the victim for 40 minutes.

The counselors also accompanied and assisted the family throughout the next few days. They helped arrange lodging, accompanied them to their son's residence hall, and sat with them at the memorial service. At all times, the counselors endeavored to be available and supportive to the family while respectfully avoiding intrusion or control.

In subsequent discussions, the families indicated they highly valued and needed the support and assistance offered by the counselors, just as RAs said they valued that counselors were involved, that they were a part of the experience, and that they cared.

Consultation. Following direct service, such as providing counseling and support to individuals and groups, consultation was the second major activity undertaken by the counseling center staff to assist the university community. As mentioned earlier, extensive work was done with RAs to help them deal with their own reactions and prepare them to work with affected residents. Similarly, consultation was offered briefly to the medical staff at the hospital after the death of the victims and as they prepared to meet with one victim's family. Counselors also offered consultation to the staff of the Health Center on campus, to the Division of Student Affairs staff, to the president's office, and to faculty seeking assistance. In each case the consultation followed a similar pattern as follows:

1. *An indepth review of what happened so that consultees had an opportunity to ask questions that remained unanswered for them*, was seen as important because, if they were left with unanswered questions, consultees might ignore their own emotions and be distracted when responding to the needs of their constituents.
2. *A full airing of consultee's emotions* was seen as important because failure to acknowledge their own emotions might prevent consultees from being aware of and addressing their constituents' emotions.
3. *A discussion of typical responses to trauma* was offered so that consultees could understand themselves and their constituents' responses.
4. *Problem solving how the consultees could best address the needs of their constituents* typically included understanding their feelings and allowing them time and space to deal with their reactions (for example, requesting that faculty delay

exams or due dates for assignments). In the case of the president's office, problem solving included examining what would be the most helpful comments the president might include in his address at a memorial service and assistance in generating a letter from the president personally addressed to every student expressing emotions about the tragedy and inviting all students to offer and seek support.

The effectiveness of consultation is difficult to assess because the persons it is intended to help may not come in direct contact with the counselors. However, the consultees consistently indicated they found the consultations to be helpful both for themselves and in their service to their constituents.

A YEAR LATER

Since the murders occurred toward the end of the spring quarter, many students left for summer vacation shortly afterward. Throughout the following year and as the anniversary date neared, a few students came for counseling noting their affiliation with the victims or event but viewing it as secondary to their presenting problem.

The counseling center staff involved with the event continued to process their experience. As the trial and sentencing of the homicidal student and the anniversary date of the murders has come and gone, the counselors have processed their own personal feelings and thoughts, and responses to clients involved in the homicides during weekly staff meetings.

RAs also continued to process their feelings and were aware of a potential increase in emotional reactions among students as the anniversary of the homicides approached. In consultation with the counseling center, they wrote a letter describing the emotions they were experiencing and sent it just prior to the anniversary to students who were residents when the murders occurred. The letter also invited the students to a memorial service with the counseling center and residence life staffs offered by campus ministry on the anniversary date. Counseling center staff met with the first responders to the crime scene and RAs on the anniversary date to discuss their emotions and support one another. Together, they attended the memorial service.

The letter, discussions and memorial on the anniversary were seen as valuable for helping students and staff acknowledge and work through their feelings. As one student expressed it, "It was important to have a memorial . . . to show this was not just another day . . ."

For the most part, the university community has appeared to reorganize itself in an adaptive fashion. However, because no research or evaluative efforts were in place prior to the violent traumatic event, assumptions of successful intervention can only be tentatively made.

RECOMMENDATIONS FOR COUNSELING CENTERS RESPONDING TO TRAUMATIC EVENTS

What follows are recommendations for counseling center staff for dealing with traumatic events on campus. These recommendations are based on literature cited earlier in this paper and on our experience assisting the university community after the murders.

Training/Preparations

1. *Provide critical incident training for staff as a component of yearly inservice.* Knowledge of the most current conceptions of critical incident debriefing and proactive intervention will provide for skilled rather than haphazard intervention.
2. *Network with medical and social work agencies on a regular basis.* Sharing of theories and ideas during non-crisis times may provide better understanding among professionals during the crisis and make it easier to communicate concerns and reservations.
3. *Establish methods for evaluating likely interventions.* Prior planning will provide for skilled rather than haphazard evaluation.

In the Event of a Trauma

1. *Provide time for the counseling staff to process reactions.* Since it has been established that counselors will likely be sec-

ondary victims, it is crucial that staff care for themselves as they care for their clients. Also, understanding their own reactions can provide insight and sensitivity to victims' responses.

2. *Be available.* Many persons traumatized by a violent act may not seek help in a counseling center. Going to the victim's location is a crucial first step in service delivery.

3. *Be flexible.* Traditional therapy may not be the most practical course. Providing for basic physical needs may be as important as providing for emotional needs.

4. *Being may be more important than doing.* One counselor reminded herself to just be human with the family. Natural reactions may create a permissive atmosphere for others to react naturally, also.

5. *Follow-up.* Response to trauma is an on-going process. Assistance could offer important benefits long after the traumatic event, particularly at sensitive times like anniversaries.

> On this day
> I live wounded in the aftermath
> On this day
> my heart
> cries red tears[1]

NOTE

1. Excerpted from a poem written shortly after the murders; cited with the permission of Casey McVay, a student who lived in the residence halls.

REFERENCES

Anderson, W. & Bauer, B. (1987). Law enforcement officers: The consequences of exposure to violence. *Journal of Counseling & Development,* *65,* 381-384.

Collins, B.B., Bowden, S., Patterson, M., Snyder, J., Sandall, S., & Wellman, P. (1987). After the shooting stops. *Journal of Counseling & Development, 65,* 389-390.

Davis, R.C. & Friedman, L.N. (1985). The emotional aftermath of crime and violence. In C.R. Figley (Ed.), *Trauma and its wake: The study and treatment of post-traumatic stress disorder.* New York: Brunner/Mazel Inc.

Downing, N.E. (1988). A conceptual model for victim services: Challenges and opportunities for counseling psychologists. *The Counseling Psychologist, 16,* 595-629.

Feinberg, L. (January 7, 1991). Personal communication.

Figley, C.R. (1983). Catastrophes: An overview of family reactions. In C.R. Figley & H.I. McCubbin (Eds.), *Stress and the family: Vol. 2. Coping with catastrophes.* New York: Brunner/Mazel Inc.

Figley, C.R. (1988). Victimization, trauma, and traumatic stress. *The Counseling Psychologist, 16,* 635-641.

Gilliland, B.E. & James, R.K. (1988). *Crisis intervention strategies.* Pacific Grove, CA: Brooks/Cole.

Kalette, D. (1990, November 29). Dangerous lessons: Violent crimes no stranger on campuses. *USA Today,* pp. 1, 2.

Lipp, M.R. (1980). *The bitter pill: Doctors, patients, and failed expectations.* New York: Harper & Row Pub., Inc.

Nuttall, E.V. & Kalesnik, J. (1987). Personal violence in the schools: The role of the counselor. *Journal of Counseling & Development, 65,* 389-390.

Roark, M.L. (1987). Preventing violence on college campuses. *Journal of Counseling & Development, 65,* 367-371.

Rose, K.D. & Rosow, I. (1973). Physicians who kill themselves. *Archives of General Psychiatry, 29,* 800-805.

Scurfield, R.M. (1985). Post-trauma stress assessment and treatment: Overview and formulations. In C.R. Figley (Ed.), *Trauma and its wake: The study and treatment of post-traumatic stress disorder.* New York: Brunner/Mazel Inc.

van der Kolk, B.A. (1987). The psychological consequences of overwhelming life experiences. In B.A. van der Kolk (Ed.), *Psychological Trauma.* Washington, D.C.; American Psychiatric Press, chapter 1, pp. 1-30.

White, S.G., & Hatcher, C. (1988). Violence and trauma response. *Occupational Medicine, 3,* 677-694.

Chapter 14

Cures for Campus Violence,
If We Want Them

Jeffrey W. Pollard
Leighton C. Whitaker

WHY WE DON'T WANT CURES GENERALLY

The fateful question for the human species seems to me to be
whether and to what extent their cultural development will
succeed in mastering the disturbance of their communal life by
the human instinct of aggression and self-destruction.

–Sigmund Freud ([1930] 1961)

By this criterion of cultural success, the United States is far and
away the greatest failure among the world's industrialized nations.
And our failure rate continues to increase with each decade. Suicide, homicide and the many forms and gradations of self-destructive and other-destructive behaviors have been proliferating rapidly
in this nation. Inevitably, so has campus violence.

We should be clear by now that the problem of violence and its

Jeffrey W. Pollard, PhD, is Director of Counseling and Health Services, Denison University, Granville, OH 43023. Leighton C. Whitaker, PhD, is Director of
Psychological Services for Swarthmore College.

[Haworth co-indexing entry note]: "Cures for Campus Violence, If We Want Them." Pollard,
Jeffrey W., and Leighton C. Whitaker. Co-published simultaneously in *Journal of College Student
Psychotherapy* (The Haworth Press, Inc.) Vol. 8, No. 3, 1993, pp. 285-295: and: *Campus Violence:
Kinds, Causes, and Cures* (ed: Leighton C. Whitaker and Jeffrey W. Pollard) The Haworth Press, Inc.,
1993, pp. 285-295. Multiple copies of this article/chapter may be purchased from The Haworth Docu-
ment Delivery Center [1-800-3-HAWORTH; 9:00 a.m. - 5:00 p.m. (EST)].

motivations in our culture are not limited to the people who are criminals, even if we include not only those who are convicted but the vastly greater number of people who commit criminal acts but are not caught, *and* all of us who motivate violence. The problem is endemic to our culture. We can see it on our large and small screens, and in our newspapers, magazines, billboards, best-selling books, and gun stores, and we can hear it in our music. Our culture rewards the purveyors of violence with money and prestige. What we fail to see is that we all are motivators of violent behavior. As psychiatrist Karl Menninger said:

> The inescapable conclusion is that society secretly *wants* crime, *needs* crime and gains definite satisfactions from the present mishandling of it! We condemn crime; we punish offenders for it; but we need it. The crime and punishment ritual is a part of our lives. We need crimes to wonder at, to enjoy vicariously, to discuss and speculate about, and to publicly deplore. We need criminals to identify ourselves with, to secretly envy, and to strictly punish. Criminals represent our alter egos–our "bad" selves–rejected and projected. They do for us the forbidden, illegal things we *wish* to do and, like scapegoats of old, they bear the burdens of our displaced guilt and punishment–"The iniquities of us all."
>
> –Menninger, 1968, p. 153

Unless we cease *our* denial that disidentifies us with *our* criminals, we will surely never have enough jails, prisons, guards, security officers, locks, alarm systems, judges, lawyers, probation officers, emergency rooms, or as many and as powerful guns as we are told we need. What do we really need to cure the violence problem? We need, first, to become witting about our own selves.

> Simply stated, most Americans, including those at all levels of education and government as well as most social scientists, seem convinced that aggression either cannot or should not be controlled. As a result, they fail even to consider a variety of potentially effective measures that could reduce violence in the United States.
>
> –Lore and Schultz, 1993, p. 16

We must ask, in all seriousness, whether we want to reduce violence in our national culture or in the campus cultures which are its microcosms. The answer, nationally, has been slow in coming. Even if the majority of U.S. citizens say they want violence reduced, major segments of our national culture–including educators–can be counted upon to resist by whatever means they have at their disposal. As this chapter is being written, Janet Reno, who is known to favor legislation to curb gun proliferation, including the Brady bill, has become the first woman U.S. Attorney General. In an effort to block her confirmation, a high official of the National Rifle Association (NRA) falsely reported to federal officials that she had been stopped for drunk driving.

Ostensible reasons for not wanting to limit violence span the gamut of constitutional arguments and personal protection issues. Considered together, these reasons are often clearly in conflict with one another. For example, certain freedoms of expression and the right to bear arms hazard people's personal safety. Ironically, the right to bear arms may mean that people feel compelled to be armed because others are armed. This psychology clearly applies to gangs and has spread into schools to which children and teenagers now bring weapons to defend themselves against other students. The fact that guns are so easy to obtain makes many people escalate their own armamentarium. Thus guns–ever more massively destructive by their numbers and firepower–are multiplying because people see that they are multiplying.

Powerful resistances to violence reduction include commercial interests, as well as bigotry, since violence promotion is enormously profitable to major segments of society. Thus wars, ranging from national to gang wars, are much valued by the weapons industry. Since violence presentations in movies, television, magazines, newspapers, and certain sports, are extremely lucrative, we can expect powerful resistance in American society, including in educational institutions which, for example, have commercially successful big-time football. Violence reduction means restraints on personal and group expressions which hurt others, whether such expression is commercially motivated or motivated by bigotry which aims to scapegoat others to raise one's own status.

We must also take into account that destruction is vastly easier and more sensational than construction. To nurture a human being into adulthood requires enormous effort and time; the process is not sensational. But destroying human beings is easy and sensational. Similarly, it is easier to neglect a child than to be nurturant. So, limiting violence means having to be constructive, an infinitely greater challenge than being destructive. Death is not an accomplishment; all living creatures have died eventually whether they tried to or not.

WHY WE DON'T WANT CURES ON CAMPUS

Even before the decline of *in loco parentis* beginning in the fifties, colleges were supposed to be ivory towers, not merely as bastions of freedom for learning but as places wherein the student was free to be more irresponsible than in the world outside. Thus fraternity initiations that were clearly destructive–resulting in severe injury or death–rarely if ever resulted in criminal or civil prosecution of the initiators. For example, even in the fifties, a freshman who was stabbed in a kidney during an initiation rite was considered merely an unfortunate accident, and neither he nor his parents filed a serious complaint. More extremely, a student, blindfolded and then dropped off on a dark road at 3 a.m. and soon killed by a motorist who didn't see him in time, was not viewed as a case of lawless endangerment by his fraternity. Those responsible were not prosecuted under the law. But the image, if not always the reality, was that colleges were safe.

Among colleges and universities, competition for traditional age students has never been higher and, for many schools finding that the national demographics are shifting away from their traditional applicant pool, it is becoming a matter of survival. Colleges and universities are therefore negatively motivated to restrict students' behavior through application of existing societal norms. Higher education may be generally afraid to see just how well it would survive in a world of fewer available traditional students if prospective students can not count on four years of suspended consequences for their behavior.

Yet only a generation ago American campuses were tranquil enclaves in both image and fact. Most still feel like privileged and peaceful islands, the nearest thing in secular society to sacred ground, but since the early 1980's image has less and less to do with reality.

–Matthews, 1993, p. 41

Members of Boards of Visitors, Regents, and Directors attended college when institutions of higher education were in fact *usually* "tranquil enclaves" and their memories of their *alma maters* are distorted through euphoric recall. They are generally reasonable people and were they to experience the campus of today with its pandemic of drunken violence and date rape, they would probably be inclined to act to change it. But because administrators are held accountable to their Boards, administrators can be viewed by those same reasonable board members as failing in their mission if they report accurately the ethos of violence on campus. Administrations are caught in the bind of needing additional students and money to continue programs which favor their institutional reputation while, at the same time, campus violence continues to haunt their efforts. Pinched between the rock of financial survival and the hard place of violent behavior, university officials genuinely feel coerced to respond in ways that compromise safety and security.

As the protective orientation of college and university administrators has declined since the fifties, campus life has become far more hazardous. Lately, as colleges and universities have begun to be required to report the crime figures for their campuses by the Student Right to Know Campus Security Act (1993), on behalf of prospective students and their parents, they have clearly lost their ivory tower image of ensuring student safety. Accordingly, local police are now more likely to come onto campuses as crimes have escalated in numbers, severity and obviousness. In this atmosphere, colleges are less able to present themselves as safe places and may resist reporting. As was recently observed, when asked for just such information,

The University of Florida, four of whose students were murdered by unknown assailants in off-campus housing in 1990, dawdled two months, then sent nearly a pound of perky but largely unrelated brochures. The security office of the City

University of New York said testily, that they had never heard of the Campus Security Act. Adelphi University, on Long Island went into a frenzy; "Why do you want to know? We can't release that. Can you prove authorization from the legal department?"

–Matthews, 1993, p. 42

It is ironic indeed to recall the demise of *in loco parentis* as having resulted from student demands to be treated as adults, only now to discover that they are being treated as though they need not be responsible adults. What response academe will eventually generate, and just how to implement that response is the challenge, for it is clear with the growth in governmental regulation that if the campus doesn't respond, the congress will. The Campus Sexual Assault Victims' Bill of Rights (1993), clarification of the Buckley Family Educational Rights and Privacy Act (1993) which affords victims of campus violence greater access to the criminal records of student perpetrators, and the Student Right to Know Campus Security Act (1993) are at once reflections of the state of affairs on the college campus and examples of the change within the legislatures which promise to reduce the isolation of the campus from the consequences of society's law.

Caught between wanting to present a picture of safety and not wanting to discourage enrollment, the campus community must take stock and face this most serious dilemma.

WHAT COLLEGES CAN DO TO REDUCE VIOLENCE

Parallel studies of aggression in children, assaultive adults, and even entire societies have suggested that humans are exquisitely sensitive to subtle social controls that could be used to reduce the frequency of individual acts of violence.

–Lore and Schultz, 1993, p. 16

The social atmosphere. The effectiveness of methods for reducing campus violence depends on the specific strategies employed, how they are implemented, and the atmosphere in which they are implemented.

One of us (LW) remembers vividly a high school teacher who demonstrated maximum effectiveness and efficiency on all counts. Ms. Hutchins, a slightly built older woman, taught mathematics students who went on to distinguish themselves in state competitions. She made her serious dedication quite obvious at the outset of the academic year. Standing in front of the class, she made two brief remarks. The first expressed her own pleasure and pride in her students. The second expressed her view of discipline. She would say tersely: "I never send students to the principal for discipline!" For a fleeting moment, a new student might have the impression that she was lax about discipline, until he or she took in Ms. Hutchin's facial expression and stance. Whereas this petite woman rarely had to speak thereafter about discipline, a burly man who taught physics and was also the wrestling coach, had many disciplinary problems with the same students whom he often sent to the principal.

No method will work if it is not "owned" by its implementer. We make the following suggestions for those who can own them, deliberately emphasizing atmosphere first.

The college catalogue can convey the serious dedication of the college and all of its members to optimizing the academic and social learning atmosphere. Such an atmosphere is characterized by an air of respect for everyone in the college and an understanding that the diversity of its constituents and their differences of opinion are not merely to be tolerated but provide essential opportunities for all forms of learning.

The catalogue should distinguish its *leadership role* from that of general social "norms" about what behavior is acceptable. Colleges aim to provide higher levels of academic achievement. Why not state out front that the college also aims higher in social learning in order to maximize its benefit both to society and the students it helps to educate? Currently, colleges may have a lower standard than the surrounding community, as exemplified in not prosecuting drunk and disorderly behavior. Once stated, these policies must be supported through a series of consequences needed for successful behavior change.

Orientation of newly matriculating students ought to emphasize that they must match the new freedoms, encountered on leaving home and coming to college, with new levels of responsibility. Yes, you can stay up late if you wish, but not at others' expense. Yes, you can determine your work pace, eating habits, and social ventures but you have to bear the consequences too. The college should point out that these realizations are necessary to make the new freedoms work.

Alcohol and other drugs. Since a great preponderance of destructive behaviors in our society generally and on campuses particularly occurs under the influence, colleges must not deny the crucial importance of strongly discouraging underage alcohol use, alcohol abuse, and other drug use. We must not be like the dean of one university who, told that all of the recent reported sexual assaults on her campus had been found to occur under the influence, insisted that the two problems were quite separate, meaning that we should look the other way when adults' favorite drug–alcohol–is involved.

Since all states have a minimum alcohol drinking age of 21, the law provides colleges with an *opportunity* to discourage underage alcohol use. Programming which specifically targets risk-reduction, by reducing availability and discouraging use, is an effective approach to prevention. Colleges can offer truly drug free residence halls that students can choose to live in, and they can cite and assist in enforcing the law when students are underage and/or drunk and disorderly. In fact the Drug Free Schools and Communities Act Amendments of 1991 and the Drug Free Workplace Act of 1988 require universities to enforce the law regarding alcohol and other drugs. The Fund for the Improvement of Post-Secondary Education (FIPSE), administered through the U.S. Department of Education has provided grants to seed substance abuse prevention programs on hundreds of university and college campuses, and each of those recipient institutions has promised to implement the Drug Free Schools and Drug Free Workplace Acts. Colleges and universities do not have to be havens for the vast profusion of destructive behaviors that are so strongly associated with alcohol and other drug use. But–and here lies the source of much difficulty–the enforcing adults must practice what they preach.

As Matthews (1993) notes, "After 10 p.m., the campus with its wild drinking and reckless sex, is almost entirely adultless" (p. 47). As a result there are no disciplinary consequences for perpetrators who are abusive, violent, or generally disregard the welfare of fellow students. Student affairs professionals should be encouraged to be present during these times of high-risk behavior, and security forces must be better trained, equipped and supported if they are to truly provide security.

Treatment of perpetrators. University and college administrators who become aware of violent students on campus should insure discipline and provide treatment for perpetrators, as well as victims, to protect the student body, faculty and staff. If colleges expel known offenders without insuring that they receive appropriate treatment either on or off-campus, in addition to discipline, they are simply passing the problem on and adding to society's pool of untreated violent individuals. It would be as if a state identified, tried, and convicted a perpetrator only then simply to banish him from that state, leaving the rest of the nation to deal with the problem. To simply expel perpetrators from campus will in no way change their pattern of violence; it only passes the problem on to another community or campus. We cannot end the cycle of violence by treating perpetrators as though they are toxic waste that can simply be dumped elsewhere. We need to establish effective treatment programs for the growing population of violence perpetrators as well as victims.

As discussed in Chapter 5, the issue of mandatory psychotherapeutic treatment is problematic ethically and clinically and perhaps legally as well. Yet institutions of higher education must be willing to treat not only the victims/survivors of violence but also the perpetrators. We need to create treatment opportunities that educate and rehabilitate and not simply punish offenders. We cannot guarantee that every violent person will benefit from such treatment, but without it we can guarantee that they will continue to violate others. Though much has been written about treating victims, little treatment programming for offenders exists currently on campuses. Those who commit violent acts often remain on campuses and continue to perpetrate or are dumped elsewhere to continue to perpetrate. We emphasize that treatment is broader than psychotherapy.

Because mental health practitioners, whether psychologists, social workers, psychiatrists, or counselors, are often unfamiliar with the process and techniques involved in batterer treatment, they often mistakenly assume that treatment for violence is a form of traditional psychotherapy including the elements of transference and counter-transference. It is usually on this view of treatment as psychotherapy that their resistance to mandatory referral is based. It would be hard indeed to refute the concerns expressed in requiring someone to enter psychotherapy.

Court-mandated programs for treatment of the domestically violent exist in virtually every major community across the nation. Treatment of the violent offender, whether performed individually or in group, typically begins in a psycho-educational mode. Such programs resemble the process commonly used to deal with those who are required by the courts to participate in programs when found guilty of driving under the influence of alcohol or other drugs.

Perpetrator treatment programs commonly comprise two phases, the first a mandatory, open-ended, and revolving curriculum. The curriculum can be started at any point and is attended until each element has been completed. Topics in this mandatory phase typically deal with such issues as the escalating cycle of violence, anger reduction techniques, definitions of abuse and violence, and male and female gender roles and how they relate to violence. The second phase offers voluntary psychotherapy for those who wish to enter this form of treatment. The first phase of treatment is based partially on the fact that most individuals who are violent have a history of psychological difficulty which the mandatory curriculum may help them identify.

Admitting to and deconstructing the violence culture. Last but not least, we suggest that all colleges and universities acknowledge that both present campus culture and United States culture, of which it is part, perpetrate violence, and that our institutions of higher education must deconstruct the myths that serve to welcome the violence culture onto campuses. Administrators should admit to violence on their campuses just as they should admit to violence in the broader culture. The current situation, however, is like that of the adult who protests proudly that he or she had a perfect upbringing as if, as a child, he or she and not others determined that upbringing. Administrators do not have to be defensive as though they personally invented the phenomenon of increasing violence in our culture or on our campuses. Nor do they need to fatalistically assume that nothing can be done about it. As Myriam Miedzian says in *Boys Will Be Boys: Breaking the Link Between Masculinity and Violence,* "People who live in violent societies tend to assume that high levels of violence are inevitable. Now that we have, hopefully, been cured of this mistaken belief, we shall focus our attention on what can be done to make our society less violent" (Miedzian, 1991, p. 76).

The authors of this book have shown much of what needs to be deconstructed; let us not be too timid to do it.

REFERENCES

Campus Sexual Assault Victims' Bill of Rights, 20 U.S.C. § 1092 (1993).

Drug-Free Schools and Communities Act Amendments of 1991, 42 U.S.C. §§ 5105a-1 (1991).

Drug-Free Workplace Act of 1988, 41 U.S.C. § 701 (1988).

Family Educational Rights and Privacy Act (PC 93-380), 20 U.S.C. § 1232 G, (1974, a. 1993).

Freud, S. (1961). Originally published in 1930. Civilization and its discontents. In *The complete works of Sigmund Freud,* Vol. 21 (J. Strachey, Trans.). London: Hogarth Press, p. 145.

Lore, R.K. & Schultz, L.A. (1993). Control of human aggression. *American Psychologist,* 48, 1, 16-25.

Matthews, A. (1993). The campus crime wave. *New York Times Magazine,* March 7, 1993, 39-47.

Menninger, K. (1968). *The crime of punishment.* New York: Viking Press.

Miedzian, M. (1991). *Boys will be boys: Breaking the link between masculinity and violence.* New York: Doubleday.

Student Right to Know Campus Security Act, 20 U.S.C. § 1001, (1993).

Index

Academic achievement, ethnic
stereotyping regarding,
156
Academic harassment, 3
Academic institutions. *See also*
individual colleges and
universities
effect of violence on, 24
football promotion by, 287
homophobia of, 180-183,184-185
preventive policies for,
194-197
role in campus violence, 80
substance abuse tolerance by,
80,84
Accidents, alcohol use-related, 72
Accountability, relaxed standards for,
84
Acquired immune deficiency
syndrome (AIDS),
92,179,186-187
Addiction. *See also* Alcohol use;
Drug use; Substance abuse
commercial promotion of, 57
Adelphi University, failure to
provide campus crime
statistics, 290
Administration
attitudes towards campus
violence, 288-290
denial of campus violence by, 17
disruptive student conduct
responses of, 29-44
codes of conduct, 32-35
evaluation of conduct
violations, 35-39
institution's characteristics
and, 32-33

failure to control campus
violence, 288-289
failure to report campus crime
statistics, 288-289
of minority-affairs offices, 169
Admissions criteria, for minority
groups, 155,156
Adolescents, homicide rate of, 48
Advertising
of alcoholic beverages and
tobacco, 52,53-55,82-83,96
children's viewing of, 104
anti-smoking, 59,67
freedom of speech in, 65-66
Affirmative action programs, 169
Affirmative action statements, about
sexual orientation, 194
African-Americans
as cigarette advertising target
audience, 60
educational loans to, 156
financial aid to, 155-156
homophobia of, 189
homosexual/lesbian, 189
Aggression
alcohol-related, 141
of children, 77
children's exposure to, 79-80
of male gender role, 100-101
as personal right, 82
sports-related, 104
suicide and, 47
as violence component, 9,10
Alabama A&M University, shooting
incident at, 274
Alcohol advertising, 52
alcohol industry's expenditures
on, 54

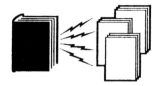

Haworth
DOCUMENT DELIVERY
SERVICE
and Local Photocopying Royalty Payment Form

This new service provides (a) a single-article order form for any article from a Haworth journal and (b) a convenient royalty payment form for local photocopying (not applicable to photocopies intended for resale).

- *Time Saving:* No running around from library to library to find a specific article.
- *Cost Effective:* All costs are kept down to a minimum.
- *Fast Delivery:* Choose from several options, including same-day FAX.
- *No Copyright Hassles:* You will be supplied by the original publisher.
- *Easy Payment:* Choose from several easy payment methods.

Open Accounts Welcome for . . .
- Library Interlibrary Loan Departments
- Library Network/Consortia Wishing to Provide Single-Article Services
- Indexing/Abstracting Services with Single Article Provision Services
- Document Provision Brokers and Freelance Information Service Providers

MAIL or *FAX* THIS ENTIRE ORDER FORM TO:

Attn: **Marianne Arnold**
Haworth Document Delivery Service
The Haworth Press, Inc.
10 Alice Street
Binghamton, NY 13904-1580

or **FAX:** (607) 722-1424
or **CALL:** 1-800-3-HAWORTH
(1-800-342-9678; 9am-5pm EST)

PLEASE SEND ME PHOTOCOPIES OF THE FOLLOWING SINGLE ARTICLES:

1) Journal Title: _____
    Vol/Issue/Year:_____Starting & Ending Pages:_____
Article Title:_____

2) Journal Title: _____
    Vol/Issue/Year:_____Starting & Ending Pages:_____
Article Title:_____

3) Journal Title: _____
    Vol/Issue/Year:_____Starting & Ending Pages:_____
Article Title:_____

4) Journal Title: _____
    Vol/Issue/Year:_____Starting & Ending Pages:_____
Article Title:_____

(See other side for Costs and Payment Information)

COSTS: Please figure your cost to order quality copies of an article.

1. Set-up charge per article: $8.00
   ($8.00 × number of separate articles) _____

2. Photocopying charge for each article:
   1-10 pages: $1.00 _____
   11-19 pages: $3.00 _____
   20-29 pages: $5.00 _____
   30+ pages: $2.00/10 pages _____

3. Flexicover (optional): $2.00/article _____

4. Postage & Handling: US: $1.00 for the first article/
   $.50 each additional article _____
   Federal Express: $25.00 _____
   Outside US: $2.00 for first article/
   $.50 each additional article _____

5. Same-day FAX service: $.35 per page _____

6. Local Photocopying Royalty Payment: should you wish to copy the article yourself. Not intended for photocopies made for resale. $1.50 per article per copy (i.e. 10 articles x $1.50 each = $15.00) _____

GRAND TOTAL: _____

METHOD OF PAYMENT: (please check one)

❑ Check enclosed   ❑ Please ship and bill. PO # _____
(sorry we can ship and bill to bookstores only! All others must pre-pay)

❑ Charge to my credit card: ❑ Visa; ❑ MasterCard; ❑ American Express;

Account Number:_____ Expiration date:_____

Signature: ✗_____ Name: _____
Institution: _____ Address: _____
City: _____ State:_____ Zip:_____
Phone Number: _____ FAX Number: _____

MAIL or *FAX* THIS ENTIRE ORDER FORM TO:

Attn: **Marianne Arnold**
Haworth Document Delivery Service
The Haworth Press, Inc.
10 Alice Street
Binghamton, NY 13904-1580

or FAX: (607) 722-1424
or CALL: 1-800-3-HAWORTH
(1-800-342-9678; 9am-5pm EST)